# Success as an Introvert

## FOR DUMMIES
A Wiley Brand

# Success as an Introvert

## FOR DUMMIES®

### A Wiley Brand

**Joan Pastor, PhD**

FOR DUMMIES®
A Wiley Brand

**Success as an Introvert For Dummies®**

Published by: **John Wiley & Sons, Inc.,** 111 River Street, Hoboken, NJ 07030-5774, www.wiley.com

Copyright © 2014 by John Wiley & Sons, Inc., Hoboken, New Jersey

Published simultaneously in Canada

No part of this publication may be reproduced, stored in a retrieval system or transmitted in any form or by any means, electronic, mechanical, photocopying, recording, scanning or otherwise, except as permitted under Sections 107 or 108 of the 1976 United States Copyright Act, without the prior written permission of the Publisher. Requests to the Publisher for permission should be addressed to the Permissions Department, John Wiley & Sons, Inc., 111 River Street, Hoboken, NJ 07030, (201) 748-6011, fax (201) 748-6008, or online at http://www.wiley.com/go/permissions.

**Trademarks:** Wiley, For Dummies, the Dummies Man logo, Dummies.com, Making Everything Easier, and related trade dress are trademarks or registered trademarks of John Wiley & Sons, Inc., and may not be used without written permission. All other trademarks are the property of their respective owners. John Wiley & Sons, Inc., is not associated with any product or vendor mentioned in this book.

LIMIT OF LIABILITY/DISCLAIMER OF WARRANTY: WHILE THE PUBLISHER AND AUTHOR HAVE USED THEIR BEST EFFORTS IN PREPARING THIS BOOK, THEY MAKE NO REPRESENTATIONS OR WARRANTIES WITH RESPECT TO THE ACCURACY OR COMPLETENESS OF THE CONTENTS OF THIS BOOK AND SPECIFICALLY DISCLAIM ANY IMPLIED WARRANTIES OF MERCHANTABILITY OR FITNESS FOR A PARTICULAR PURPOSE. NO WARRANTY MAY BE CREATED OR EXTENDED BY SALES REPRESENTATIVES OR WRITTEN SALES MATERIALS. THE ADVISE AND STRATEGIES CONTAINED HEREIN MAY NOT BE SUITABLE FOR YOUR SITUATION. YOU SHOULD CONSULT WITH A PROFESSIONAL WHERE APPROPRIATE. NEITHER THE PUBLISHER NOR THE AUTHOR SHALL BE LIABLE FOR DAMAGES ARISING HEREFROM.

For general information on our other products and services, please contact our Customer Care Department within the U.S. at 877-762-2974, outside the U.S. at 317-572-3993, or fax 317-572-4002. For technical support, please visit www.wiley.com/techsupport.

Wiley publishes in a variety of print and electronic formats and by print-on-demand. Some material included with standard print versions of this book may not be included in e-books or in print-on-demand. If this book refers to media such as a CD or DVD that is not included in the version you purchased, you may download this material at http://booksupport.wiley.com. For more information about Wiley products, visit www.wiley.com.

Library of Congress Control Number: 2013949557

ISBN 978-1-118-73837-5 (pbk); ISBN 978-1-118-73832-0 (ebk); ISBN 978-1-118-73843-6 (ebk); ISBN 978-1-118-73866-5 (ebk)

Manufactured in the United States of America

10 9 8 7 6 5 4 3 2 1

# Contents at a Glance

*Introduction* .................................................................. *1*

*Part 1: Getting Started Understanding Introversion* ......... *5*

Chapter 1: Introverted? Good for You! ..............................................................7

Chapter 2: Are You Really an Introvert? ..........................................................15

Chapter 3: What Makes You an Introvert, and Will You Always Be One? ...............31

*Part 11: Triumphing in an Extrovert's Work World* ......... *45*

Chapter 4: Playing to Your Strengths: How to Shine in the Workplace ...................47

Chapter 5: Making Your Mark as a Quiet Leader ..............................................63

Chapter 6: Keeping a Team Happy and Productive ...........................................79

Chapter 7: Becoming a Confident Public Speaker ...........................................101

Chapter 8: Managing Up ..............................................................................127

Chapter 9: Moving On: Acing a Job Interview the Introvert Way .......................143

Chapter 10: Succeeding as an Entrepreneur ..................................................159

*Part 111: Finding Personal Happiness as an "Innie"* ..... *177*

Chapter 11: Being Your Personal Best .............................................................179

Chapter 12: Falling in Love and Staying in Love ...............................................199

Chapter 13: "Cheers!" Taking the Stress Out of Big Social Events.........................217

*Part 1V: Supporting Introverts* ................................... *227*

Chapter 14: Being an Understanding Friend to an Introvert ...............................229

Chapter 15: Parenting an Introverted Child .....................................................239

*Part V: The Part of Tens* ............................................ *263*

Chapter 16: Ten Notable Innies.....................................................................265

Chapter 17: Ten Tips for Making a Networking Event Work for You .....................271

Chapter 18: Ten Things an Introvert Doesn't Want to Hear................................277

Chapter 19: Ten Ways to Make a Workplace Innie-Friendly...............................283

*Index* ..................................................................... *289*

# Table of Contents

**Introduction** ............................................................. 1

    About This Book ........................................................ 1
    Foolish Assumptions .................................................. 2
    Icons Used in this Book ............................................. 2
    Beyond the Book ....................................................... 3
    Where to Go from Here ............................................. 3

**Part 1: Getting Started Understanding Introversion** ......... 5

**Chapter 1: Introverted? Good for You!** ...................... 7

    How Introverts and Extroverts Differ .......................... 8
        The biggest difference between introverts and extroverts ... 8
        Other ways introverts are different from extroverts ....... 8
    Why Being an Introvert Is Cool .................................. 9
        Introverts are great friends .................................... 10
        Introverts are creative .......................................... 10
        Introverts are natural leaders ................................ 11
        Introverts are studious ......................................... 11
    If Being an Introvert Is So Great, What's the Problem? .... 12
    Thriving in an Extroverted World .............................. 13

**Chapter 2: Are You Really an Introvert?** .................... 15

    Qualifying as an Introvert ........................................ 15
        Exploring the introvert continuum ......................... 16
        Taking the test: Do you score as an introvert? .......... 16
    Considering Shyness ............................................... 20
        Separating shyness from introversion ..................... 20
        Taking the test: Are you shy? ................................ 21
        Dealing with shyness ........................................... 23
        Comparing normal, healthy shyness to serious disorders ... 24
    Getting in Touch with Sensitivity .............................. 25
        Identifying the difference between sensitivity and introversion ... 25
        Taking the test: Are you highly sensitive? ............... 26
        Managing sensitive issues .................................... 27
        Meditating your stress away .................................. 28

**Chapter 3: What Makes You an Introvert, and Will You Always Be One?** ...................................31

Nature or Nurture: Determining What Makes You an Introvert .............31
Your genes ...........................................................................32
Your brain's wiring ...............................................................33
The influence of culture .......................................................35
The effects of upbringing ....................................................35
Acting Like an Outie: When Temporarily Playing the
Extrovert Can Work .............................................................36
Mastering the skills of the pretend extrovert .......................38
Recognizing the pros and cons of being a pretend extrovert........41
Can You (and Should You) Become a Real Extrovert? ...........................42
Can you truly change your stripes? ......................................43
Will you get more innie or outie as you age? ........................44

## Part II: Triumphing in an Extrovert's Work World ......... 45

**Chapter 4: Playing to Your Strengths: How to Shine in the Workplace** ..........................................47

The Facts of Office Life ..............................................................48
Thriving in a Noisy Workplace ...................................................49
Making a break for it ...........................................................49
Creating an innie oasis in your cubicle ................................50
Scheduling blocks of "alone" time .......................................51
Getting physical ..................................................................51
Telecommuting ....................................................................52
Establishing Yourself at Work .....................................................53
Shining a light on your successes .......................................53
Flexing your quiet power at meetings ..................................54
Standing up to workplace troublemakers ............................55
Making allies in the workplace ............................................57
Finding Your Niche: Jobs that Appeal to Introverts and Extroverts ......58
Identifying careers that are a natural fit for innies or outies ..........59
Picking the career that fits you best ....................................61

**Chapter 5: Making Your Mark as a Quiet Leader** ....................63

Assessing Your Leadership Strengths ..........................................63
Your research and decision-making skills .............................64
Your knack for encouraging independence ...........................64
Anticipating the Challenges of Leading as an Introvert .....................66
Setting the Stage for Success .....................................................67
Building your transformational skills ....................................67
Reinforcing effectively .........................................................69

Acing the art of structured brainstorming ........................70
Boosting your emotional intelligence ........................72
Mastering the art of focused conversation ........................74
Six Survival Tips for Innie Leaders ........................75
Delegating more ........................75
Outing yourself as an innie ........................76
Guarding your internal energy by scheduling wisely ........76
Wearing "power clothes" ........................77
Creating a battery-recharging retreat ........................77
Pairing up with an extrovert ........................77

**Chapter 6: Keeping a Team Happy and Productive ...............79**
Understanding the Stages of Team Development ........................79
Taking Charge in the Forming Stage ........................80
Creating a contract with your team ........................81
Establishing accountability ........................84
Projecting quiet confidence ........................86
Getting your team members acquainted ........................87
Leading in the Storming Stage ........................87
Creating a team support agreement ........................88
Analyzing team dynamics ........................90
Communicating clearly and beware the innie "cone of silence" ...92
Troubleshooting effectively ........................92
Leading in the Norming Stage ........................97
Focusing on key results ........................97
Keeping an eye on your norms and goals ........................98
Building relationships ........................98
Leading in the Performing Stage ........................99
Ending on a High Note in the Adjourning Stage ........................99

**Chapter 7: Becoming a Confident Public Speaker ...............101**
Calming Your Innie Nerves: Preparation Is the Key ........................102
Visualizing success ........................102
Identifying your pivotal points ........................104
Mastering your material ........................104
Focusing on your priorities ........................108
Getting the details down pat ........................110
Practicing your technique ........................111
Grabbing Your Audience: Six Ways to Win Them Over ........................113
Making your listeners feel comfortable and connected ........114
Grabbing their attention with stories and humor ........................116
Persuading with power ........................117
Changing things up to keep your listeners' attention ........................121
Handling hecklers with ease ........................121
Being yourself ........................123

Catching Your Breath and Briefly Taking the Spotlight Off Yourself....123
    Asking your audience for input................................................123
    Offering handouts .....................................................................124
    Scheduling battery-recharging breaks ....................................125

**Chapter 8: Managing Up** ..............................................**127**
The First Step in Managing Up: Knowing Your Manager ......................128
    Responding to your manager's style.......................................128
    Identifying your manager's goals.............................................130
    Earning your manager's trust...................................................132
The Second Step in Managing Up: Expanding Your Role .....................134
    Spotting avenues for growth ....................................................134
    Becoming a problem solver.......................................................135
    Stepping outside your comfort zone ........................................135
    Volunteering as a peer coach...................................................135
Avoiding Pitfalls When You're Managing Up .......................................140
Making a Habit of Managing Up ...........................................................141

**Chapter 9: Moving On: Acing a Job Interview the Introvert Way** ...**143**
Identifying Your Strengths and Challenges.........................................144
Prepping for an Interview......................................................................145
    Doing your detective work .......................................................145
    Creating a powerful portfolio ..................................................145
    Rehearsing with a friend who won't go easy on you..............146
    Writing down your key points...................................................148
    Making a wish list......................................................................148
Scoring in a Phone Interview ................................................................149
Performing on the Big Day .....................................................................150
    Getting ready for your interview ..............................................150
    Looking assertive at interview time .........................................150
Assessing Fit: Are the Job and the Workplace Right for You?.............152
    Asking the right questions........................................................152
    Gathering clues on a tour .........................................................153
    Weighing the pros and cons .....................................................153
Handling a "No"......................................................................................153
Responding to a "Yes" ...........................................................................154
    Negotiating salary......................................................................154
    Talking about vacations, schedules, and benefits..................155
    Setting a start date...................................................................156
Planning Your Path to Career Success .................................................156
    Setting smart goals ...................................................................156
    Gaining the job skills you need ................................................158

**Chapter 10: Succeeding as an Entrepreneur**....................**159**
Starting Off on the Right Foot ...............................................................160
    Creating your business plan.....................................................160
    Strengthening your entrepreneurial skills...............................160
    Overcoming the urge to procrastinate ....................................161

Marketing Yourself .................................................................................. 162
  Building your reputation as an expert ....................................... 162
  Teaming up with other entrepreneurs (especially outies) ......... 164
  Asking extroverts to help you make contacts............................ 164
  Integrating Internet and face-to-face marketing...................... 165
  Polishing your online presence.................................................. 165
Creating Long-Term Loyalty.................................................................. 166
  Being available ............................................................................ 166
  Influencing in the right way ...................................................... 166
  Building deeper relationships with your clients........................ 167
  Giving back to your community.................................................. 168
  Thanking your clients in small ways ......................................... 168
  Avoiding marketing approaches that irritate clients ............... 169
Coping When Prospects Don't Pan Out ............................................... 169
  Dealing with disappearing acts................................................. 170
  Handling rejection ....................................................................... 171
Building Your Dream Team .................................................................. 171
  Interviewing wisely when you're hiring staff............................ 172
  Choosing employees who can complement your skills.............. 173
  Hiring the right person to make your website sparkle ............. 174
  Considering a business coach..................................................... 174

## Part III: Finding Personal Happiness as an "Innie" ..... 177

## Chapter 11: Being Your Personal Best . . . . . . . . . . . . . . . . . . . . . . . . .179
Being Kind to Yourself ......................................................................... 179
  Using the dump-sheet-and-flower technique............................. 180
  Reframing your thoughts ............................................................ 184
  Practicing thought-stopping....................................................... 184
  Treating life as an experiment................................................... 185
  Visualizing your happy, healthy inner child and inner adult....... 185
Gaining More Control Over Your Life ................................................. 186
  Taming self-pity........................................................................... 186
  Taking charge of your problems................................................. 187
  Cultivating optimism .................................................................. 188
  Harnessing the power of gratitude ........................................... 190
Getting Your Stress Under Control ..................................................... 190
  Interpreting stressful events accurately................................... 191
  Understanding your stress threshold ....................................... 192
  Considering a personal coach or mental health professional ..... 193
Making New Friends ............................................................................ 194
  Looking for friends in all the right places................................. 194
  Setting realistic goals ................................................................ 195
  Breaking the ice.......................................................................... 196
  Keeping friendships healthy...................................................... 196

### Chapter 12: Falling in Love and Staying in Love . . . . . . . . . . . . . . . .199

Navigating the Dating Scene.................................................................199
  Spotting people you'd like to date......................................................199
  Making a first date work........................................................................201
  Addressing expectations ......................................................................201
Enjoying a Deep and Healthy Relationship .........................................202
  Grasping the basics of a good relationship.......................................202
  Recognizing how different personalities mesh in relationships ....204
Handling Innie-Outie Differences Successfully ...................................205
  Identifying each other's needs and interests ...................................206
  Figuring out how to talk with each other...........................................207
  Looking for win-win solutions .............................................................209
  Analyzing your different arguing styles ............................................210
  Being wary of perfectionism................................................................212
  Identifying the real source of your issues ........................................214
Splitting Up Sanely.................................................................................214
  When you're getting dumped ...............................................................215
  When you're doing the dumping .........................................................216

### Chapter 13: "Cheers!" Taking the Stress Out of Big Social Events. . .217

Understanding Why Social Occasions Stress You Out .......................218
Coping When You're an Innie Guest ......................................................218
  Planning ahead........................................................................................219
  Escaping the crowd ...............................................................................219
  Breaking the ice......................................................................................220
  Scheduling some unwinding time — before, during, and after....220
Coping When You're an Innie Host ........................................................221
  Taking the focus off yourself..............................................................221
  Creating innie sanctuaries ..................................................................221
  Teaming up with a cohost ....................................................................222
  Recharging your batteries ...................................................................222
  Getting those last guests to go home ...............................................223
Deciding Whether to Say Yes or No to an Invitation ..........................224
  Determining which invitations to accept...........................................224
  Declining invitations tactfully ............................................................225

## Part IV: Supporting Introverts.............................. 227

### Chapter 14: Being an Understanding Friend to an Introvert. . . . . . .229

Accepting Innies Just as They Are ........................................................230
  Recognizing that introversion is healthy..........................................230
  Recognizing the special strengths of the innies you know ..........231
Making an Innie-Outie Relationship Work............................................231
  Respecting an introvert's need for "alone" time..............................232
  Allowing an introvert to think before talking...................................232
  Minimizing multitasking demands.......................................................233

Understanding an introvert's desire to stay out of the spotlight..... 233

Grasping an introvert's approach to new activities..................... 235

Partying in Ways That Suit You Both........................................... 235

Getting the introvert's perspective on social occasions ............. 235

Being okay with early departures............................................... 236

Accepting an introvert's right to skip some events ..................... 237

**Chapter 15: Parenting an Introverted Child . . . . . . . . . . . . . . . . . . . . .239**

Identifying Introversion in a Child................................................ 239

Distinguishing Between Introversion and Medical Conditions ............ 240

Considering ADD and ADHD......................................................... 241

Ruling out autism spectrum disorders ....................................... 242

Creating an Innie-Friendly Home for Your Child ............................. 243

Appreciating your child's innie-ness......................................... 243

Steering clear of the overscheduling trap ................................. 244

Helping your innie child handle change ..................................... 245

Bridging the communication gap................................................ 247

Keeping sibling relationships positive......................................... 247

Giving your innie her own private space..................................... 248

Encouraging Friendships.............................................................. 249

Helping a younger child make friends......................................... 249

Helping an older child or teen make friends ............................... 250

Helping an introverted teen handle romance —

or the lack of it........................................................................ 252

Enhancing Your Child's Self-Image............................................... 253

Explaining introversion to your child ......................................... 253

Avoiding the urge to praise outie behaviors............................... 254

Acknowledging your child's emotions......................................... 254

Helping Your Young Innie Have a Good School Experience ................. 255

Working with your child's school and teachers ........................... 256

Considering alternatives to public schools................................. 257

Protecting Your Child from Bullies ............................................... 259

Making sure your child's school has an anti-bullying plan .......... 260

Teaching your child ways to handle bullies................................. 260

**Part V: The Part of Tens ............................................... 263**

**Chapter 16: Ten Notable Innies . . . . . . . . . . . . . . . . . . . . . . . . . . . . . .265**

Charles Darwin............................................................................ 265

Neil Armstrong............................................................................ 266

Elizabeth Barrett Browning.......................................................... 266

Johnny Depp ............................................................................... 267

Eddie Murphy.............................................................................. 267

Johnny Carson ............................................................................ 267

Jerry Seinfeld.............................................................................. 268

Tom Smith .................................................................................. 268

Calvin Coolidge ........................................................................... 269

Abraham Lincoln ......................................................................... 270

**Chapter 17: Ten Tips for Making a Networking Event Work for You . . .271**

Be Picky ................................................................................................271
Do Your Homework...............................................................................272
Set SMART Goals for Each Event .......................................................272
Think about Trout Fishing (Really!) ...................................................273
Arrive Early ..........................................................................................273
Focus on One Person at a Time...........................................................274
Grab a Plate ..........................................................................................274
Manage Your Leads ..............................................................................275
Be the One Who Reaches Out .............................................................276
Say Thanks ...........................................................................................276

**Chapter 18: Ten Things an Introvert Doesn't Want to Hear .......277**

"We were just in the neighborhood and thought we'd drop in." ..........277
"Turn to the person next to you and introduce yourself." ....................278
"Guess what — I told the waiter it's your birthday!" .............................279
"We're having so much fun; can we stay with you a few more days?" ...279
"Oh, I just thought of one more great story. . . ." ...................................280
"Surprise!" ............................................................................................280
"Give your Aunt Ruth a big hug." .........................................................281
"You're so quiet; what's wrong?" ..........................................................281
"Yay! Our class reunion is coming up!" ................................................282
"I'm so glad you returned my call; we have a lot to catch up on." ........282

**Chapter 19: Ten Ways to Make a Workplace Innie-Friendly .......283**

Let Innies Migrate to the Edges of Your Office .........................................283
Cut Down on Meetings .........................................................................284
Make Your Meetings Better..................................................................284
Provide Privacy Screens ......................................................................285
Ask about Acoustics.............................................................................285
Create Private Zones ...........................................................................286
Give a Thumbs-Up to Headphones......................................................286
Let Your Workers Telecommute Part of the Time ..............................287
Offer Innies Opportunities to Work Independently ..........................287
Rethink Your Interview Process ..........................................................288

*Index* ...................................................................**289**

# Introduction

. . . . . . . . . . . . . . . . . . . . . . . . . . . . . . . . . . . . . . . . . . . . . . . . .

**A**re you an introvert? If so, I have good news: It's your time to shine!

Yes, you're still living in a world that's geared for extroverts. From cocktail parties to crowded cubicle farms, the universe seems to be designed for social butterflies. But behind the scenes, a "quiet power" revolution is going on. Introverts are coming into their own, both personally and professionally — and in the process, they're starting to remake the world so it works for them.

*Success as an Introvert For Dummies* is part of that revolution. In these pages, you discover why introverts are so wonderful and why the world couldn't get along without them. Better yet, I show you how to use your introverted strengths to reach your full potential. And I also tell you how to redesign your professional and personal environments so they empower you to be happy, healthy, and successful.

## About This Book

*Success as an Introvert For Dummies* is all about introverts. (You guessed that, right?) But one thing I want to say right upfront is that although I'm a huge fan of introverts, I'm a huge fan of extroverts, too.

Why do I mention this? Because I'm surprised by the number of books and websites that pit introverts and extroverts against each other, as if one personality type is "right" and the other is "wrong." That's a big mistake, because the truth is that both introverts and extroverts are terrific. And they're both more successful when they're trying to understand and help each other, not when they're at war with each other.

So I've written this book to empower both *innies* (introverts) and the *outies* (extroverts) who support them. Whether you're an innie or an outie, I hope you'll feel welcomed and respected as you read these pages.

By the way, I use the terms *innie* and *outie* frequently in these pages. I've borrowed the terms from psychologist Marti Laney, who deserves a hat tip because I think she's the first person to come up with them.

# Foolish Assumptions

As I wrote this book, I tried to imagine who its readers would be and what they'd want to know. And here's what I'm assuming about you:

✔ You're an introvert — or you have an introverted partner, relative, or friend who you want to understand better.

✔ You're more interested in practical advice than in scientific theories. However, you're also a little bit curious about what makes introverts tick.

✔ You lead a busy life, so you want information you can quickly translate into action.

✔ You're interested both in personal fulfillment and in career advancement. (And here's good news: The information in this book is geared for introverts, but whether you're an introvert or an extrovert, you'll find tips that will help you both professionally and personally.)

# Icons Used in this Book

To make this book even more useful for you, I include special icons to help you spot ideas and information you may find particularly useful. Here's what each one means.

This icon draws your attention to a piece of advice that's worthy of special attention.

This icon flags important information to keep in mind as you expand your knowledge about introverts.

I use this icon to help you steer clear of mistakes that can cause problems at work or in your personal relationships.

If you're interested in the science behind introversion, keep an eye out for this icon.

# Beyond the Book

You got more than you bargained for when you bought this book. You can access bonus material online at www.dummies.com:

✔ You can download the book's Cheat Sheet at www.dummies.com/cheatsheet/successasanintrovert. It's a handy resource to keep on your computer, tablet, or smartphone.

✔ You can read interesting companion articles that supplement the book's content at www.dummies.com/extras/successasanintrovert. There's even an extra top-ten list for your amusement.

# Where to Go from Here

If you want to skip around as you read this book, feel free! You can read each chapter on its own, and I include handy cross-references. So dive into any chapter or section that interests you. Here are some suggestions:

✔ If you're fascinated by what makes you an introvert — or you're wondering whether you really *are* an introvert — you may want to jump into Chapters 2 and 3.

✔ If you're more interested in making your introverted nature work for you in the business world, Chapter 4 is a good place to start. And if you want to climb the career ladder quickly, check out Chapters 5 through 10 as well.

✔ If you want to increase your personal satisfaction, make new friends, and find true romance the introverted way, check out Chapters 11 and 12.

✔ If you're seeking tips for surviving (or even enjoying) social occasions, take a peek at Chapter 13.

✔ If you're an extrovert who wants to be supportive of an introverted friend or child, Chapter 14 or 15 is a good jumping-off point.

No matter where you start, I think you'll enjoy discovering more about the remarkable gifts and talents that introverts possess. And if you're an introvert yourself, I hope you'll come away feeling proud about how amazing you are!

# Part I

# Getting Started
# Understanding Introversion

getting started

understanding
introversion

# In this part . . .

- ✔ Understand the differences between introverts and extroverts.

- ✔ Recognize the traits of an introvert and see whether you qualify by taking a couple of informal quizzes.

- ✔ Find out how to live in an extroverted world and explore techniques for pretending to be extroverted when you need to.

- ✔ Understand that shyness and sensitivity don't necessarily mean introversion.

- ✔ Discover what makes you an innie.

# Chapter 1

# Introverted? Good for You!

## In This Chapter

▶ Spotting the differences between introverts and extroverts

▶ Valuing the talents and assets of innies

▶ Identifying the challenges of being an introvert in an extrovert's world

▶ Knowing the five basics for succeeding as an introvert

**D**oes the following sound like you? You're happier reading a book than going to a dinner party. You love your friends, but you treasure your moments alone. And you'd rather eat nails than attend a corporate team-building event.

If any of these ring a bell, I'm guessing you're an introvert. And what's more, I'm guessing that your extroverted friends don't understand you *at all*.

Oh, sure, these people love you. But they don't get why noisy team meetings and brainstorming sessions wear you out. They can't figure out why you prefer hiking or puttering in your kitchen to singing karaoke in a crowded bar. And above all, many of them think they can (and should) change you.

Well, here's the truth: If you're introverted, odds are you're hard-wired that way. You can be wildly successful in a world that's largely geared for extroverts — and, in fact, that's what this book is all about. But deep down inside, you'll always be exactly what you are: an introvert. And as I explain shortly, that's a very, very good thing!

But before I talk about why introverts totally rock, I need to explain just what an introvert is. And to talk about that, I need to talk about extroverts as well.

# How Introverts and Extroverts Differ

Did you ever wonder why your extroverted friends think and behave so differently from you? I explain why in this section, and I also look at a wide variety of behaviors that distinguish innies from outies.

## The biggest difference between introverts and extroverts

The first thing to know about introverts and extroverts is that they charge their batteries in different ways.

For extroverts, being in the middle of a crowd of people is energizing. They can talk for hours and come away feeling refreshed and invigorated. So they surround themselves with friends and family, and they can't wait to meet even more people and try even more activities. For them, walking into a room full of strangers is like taking a shot of a high-caffeine energy drink.

If you're an introvert, this behavior is hard for you to understand. It's not that you dislike people. In fact, you truly enjoy them; however, you enjoy them in small doses. You love meeting a good friend for lunch or hanging out with close family members on the weekend. But making endless small talk at a party filled with strangers doesn't energize you. In fact, it does just the opposite: It drains you, and you can't wait to recharge your batteries with a quiet walk, an evening at home with your family, or a good book.

## Other ways introverts are different from extroverts

Because introverts look inward and extroverts look outward, they respond very differently to the world around them. If you're an introvert, here are some of the ways you're unlike your extroverted friends:

- ✔ You generally think before you talk, while outies tend to say whatever comes to mind.
- ✔ You like to focus deeply on a few interests, while extroverts tend to explore a lot of activities more superficially.
- ✔ You probably like texting or e-mailing people, while extroverts enjoy phone calls or face-to-face meetings.

# What's the ratio of introverts to extroverts?

Estimates vary widely, but many experts believe that about 30 percent of people are introverts. Some estimates run as low as 25 percent, while others are as high as 50 percent.

But just for the record, not everyone is an introvert or an extrovert. Many people are *ambiverts*, which means they land in the middle of the introvert-extrovert spectrum and can fit comfortably into either world.

✔ You may find multitasking stressful, while extroverts are usually pretty good at it.

✔ You likely weigh risks more carefully than an extrovert.

✔ You have a few very deep friendships rather than a lot of casual acquaintances.

✔ You tend to dress in colors and act in ways that help you blend in rather than stand out.

People often attribute a lot of other behaviors to introverts, but some of these behaviors actually stem from two other traits: shyness and sensitivity. In Chapter 2, you can test yourself to see whether you're introverted, shy, or sensitive — or a combination of these three.

# Why Being an Introvert Is Cool

Because you're very different from your outgoing friends, it's all too easy to think that something's wrong with you. And it's even easier to feel like an oddball if you're surrounded by social butterflies who tease you about being a "loner" or a "party pooper." (I talk more about this in Chapter 14.)

But here's the most important message of this entire book: Innies and outies are equally great. The world needs both, and smart people recognize this fact. So does Mother Nature, who has good reasons for wiring innies and outies in different ways biologically (see Chapter 3).

And here's another fact: As an introvert, you're amazing! You're likely to be a loyal friend, a creative and independent thinker, and a true scholar — and you can also be a natural-born leader. The following sections give you a closer look at why you're so terrific.

## Introverts are great friends

An extrovert can walk into a room full of strangers and walk out a few hours later with five new best buddies. If you're an introvert, on the other hand, making new friends is a challenge (which I address in Chapter 11). So at first glance, it sounds like your outgoing friends have the advantage here.

But what happens when you do make a new friend? That's where you clearly shine.

First of all, you're as loyal as they come. Because you work hard for each friendship, you highly value your relationships. You're likely to be forgiving when disputes arise, and you'll probably never dump a friend for someone who's more trendy or interesting. For you, a friendship lasts for life, and any time a friend needs your help, you'll give your all.

And here's another area in which you excel as a buddy: You're a listener, not a talker. So if your friends come to you with their problems, you'll be happy to let them vent (as long as they don't go on forever!). In fact, your friends may be more likely to open up to you than they are to bare their souls to their extroverted friends. That's because they know you're sensitive, you're thoughtful, and you'll keep their secrets safely tucked away.

Want another pat on the back? As a quiet innie, you're not a drama queen or a spotlight-stealer. That guy arguing loudly with his girlfriend at a restaurant? Not you. That woman showing off her belly-dancing skills at your company's holiday party? Nope, not you either. Because you hate making a scene, your friends know you'll never embarrass them in public.

## Introverts are creative

What do movie star Michelle Pfeiffer, *Star Wars* director Steven Spielberg, and Harry Potter creator J. K. Rowling have in common? All three of them are introverts. So is Apple cofounder Steve Wozniak, who invented the first Apple computer all by himself.

Of course, there are plenty of creative extroverts, too. (For example, it's a good bet that Snoop Dogg doesn't have an introverted bone in his body!) But the credit for many of the world's greatest paintings, books, symphonies, and scientific ideas and inventions goes to introverts.

One reason that introverts are good at translating creative ideas into reality is that they're able to work hard for long periods of time. Unlike outies, they don't need to stop every couple of hours and call a friend to recharge their batteries.

Also, introverts are independent thinkers. That means they're less likely to go along with the crowd and more likely to come up with new and novel ideas. In a team-oriented world, this tendency can make life difficult for them (something I talk about in Chapter 4), but it also gives them the power to come up with brilliant ideas like the light bulb and $E = MC^2$.

And finally, while outies are frequently out partying, innies tend to spend a lot of time delving deeply into the topics that interest them. As a result, they're building the knowledge base they need to translate their creative ideas into reality. For example, one study measuring college students' knowledge about 20 wide-ranging topics found that the introverts knew more about every single topic than the extroverts did.

## Introverts are natural leaders

In Chapters 5 and 6, I talk about the introverted traits that can translate into powerful leadership skills, including a willingness to let other people shine and a talent for gathering facts and doing research. In addition to propelling many introverts to the top of the leadership chain, these traits can also help you shine as an entrepreneur — especially if you center your marketing approach around them (something I talk about in Chapter 10). And they can also help you climb the corporate ladder by using a technique called *managing up*. (You can find out all about this in Chapter 8).

## Introverts are studious

Are you an introvert who's really smart or even gifted? If so, you have a lot of company. Fifty percent of gifted children are introverts, and three-quarters of the "super-gifted" — those with IQs above 160 — are innies.

Overall, introverts and extroverts are equally smart. But even when their IQs are comparable, introverts are more likely to do well in college and to get graduate degrees.

What's the reason for this? My guess is that because introverts enjoy the life of the mind, learning and studying come more naturally to them. They're also able to focus longer and more intently on complex material.

In addition, introverts may be better at delaying gratification. (In Chapter 3, I explain why they appear to have a biological advantage here.) So when they're facing a choice like "Should I study for tomorrow's final or go to a party?" they're more likely than extroverts to make the sensible decision.

# If Being an Introvert Is So Great, What's the Problem?

If you're an introvert, I hope you're feeling pretty good about yourself by now. As you can see, you don't need to be "fixed," because you're perfectly fine as you are. In fact, a world without introverts like you would be a pretty awful place! We wouldn't have Charlotte Brontë's books, Emily Dickinson's poems, or Beethoven's music. And if extroverts didn't have introverts to put the brakes on, their meetings may simply never end — ever. (Shudder.)

But — you knew there was a *but,* didn't you? — psychologists like me talk about *goodness of fit,* which means that it's easiest to succeed in life when your personality and your environment match well. And here's where things can get a little tricky for you as an introvert.

You see, if introverts made the rules, you'd live in a perfect world. You'd have your own private office at work. Holiday parties would be short and small. Neighbors would always call before dropping by. Family events would be optional, all-day office meetings would be illegal, and team-building events would be punishable by death.

But in the real world, extroverts seem to be running the show, which means they get to call the shots. So you're likely to wind up in a jam-packed open office with a boss whose chief concern is, "Are you a team player?" Your job may require you to do things that introverts hate, such as give speeches (which I discuss in Chapter 7). Your friends and family members will be miffed if you miss a single wedding, birthday bash, or baby shower (see Chapter 13 for how to handle these). And job interviewers will expect you to answer rapid-fire questions instead of giving you the time you need to think (I discuss this in Chapter 9).

For introverted children, still more problems occur. Today's noisy classrooms focus on group activities, and bright innie kids often get lower grades just because they don't like to speak up.

And then, of course, there's the world of romance, which I discuss in Chapter 12. Dating can be a big challenge for introverts, who hate the bar scene and crave the kind of real, old-fashioned intimacy that's rare these days.

# *Thriving in an Extroverted World*

Clearly, your world isn't custom-tailored to you as an introvert. So the big question is, can you still succeed in it? Luckily, as you'll see in these pages, the answer is a resounding "yes." Of course, it'll take some work, but as an introvert who's good at reasoning, planning, and tackling big projects, you're the perfect person for the job!

As you read this book, you'll find hundreds of tips for getting ahead in a world geared for extroverts. You'll get the most from these tips if you keep these five underlying principles for introverted success in mind:

✔ **You have the right to be yourself.** Introversion is normal and healthy, just like extroversion. It would be a boring world if we all felt and behaved the same way, so don't think that you *or* your introverted friends need to change your inner selves. Instead, focus on ways in which you can complement each other.

# Chapter 2

# Are You Really an Introvert?

*In This Chapter*

▶ Recognizing introversion

▶ Identifying shyness

▶ Understanding sensitivity

Your best friend says you're an introvert. Your mom calls you sensitive, and your dad tells people you're shy.

So who's right, and who's wrong? As you find out in this chapter, the answer isn't as simple as you may think. *Shy, sensitive,* and *introverted* all mean very different things, but in many cases, they overlap.

For example, you may have many traits of an introvert, some traits of a shy person, and a few traits of a sensitive person. People don't fit easily into cookie-cutter molds, which is what makes them so interesting. The tips I offer in this book for succeeding as an introvert can also be helpful for people who are shy or sensitive. So whether you're a clear-cut innie, a shy person, or a sensitive soul, there's something in these pages just for you.

To help you find out which of these terms describes you best, this chapter takes a look at each one. First, you find out whether you're really the introvert you think you are. After that, I discuss the two kissing cousins of introversion: shyness and sensitivity. And I also talk a little about the difference between normal, healthy introversion or shyness and problems such as social anxiety disorder, avoidant personality disorder, and agoraphobia.

## Qualifying as an Introvert

In Chapter 1, I talk about what introversion is. Here, I look at the introvert-extrovert spectrum and give you a chance to test yourself and see just how introverted you really are.

## Exploring the introvert continuum

The first thing to realize about introversion is that almost nobody's a total innie. (Well, hermits come pretty darned close, but not many of them exist.) In reality, everyone falls somewhere on a continuum between extroversion and introversion, with the ambiverts I talk about in Chapter 1 landing somewhere in the middle.

Also, you may find that you're very introverted in some ways and not in others. For example, my friend Jeff is a very private guy who hates parties and loves to read for hours. But he dresses like a total outie, in bright colors and bold styles, and I can spot him instantly in a crowded restaurant.

So don't think "all or nothing" when you're analyzing your own personality. Instead, realize that every innie has a little bit of extrovert inside, and every outie has a little bit of introvert inside. There are a lot of shades of gray when it comes to introversion and extroversion.

## Taking the test: Do you score as an introvert?

You can take many "official" tests to find out whether you're an innie (I include the quotes because I'm skeptical about how valid some of these tests are).You may even run across one of these tests at work because a lot of companies use them. However, you can get a ballpark idea of whether you're introverted or extroverted just by taking the following quick little test. Although not scientific, it's pretty accurate! To get the best results, be sure to answer every question — don't skip any.

**Informal Innie/Outie Test**

As you answer these questions, think about what's generally true for you (not just how you feel right now).

1. Which would you rather do at work?

    ⊀ A. I prefer to work independently.

    B. I prefer to collaborate with a team.

2. How do you feel after spending two and a half hours at a party with your friends?

    ⊁ A. I feel exhausted.

    B. I feel energized.

3. How do you react if you're giving a short speech on a subject you know well and the audience is responding enthusiastically?

   A. I stay energized by focusing on my topic.

   B. I focus on my topic, but I also gain positive energy from my audience.

4. How do you solve personal problems?

   A. I like to think things through first and come up with a solid plan, even if it creates delays.

   B. I usually talk to other people about my problems, and I may start taking action before I have a full plan in mind.

5. At a meeting, which do you typically do?

   A. I sit quietly and talk only if I'm pretty sure I have an intelligent idea.

   B. I speak up on any topics I'm interested in

6. When you were a child in school, what did you do when you didn't understand something the teacher said?

   A. I kept my confusion to myself and tried to figure it out later on my own.

   B. I'd look confused or ask a question.

7. Which of the following best describes you?

   A. I prefer to have a few close friendships, and I've never felt much need to have a lot of people "like" me.

   B. I enjoy having a lot of friends.

8. What's your favorite way to learn new things?

   A. I enjoy going to books or the Internet and reading for hours.

   B. I enjoy going to lectures or seminars where I can be with people and learn from experts.

9. When you're working on a complex task, how long can you stay focused?

   A. I can work for hours and lose all track of time.

   B. I need frequent "people" breaks.

10. What do you do if you have a problem you can't solve?

    A. I tend to dwell on it.

    B. I'm good at letting go and moving on.

11. How do you feel about spending time at home alone or with your family?

    A. It makes me feel completely content.

    B. I love my home life, but I begin to feel restless or "down" if I don't have any outside activities.

12. Which of the following sounds most like you?

    A. I'm reserved.

    B. I'm outgoing.

13. What makes you feel energized?

    A. I feel energized after I've been mulling over some new ideas in my mind or on paper.

    B. I feel my energy pick up after I've been around people.

14. Which of these describes how you're likely to react in a noisy, high-pressure meeting?

    A. I'll probably shut down mentally and want to escape.

    B. I'll be in the middle of the fray — and I'll feel excited by all the energy in the room.

15. If a distant relative calls, what are you most likely to do?

    A. I'll let the answering machine get it, so I can find out what she wants before I talk with her.

    B. I'll grab the phone.

16. What are your main goals when you shop for clothes, shoes, or accessories?

    A. I go for something comfortable that will allow me to blend in.

    B. I go for something that will make people look at me and say, "Wow!"

17. Which of the following describes you best?

    A. I select a few interests and explore them deeply.

    B. I try a lot of new activities.

18. When you meet new people, do you share a lot of personal information with them?

    A. No. I open up to only close friends.

    B. Yes, because it's a good way to get to know them.

19. How do you feel about making small talk at parties?

    A. I hate it.

    B. I enjoy it.

20. Can you multitask easily?

    A. No. I prefer to tackle one project at a time and give it all my attention.

    B. Sure, no problem!

21. How would you react if you found out that your company was paying to send you to a two-day team-building exercise?

     ⤡ A. I'd think, "Is there any way I can get out of this?"

     B. I'd think, "Oh, boy! But only for two days?"

As you probably guessed, introverts typically answer "A" to these questions, and extroverts answer "B." So if you said "A" most of the time, it's a good bet that you're the real deal when it comes to introversion.

And because introverts like to think deeply, here's another exercise you may enjoy.

**The Innie/Outie Interests Questionnaire**

Take a few minutes to ponder each of the following questions:

1. What activities did you enjoy most as a 5-year-old? As a 10-year-old? As a teenager? Don't think about what your parents wanted you to do but rather the activities that *you* liked the best.

2. What activities did you wish you could do when you were a child?

3. What are your favorite activities now?

4. If you had the time and money to do anything you wanted to do, what would your favorite activities be?

5. If you couldn't use your TV, computer, smartphone, or other electronic devices for a week, what would you want to do with your time?

6. What were your parents, grandparents, aunts, and uncles interested in as adults (especially those who retired and could do what they pleased)? If you have siblings, what are they interested in?

As you review your answers, you'll likely spot patterns, such as the following:

✔ Most introverts show their colors early in childhood by preferring innie hobbies, such as reading or art. So if you've always loved innie pursuits, odds are you're an introvert.

✔ When asked the question, "What would you do if you were rich and could do anything?" most introverted adults immediately choose an innie interest. For example, one friend of mine instantly said, "I'd buy a farm out in the middle of nowhere and raise chickens."

✔ Most people can trace their innie or outie genes back at least a few generations by identifying what their relatives liked to do best. For instance, my introverted friend Sarah says that when her dad retired, he spent a year trying to read Norse mythology in the original language. If that's not an innie pursuit, I don't know what is!

After taking the informal innie/outie test and doing the interests questionnaire, you should have a pretty good sense of where you fall on the innie/outie scale. But there are two more traits to consider if you want to truly know yourself: shyness and sensitivity. I talk about shyness in the next section and sensitivity later in this chapter.

# Considering Shyness

Many people think that introversion and shyness are synonyms, but they're actually two different things. In fact, as you see in this section, a lot of extroverts are shy, and a lot of introverts aren't.

To find out whether you're shy yourself, you can take the quick test I offer in this section. And if you discover that you're on the shy side, you'll appreciate these tips for thriving in social situations.

## Separating shyness from introversion

What's the difference between being shy and being an introvert? Introverts are happier alone than in a crowd, but they can be perfectly confident in social situations. Shy people, on the other hand, *want* to socialize, but their anxiety gets in their way. Here are two scenarios that help show the difference:

- Jill gets an invitation to a holiday party hosted by her friend Kate. She'd rather curl up on the couch with her husband and watch *It's a Wonderful Life,* but she knows that Kate expects her to show up, so she goes. At the party, Jill meets some interesting people and has a great time chatting with them, but after two hours, she gives her hubby the "time to go home" signal.

- Alex gets an invitation to the same holiday party. He's excited, because he thinks Kate is a lot of fun and he'd like to get to know her better. But at the party, he's flustered and anxious. When Kate says, "You look handsome tonight," he blushes beet-red. Other guests try to make small talk with him, but he's totally tongue-tied. When he gets home, he mentally kicks himself for being so awkward.

Jill, the first party-goer, is an introvert; however, she's not shy. She's not a mingler by nature, but when she does go to a social event, she chats easily with people and often has fun (as long as she can escape after a few hours). If you asked Kate's other guests about her, they'd probably say, "Jill? She's really interesting. I had a great time talking with her."

## A few facts about shyness

Just about everyone feels shy once in a while. In fact, one famous study found that 80 percent of people said they were shy at some time in their lives, and more than 40 percent said they were currently shy. And by the way, these numbers point to an interesting fact about shyness: It's not as "permanent" as introversion. Kids who are shy often outgrow it, and sometimes people who aren't shy in the first place get shyer as they age.

What makes someone shy? Genes play a role, but so does culture. For example, people in Asian cultures tend to be shyer than people in some other cultures . One study found that 31 percent of people in Israel were shy, compared to 57 percent in Japan and 55 percent in Taiwan. However, cultures change, and often, younger generations are less shy than their parents or grandparents.

Now, what about Alex? He's very shy, but he's not introverted. He wants to mingle, but he gets anxious when he's meeting new people. He worries that they'll form a negative impression of him, and that makes it hard for him to speak up. If you asked Kate's guests about him, they'd probably say, "Alex is a sweet guy, but he sure is quiet, isn't he?"

Alex exhibits the classic signs of shyness. However, like most shy people, he's not always shy. At work, where he's confident and highly respected, he can chat easily with anyone. And at family gatherings, he can be the life of the party! But at a job interview, at a party, or on a date, he feels self-conscious, gets butterflies in his stomach, begins stammering, and finds his palms getting sweaty.

## *Taking the test: Are you shy?*

If you're curious about how shy you are, here's a quick test that can help you find out. This test isn't scientific, but it's fun and pretty accurate. Just answer "A" or "B" to each question.

**Informal Shyness Test**

1. Do you generally feel nervous or tongue-tied when you're socializing with people you don't know well?

    ⋆A. Yes

    B. No

2. Do you worry a lot about being rejected by other people in a social situation?

    A. Yes

    B. No

3. Do you often replay social events in your head and feel embarrassed or ashamed about something you said or did?

    A. Yes

    B. No

4. Do you often feel lonely and wish you could socialize more with other people?

    A. Yes

    B. No

5. Do you frequently let people take advantage of you because you're afraid of standing out or drawing attention to yourself?

    A. Yes

    B. No

6. Is it hard for you to talk with other people about your personal feelings?

    A. Yes

    B. No

7. If someone rejects you, do you automatically assume that it's your fault?

    A. Yes

    B. No

8. Do you spend a lot of your time thinking about ways to avoid being rejected or about ways to get people to like you?

    A. Yes

    B. No

Shy people typically answer "A" to these questions, and people who aren't shy usually answer "B." So the more "A" answers you have, the shyer you probably are.

# Dealing with shyness

If you're shy and you're happy being that way — hurray! Shyness isn't a problem if it's not interfering with your life. As the famous (and shy) humorist Garrison Keillor says, "Shyness is not a disability or disease to be 'overcome.' It is simply the way we are. And in our own quiet way, we are secretly proud of it."

And shy people should be proud! They include some of the world's most famous writers, painters, scientists, teachers, doctors, nurses, and — surprisingly — entertainers. (Barbra Streisand, an extrovert, is notoriously shy.) Shy people are often high achievers, and they're typically quite happy being who they are.

But what if you're *not* happy being shy? If you're a student, extreme shyness can hold you back by making it difficult for you to speak up in class. If you're trying to move up the career ladder, you may find it challenging to be assertive in meetings. And being shy may prevent you from making connections with the people you want to know.

If you do find that shyness is a problem, there's good news. Most experts believe that you can overcome your shyness — or at least figure out how to work around it — if you want to.

If you think your shyness is causing problems for you, here are some tricks to try:

- ✔ Before you go to a party or a meeting, visualize yourself having fun. Picture yourself making eye contact easily with other people, telling them about yourself or your ideas, and enjoying their attention.

- ✔ Overcome your fear of rejection. Here's a simple exercise that can help you do this. At a mall or grocery store, go up to at least five strangers and ask a question — for example, "What time is it?" or "Can you tell me where the toy store is?" Most likely, some people will respond in a friendly way, while a few will be brusque or even ignore you. No matter how they respond, you'll find that your anxiety decreases with practice.

- ✔ Practice deep-breathing exercises. One good one is the *five-two-five method.* Breathe in slowly to the count of five, breathing deep from your diaphragm (so the air pushes your tummy outward). Hold the breath for two counts, and then breathe out slowly for five counts. This exercise can instantly reduce your anxiety in social situations.

- ✔ Consider joining a shyness support group in your area or online. People in the same boat as you can offer help and guidance. Also, when you see that other shy people are smart, funny, and interesting when they're relaxed, it will help you realize that you're pretty cool yourself.

If you find that your shyness is truly debilitating, therapy may be a good option. I work with shy patients to help them control their anxiety in social situations, with great success.

## Comparing normal, healthy shyness to serious disorders

Shyness is a perfectly normal trait. In fact, as I mention earlier in this chapter, just about everyone is shy at one time or another. However, some people go well beyond being shy. They suffer from such conditions as social anxiety disorder or avoidant personality disorder.

### Social anxiety disorder

Some people can actually experience sheer terror at the idea of being around other people. This reaction is called *social anxiety disorder,* and it's very common. In fact, it's the third most common psychiatric disorder! So if you have this problem, don't feel like you're alone. About 15 million Americans are in the same boat as you.

Some people with social anxiety disorder have trouble only in certain situations, such as when they have to speak up in business meetings. (That's called *circumscribed* social anxiety disorder.) Other people panic in any situation that throws them in with other people, a condition called *generalized* social anxiety disorder.

Symptoms of social anxiety disorder can include a rapid heartbeat, sweaty palms, dizziness, or nausea. Some people feel faint or even experience full-blown panic attacks. It's no fun. And if you experience social anxiety, it can put a big crimp in your social life or your career.

Luckily, this problem is treatable. Although doctors often prescribe medication for it, you can also try an approach called *cognitive behavioral therapy* (CBT). CBT helps you identify the self-defeating thoughts and behaviors you're experiencing and replace them with more effective thoughts and behaviors. Group CBT is especially helpful, because you can confront your fears in a supportive group of people who know just how you feel.

### Avoidant personality disorder

A more serious issue is *avoidant personality disorder.* If you have this problem, you're highly self-conscious, terrified of rejection, and obsessed with your own perceived shortcomings. Even the mildest criticism feels like a knife through your heart, and you're plagued by low self-esteem and feelings of inadequacy. As a result, you isolate yourself from other people. You may find it difficult to keep a job because of your symptoms, and you may become afraid to be in open spaces, like shopping malls, or even to leave the house (a condition called *agoraphobia*). Doctors can treat avoidant personality disorder or agoraphobia with medications, CBT, and other approaches, such as social skills training.

### Getting help

If you think you may have social anxiety disorder or avoidant personality disorder, or you suffer from agoraphobia, reach out and get help. Treatment takes time and hard work, but it can change your life.

One thing that therapy for any of these disorders should address is the role of perfectionism. (I talk more about this in Chapter 12.) People with these problems often set unrealistic standards for themselves or for others. As a result, they're too harsh on themselves and the people around them. Often, for real progress to occur in therapy, people need to forgive themselves and their loved ones — and they need to realize that nobody's perfect. (Think how boring life would be if we all were!)

# Getting in Touch with Sensitivity

Introverted people are often defined as "sensitive souls." But just like shyness, sensitivity is a distinct trait that sometimes — but not always — goes hand-in-hand with introversion. In this section, I explain what sensitivity is, offer you a test so you can see whether you're sensitive yourself, and talk about ways to cope as a sensitive person in a not-so-sensitive world.

## Identifying the difference between sensitivity and introversion

Do bright lights, strong scents, and crowds often overwhelm you? Do you jump when a dog barks, or get hot or cold more easily than other people? Do you become anxious when a lot is going on or often feel the need to "hide away" in a darkened room?

If so, you may be more sensitive than other people. And I don't just mean physically sensitive — although your senses may be in overdrive — I also mean that you're sensitive to the nuances in conversations, to the emotional tension in a room, and to the pain and sadness of other people. The slings and arrows that less-sensitive people shrug off can wound you deeply, and as a result, you may hesitate to expose yourself to social situations.

As a result, it's easy for highly sensitive people to get labeled as introverts. But here's the difference:

- ✔ Introverts are energized by their inner world and drained by too much contact with other people, so they prefer solitude to crowds.
- ✔ Sensitive people can be completely overwhelmed by the outside world — whether they're attending a crowded party, watching a loud movie, or driving in traffic.

Also, it's not just innies who are highly sensitive. According to research, 30 percent of very sensitive people are extroverts. Overall, it's likely that 15 to 20 percent of people are highly sensitive. Sensitivity appears to be an innate trait, so if you're highly sensitive, you're born that way.

## Taking the test: Are you highly sensitive?

To get a feel for whether you're highly sensitive, here's another quick test. It isn't scientific, but it's fun and can give you some good clues to how sensitive you really are.

**Informal Sensitivity Test**

1. Do you often feel the need to "hide out" in your bedroom or another private place because you feel overwhelmed?

    A. Yes

    B. No

2. How do you react to loud noises, bright lights, and a lot of commotion?

    A. I love the excitement.

    B. I feel overwhelmed and become anxious.

3. Are you bothered by certain fabrics or by the tags on your clothes?

    A. Yes

    B. No

4. Do you react strongly to certain smells, such as perfumes?

    A. Yes

    B. No

5. How do you react to pain?

    A. I'm very sensitive to it.

    B. I think I react pretty normally.

6. Do you tend to be strongly affected by other people's moods?

   A. Yes. If someone is upset or angry, it disturbs me a lot.

   B. No. I notice people's moods, but I don't overreact to them.

7. Do you startle easily?

   A. Yes

   B. No

8. Are you very conscientious — perhaps to a fault?

   A. Yes. I fret over even small failures.

   B. No. I try to do a good job, but I don't sweat small mistakes.

9. Do you believe that you're generally more conscientious than other people?

   A. Yes, and I get annoyed when other people aren't as conscientious as me.

   B. No, I think I'm pretty average when it comes to being conscientious.

10. How do you react to changes in your life?

    A. I get very stressed, and I may have a meltdown.

    B. I get a little stressed, but I can handle change efficiently.

11. Are you better than most people at noticing subtle things in your environment?

    A. Yes

    B. No

12. Do world problems or tragedies affect you more than they seem to affect other people?

    A. Yes

    B. No

Did you have more "A" answers than "B" answers? If so, there's a good chance that you're highly sensitive.

## Managing sensitive issues

If you're sensitive, you're observant, caring, and conscientious — all very good things! A sensitive person's ability to notice nuances and details can be handy in a lot of career fields, from interior design ("that paint color is just a little off") to psychology ("she says she's fine, but her body language tells me she's worried"). You're likely to be a deeper thinker if you're highly sensitive, and you may have a strong spiritual side. What's more, you probably appreciate the beauty of art and music more deeply than your nonsensitive buddies.

On the downside, daily life can be challenging if you're highly sensitive. You're more likely than other people to fall apart when things get chaotic. You cry more easily, and you feel guilt or shame more strongly. It's more difficult for you to jump into new situations, which is why people often think you're shy or introverted. And you may react more strongly than other people to anything from caffeine to sirens to the pain of a vaccination.

For these reasons, being highly sensitive may make it more difficult for you to cope socially or on the job. If so, don't worry: You can gain more control over your physical and emotional responses to the world by doing the following:

- **Try mindful meditation and deep-breathing exercises on a daily basis.** (See the next section for more on meditation and the earlier section "Dealing with shyness" for deep-breathing techniques.)

- **If your office has a flex-time policy, try coming in earlier than most people** so you can enjoy a little peace and quiet before the rest of the gang hits the front door. Also try earplugs or headphones to help you survive in a noisy workplace.

- **If you feel stressed at home, try aromatherapy or a long bath to help calm you down.** Also, many very sensitive people find that yoga and Tai Chi are fantastic stress reducers.

- **Identify the triggers that make you melt down.** A lot of highly sensitive people react strongly to being hungry, so try to eat regular meals. If caffeine affects you powerfully, limit your coffee and tea and even go easy on the chocolate.

- **Get regular sleep.** If you have trouble falling asleep, try dotting a little lavender oil on your bedpost or experiment with a "white noise" machine that can help you ignore traffic sounds or barking dogs. (Also avoid watching loud or disturbing movies or news programs right before bedtime.)

## Meditating your stress away

One of the best ways to de-stress if you're highly sensitive is to practice mindful meditation. Sometimes the simplest solutions are the most powerful ones — and that's true for this stress-relieving technique. One recent study involving 47 highly sensitive people found that when they practiced mindful meditation for eight weeks, their stress and social anxiety dropped dramatically. In addition, their self-acceptance scores improved.

## The common denominator

Sensitivity is more common in innies than in outies, and I'm pretty sure there are more shy innies than shy outies. But that's not surprising, because introversion, shyness, and sensitivity all have something in common. All three are called *internalizing* traits; people with these traits focus their attention inward rather than outward.

So it's no surprise for a person to be introverted and shy or introverted and sensitive — or to exhibit all three traits. But remember that your outie friends can also be shy or sensitive!

Mindful meditation is easy to do, although it takes a little practice and patience to get good at it. Here's how you do it:

1. **Find a quiet and private spot, either indoors or outdoors. Sit comfortably in a chair or on the floor or ground.**

2. **Close your eyes and slowly breathe in and out through your nose. Focus on your breathing and on the movement of air into and out of your body.**

   You may want to use the five-two-five breathing method I mention in the section "Dealing with shyness," earlier in this chapter. Also, you may find it easier to focus instead on a nonsense word, called a *mantra,* or on a visual image in your mind, such as a candle, or on a physical spot, such as the back of your hand.

3. **Notice how your body feels. (Are you warm or cold? Are your arms relaxed or tense?) Also, notice what's happening around you. (Is it raining lightly outside? Can you hear birds chirping or cars going by?)**

4. **Allow your thoughts and emotions to flow naturally without judging them.**

   When you notice that you've stopped focusing on your breathing and are instead thinking about something, simply notice the thought or feeling. Then let it go and gently return to focusing on your breathing.

At first, you may find it difficult to let go of your fears and anxiety when you meditate. But the more you practice, the easier it is to get in "the zone." When you do, you'll feel calm and relaxed, and this feeling is likely to last well after you end your session.

How powerful is mindful meditation? Research shows that it can actually change your brain structure! A recent study showed that just eight weeks of meditation increased gray matter density in several regions of the brain — in particular, the left hippocampus, which is involved in learning, memory, and emotional control.

# Chapter 3

# What Makes You an Introvert, and Will You Always Be One?

• • • • • • • • • • • • • • • • • • • • • • • • • • • • • • • • • • • • • • • • • • • • • • • • •

## In This Chapter

▶ Understanding the origins of introversion

▶ Discovering why being a pretend outie is sometimes smart

▶ Exploring your choices — stay "all innie" or move to the outie side?

• • • • • • • • • • • • • • • • • • • • • • • • • • • • • • • • • • • • • • • • • • • • • • • • •

**T**his chapter is based on the old saying, "know thyself." To understand your innie nature, it helps to trace your personality all the way back to its roots. So I start this chapter by looking at all the interesting reasons you're an introvert.

After that, I talk about how you can stay true to yourself and still put on a pretend outie face every once in a while (but only if you *want* to, because it's your choice). And finally, I dive headfirst into two controversial questions: Can introverts actually become extroverts? If so, is it a good idea for them to try?

## Nature or Nurture: Determining What Makes You an Introvert

If you're an introvert, here's something to think about: Does Mother Nature decide whether you're an innie or an outie even before you're born?

As it turns out, the answer isn't all that clear-cut. Genes strongly influence whether you're an introvert or an extrovert, but there's no single "introvert gene." And although a lot of evidence shows that you're wired differently from party animals, the way you express your personality may also depend on where you live and how you're raised. In this section, I look at how all of these influences tie in together.

## *Your genes*

If you look like a movie star, thank your genes! Those genes also help determine whether you're tall, short, smart, or athletic — and even whether you have a sweet tooth. But how much credit do they get for you being an introvert?

One way scientists investigate this question is by studying twins. Identical twins share all their genes, while fraternal twins share only half — so if genes are important, researchers will see a big difference between the two groups. Scientists can also compare twins raised together to twins raised apart, giving them clues about the roles of nature and nurture.

So far, twin studies show that the effect of genes is pretty strong. But it's equally clear that no single gene makes you an innie or an outie. Instead, your personality is the end result of a lot of genes (as well as other factors we talk about later in this chapter). In particular, scientists are zeroing in on genes that affect one brain chemical: *dopamine.*

Dopamine is a chemical that helps control your brain's reward center. It gives you that "wow" feeling when your slot machine pours out coins in Las Vegas, when you kiss someone, or when you first ski down a slope without falling on your fanny. And it also tells you, "Hey, that was fun! I want to do it again and again!" So it motivates you to keep pulling that slot machine lever, smooching your sweetie, or heading back to the ski lift.

A lot of clues hint that innies and outies differ when it comes to the genes that influence dopamine levels, activity, or sensitivity. Tiny differences in certain genes may mean that your extrovert friends get a bigger dopamine rush than you do when it comes to meeting new people or trying crazy things like bungee-jumping. On the other hand, they may make you extra-sensitive to dopamine, so you get overwhelmed when your world is buzzing with new people and new activities.

In addition, researchers are looking into the roles of genes that affect other brain chemicals. (I talk about some of them in a bit.) At this point, however, scientists don't have all the answers when it comes to the effects of genetics on introversion. And plenty of controversy exists, with today's findings often contradicting yesterday's. So the jury's still out when it comes to genes and introversion, but those identical and fraternal twins do show that heredity is a big part of the story.

# *Your brain's wiring*

Look around a room, and you may be able to tell introverts and extroverts apart on the outside. That guy over there flirting happily with all the ladies? Most likely an extrovert. The guest over in the corner hanging out quietly with the dog? Probably an introvert.

Ah, but here's the big question: Can you tell innies and outies apart on the *inside* by looking at the structure or wiring of their brains? The answer, according to scientists, may be yes. For example:

- ✔ One study found that innies had higher volumes of gray and white matter in many areas of the brain. In particular, they had more gray matter volume in areas that help them control their behavior, allow them to think deeply about themselves, and make them excel at something called *social-emotional processing*. That's a fancy term for evaluating what's going on around you and reasoning about the mental states of other people (as in, "What is that guy with the lampshade on his head thinking?").

- ✔ A different study found that outies have more gray matter on the right side of the brain in a region called the *amygdala,* which helps them regulate their response to fear. They also have more gray matter in a region called the orbitofrontal cortex, and people with more volume in this area may have a lower risk of depression. Researchers say this area may help explain why outies are less prone to depression and anxiety.

- ✔ Another team of scientists found that innies have more activity in the brain regions they use when solving problems, making plans, and recalling events. Outies, however, have more activity in areas involved in organizing and interpreting messages from the senses.

- ✔ Studies hint that the brains of innies and outies react very differently to faces. In one study, scientists studied people's brainwaves as they looked at expected or "oddball" (unexpected) faces or flowers. Outies had a stronger response to the oddball faces than to the oddball flowers, but innies didn't. The researchers say that this may be evidence that introverts can "take or leave" people — something that won't surprise you if you're an innie who's trying to decide whether to go to a party tonight or stay home and read a good book, like this one!

And here's an interesting tidbit: Innie and outie brains don't just respond differently to social cues; they even respond differently to touch. In one study, researchers measured the brainwaves of innies and outies while delivering quick pressure to their index or pinkie fingers. The innies had stronger responses than outies in a brain region that processes information related to touch.

# Do you have trouble recognizing faces?

It's such an embarrassing moment! There you are, wandering down a grocery store aisle, when someone comes up to you and says, "Hi! It's wonderful to see you again." And you don't have any clue who that person is.

This happens to everyone, but there's evidence that it happens more often to introverts. Recently, researchers compared the face recognition skills of innies and outies. They found that compared to innies, outies who scored high in gregariousness correctly recognized more faces. When it came to recognizing different flowers, however, both groups did equally well.

My guess is that as a group, innies may be a little bit "face blind" compared to their outie friends. There's also evidence linking shyness and social anxiety — which some introverts experience (see Chapter 2) — to difficulty in identifying faces. (Another group of people who often have trouble recognizing faces are people with autism.)

Of course, this discussion brings up a which-came-first question — the chicken or the egg? Are outies wired from birth to be better than innies at recognizing faces? Or do they just get more practice at identifying faces because they love being around people? It's a question scientists will have to sort out someday. But in the meantime, here are some tips that can help you out if you have trouble remembering faces.

- When you meet a new person, search for one or two features that stand out and aren't likely to change over time — for instance, a mole, a dimpled chin, or height.

- Use *mnemonic devices,* which are clever tricks to help you remember things. These can include rhymes, mental pictures, acronyms, or abbreviations. For example, if you meet a man named Jeff who has a large nose and works in a bakery, try remembering him as "big-nose Jeff, the pastry chef." Or create a mental picture of him with a gigantic nose and a huge chef's hat on his head. The sillier your mnemonic devices are, the better they'll stick in your head.

- Pay close attention to how people speak. Often, people who aren't good at remembering faces are much better at identifying voices.

- If you're meeting people at a party or business meeting, find an excuse to take photos. When you get home, scribble the people's names on the photos to help you remember them.

And innies appear to be more sensitive to taste as well. If you put lemon juice on the tongues of introverts and extroverts, the innies will salivate more.

What does this mean? It suggests that innies — much like the highly sensitive people I talk about in Chapter 2 — may be extra-responsive to the stimulation they get from the world around them. And that could explain why they need more down time than those extroverts who bounce quickly from one sensory thrill to the next.

## The influence of culture

So far, the evidence shows that biology plays a big role in dictating personality. But hold on — there's more to this story! That's because the cultures people live in can influence how successful they are as innies or outies.

For example, one study found that kids in Canada rated shy or sensitive kids more negatively than other kids. Kids in China, on the other hand, rated them more positively. (As I mention in Chapter 2, shyness and sensitivity often overlap with introversion.)

In another study, researchers asked students to read stories describing shy or socially withdrawn people. In addition, they asked them to read stories describing outgoing and confident people. Then they asked the students to predict how well each person would do socially and professionally.

The result? Students in Western countries were far more likely than people in East Asian countries to predict that shyness or social withdrawal would negatively affect people's quality of life. In addition, this study found that Westerners who described themselves as shy or withdrawn felt that this negatively affected their lives more than shy or withdrawn people in East Asian countries did.

As these studies show, thriving can be more of a challenge in societies that see social butterflies as normal and view introverted or shy people as odd. (And that's one reason I explore the benefits of occasionally playing the part of an outie later in this chapter.)

## The effects of upbringing

Those twin studies I talk about earlier make it clear that genes are major players when it comes to making you an innie. In contrast, it looks like your family life doesn't really get all that much credit or blame when it comes to forming your personality. But as it turns out, your family experiences can still have a big effect on your life. Why? Because they may help predict how happy you'll be as an introvert.

For example, if your mom or dad is a die-hard extrovert and you aren't, it may make it more difficult for you to communicate with your parent and vice versa. (I talk more about this in Chapter 15.) And if you're an innie, moving frequently when you're a kid can raise your risk of being unhappy as an adult. That makes sense, because it can be difficult for innies to constantly adjust to new situations and people.

Studies also show that genes and upbringing can interact. One gene that's attracting attention is called 5-HTTLPR. This gene regulates levels of a brain chemical called *serotonin*. The "short" variant of this gene appears to be linked to both introversion and a higher risk for depression. However, studies hint that people with the short variant aren't at much higher risk for depression unless they experience some trauma, like bullying or abuse. So supportive families who protect their wee innies from traumas (as much as possible) and give them the tools to stick up for themselves when bullies strike may help them become happy adults.

None of this means that you're doomed to be miserable as an innie if you moved a lot as a child or that you're destined to be depressed if your family was difficult. In fact, most innies turn out perfectly fine even if they moved a lot or grew up in stressful homes. However, it does show that family matters.

And needless to say, you'll probably be happier and more confident as an innie adult if your parents respect your gifts and understand your needs (I talk more about this in Chapter 15). So even if Mom and Dad don't have a whole lot to do with your innie nature, they're very important when it comes to how you express it.

# Acting Like an Outie: When Temporarily Playing the Extrovert Can Work

Are you puzzled by the heading of this section? If so, I'm not surprised! Throughout this book, I stress that it's fantastic to be an introvert; in this chapter, I explain that your genes and your brain are wired for innie-ness. So why shake things up, when you're perfectly fine as you are?

Well, as it turns out, there's a good reason — at least sometimes. Being an innie works beautifully in most situations, but occasionally it can put you at a disadvantage. At these times, temporarily acting like an extrovert may save the day.

Why camouflage your innie-ness at times? Because in some situations, such as the following, outies often win out over innies:

✔ Attracting and retaining customers as an entrepreneur

✔ Job interviews

✔ Marketing

✔ Meetings

✔ Networking events

✔ Parties

▶ Performance reviews

▶ Public speaking

Behaving like an outie in these temporary situations can be useful for two reasons. First, it can help you break the ice more quickly — and that's a big plus in a short encounter like a job interview. Second, it can make you appear friendlier, more approachable, and more confident. (And yes, I know you're all those things, but as an innie, you may not always show those sides of your personality quickly!)

If you add some pretend-extrovert skills to your own repertoire, you can pop on your outie mask whenever you need it — maybe once a month or once a year — to help you score a dream job, get a promotion, or make a key networking connection. The rest of the time, you can tuck it away and be your happy innie self. In the following sections, I tell you how to pull off this temporary outie act, and I also look at the possible emotional benefits and costs of pretending to be an extrovert.

## My story: The fainting psychologist

When I got my master's degree, I couldn't wait to begin my new career as a psychologist. And I quickly learned that the biggest secret to establishing a successful business was to get in front of people.

So I started giving talks; however, it wasn't easy for an innie like me. No matter how large or small the crowd was, I always felt the same way — absolutely terrified! In fact, at two of my presentations, I fainted on stage.

I didn't think things could get worse, but they did. After doing a pre-recorded show for a radio station for a while, I agreed to do a live call-in show on what was then the biggest AM radio show in Philadelphia. I made it through the initial questions okay, but we didn't have headphones and I had to focus very hard to understand the callers. As a result, I started to panic. And before long — bam. There I was, out cold on the floor.

The host, Wally Kennedy, smoothly covered for me and then put on a pre-recorded show. When I came to, I expected him to be angry, but instead, he said one of the kindest things I've ever heard: "Joan, you're too good to have this happen." He repeated, "You're too good to have this happen." And then he said, "so I'm going to keep having you on the show."

He kept that promise, and I never fainted on him again. And I'd like to say that I got over my stage fright quickly, but that's not the case. In reality, it took me 10 or 15 years of practice to get comfortable talking in front of people.

So when I talk about cultivating some outie skills if they can be useful to you, I'm speaking from experience. I know that it's difficult, and that it takes real motivation. But as I tell my audiences now, "If I can do it, anybody can!" Just remember that you don't need to do this if there's no payoff in it for you. It's entirely your choice.

It's important to realize that there's no reason to develop your extrovert muscles if you don't feel the need for them. For many innies, they're completely unnecessary. So listen to your heart, and do what feels right for you.

## Mastering the skills of the pretend extrovert

Picturing yourself as the life of the party or as a smooth talker in a job interview may be a bit strange. But if you practice a few pretend-outie skills diligently, you may surprise yourself! Again, however, I want to stress that it's hard work to get these skills down pat, so decide whether there's any benefit in it for you. If your answer is yes, here are the key skills to practice.

### Honing your body language

People send messages not only with their words but also with their actions — posture, smiles and frowns, and even the way they move. So to act the part of an extrovert, you need to mimic the body language of outies.

The best way to master the moves of outies is to observe them in their native habitat. So the next time you're in a meeting or at a party, keep an eye on the outgoing people. Notice these details in particular:

- **How they stand:** Typically, you'll see outies standing up tall, with their arms away from their bodies — not crossed over their chests. When they're talking or listening, they tend to lean into the conversation. Sometimes they're so excited or eager that they bounce a little on their feet. They also like to tilt their heads as they're listening.

- **How close they get to other people:** As a rule, innies like to keep a little physical distance, while outies may plop down right next to someone on a couch or in a meeting room. (Of course, this depends on their relationship to the person — so try this with friends, not with your boss!)

- **How often they make eye contact:** Extroverts tend to gaze longer at someone who's speaking, while introverts often look away fairly quickly.

- **How they gesture:** Extroverts typically use broad gestures and gesture toward other people, while innies often gesture toward themselves. Outies also tend to gesture more often and more smoothly.

- **How they smile:** When extroverts smile, they don't just move the corners of their mouths up. They also crinkle their eyes.

After you have a good feel for extroverted body language, practice it yourself at home. One fun way is to watch extroverts in movies or TV shows and imitate them. (For example, take a look at Oprah Winfrey — a confirmed outie.)

Mastering the moves of outies won't come easy to you at first. But as one innie commented in an online discussion group, "It's like sit-ups — do it every day and it gets easier."

# The power of a crinkle

A real estate firm once asked me to work on its realtors' communication skills. Early on in my conversations with the team, I learned an interesting thing about one realtor named Wendy. Everyone said she was outstanding at her job, but she never smiled.

I didn't tell Wendy what her colleagues said about her. Instead, I invited her and several of the other realtors to meet with me one at a time to talk privately about their goals and their work.

After a while, I turned to Wendy and said, "You know, you're really very good at what you do." She nodded, and then I asked, "Are you open to a little feedback?" She bristled a little, but she said yes. So I said, "We've been talking for 45 minutes, and I haven't seen you smile once."

Wendy was shocked. She immediately retorted, "What do you mean? Of course I smile. Everyone smiles."

I pulled a hand mirror out of my purse (making up some excuse to explain why I had it) and asked Wendy to look in the mirror and smile. She made a little grimace, but her face barely moved. And she said, "Holy cow. I'm not smiling. I never knew this." And then — because she was very bright and results-oriented — she said, "How do I smile?"

Wendy and I went into the restroom and practiced smiling side-by-side. (Fortunately, no one else came in to see what we were doing.) After she had a big smile down pat (including that all-important eye crinkle), she marched out of the restroom and announced to the other realtors, "I've just taken smiling lessons!" Everyone (including Wendy) burst out laughing, and the other realtors — most of whom were more extroverted than she was — congratulated her heartily.

Wendy's story illustrates why some innies benefit from cultivating a few outie skills. As a realtor, Wendy needed to win over clients quickly — and in an extroverted world, that's easier to do with a great big smile.

## Beefing up your conversational muscles

Introverts have loads of talents, but small talk isn't always one of them. So if you want to come across as an extrovert in conversations, you'll need to work at it. The best way to begin is by practicing conversation starters. Here are some of the best ways to get the conversational ball rolling:

- ✔ **Ask people for advice.** For example, if you hear someone talking about gardening, wander over and say, "I'm interested in starting a garden myself, but I don't know what grows well around here. Do you have any good tips?"

- ✔ **Get people to tell stories about themselves.** For example:
  - If you're talking with someone who loves to travel, ask, "What's the best place you ever visited? The worst?"
  - If you're speaking with a teacher, say something like, "My sister's a teacher, and she has some really crazy days. Do things ever get really wild in your classroom?"

- Are you schmoozing with a plumber? Ask what's the craziest thing he or she ever pulled out of a drain. (Of course, you may not want to hear the answer!)

✔ **Lead with a compliment.** To get more mileage, combine your compliment with a question that will keep the other person talking. For example, say, "That's a gorgeous necklace. Where did you get it?"

✔ **Focus on asking open-ended questions rather than questions that people can answer in a few words.** For example, imagine that you're talking with a realtor. Don't ask, "What area of town has the best housing prices right now?" Instead, ask questions like "What do you think of today's housing market?"

After you get a conversation started, don't just stand there quietly and listen. Remember, you're pretending to be an outie! So lean into the conversation, and smile widely or laugh if the other person makes a joke. And ask a lot of follow-up questions — as many as you can stand. (The more introverted you are, the harder you may find this, so be patient with yourself as you develop this skill.) Follow-up questions are crucial because they keep the conversation moving along and tell the other person that you're really interested.

One of the best ways to think of questions to ask people is to picture their experiences in your own mind. For example, if the world traveler tells you that she loved Spain, visualize yourself as a tourist in Madrid or Barcelona. What would you do there? What would you eat? Where would you stay? This can help you conjure up all sorts of questions to ask her — about the restaurants, the hotels, the weather, the airports, and so on. She'll wind up thinking you're a sparkling conversationalist, when in reality, she's the one doing all the talking.

### Role-playing with a friend

You may be rolling your eyes at the idea of role-playing. It doesn't sound like an innie thing at all, does it? And that's what I thought, too, when I first started working with business teams. But I quickly discovered that the introverts on those teams were brilliant at role-playing and found it very helpful.

If you decide to try it yourself, the key is to team up with someone you're very comfortable with to start. Also, decide exactly what you want to role-play. For example, you may role-play meeting a stranger at a party or giving a status report at a meeting.

As you're role-playing, try out each of the conversational and body language skills I talk about in the sections "Honing your body language" and "Beefing up your conversational muscles," earlier in this chapter. It'll be easier if you practice them one at a time before you try combining them. The more you practice these skills, the more easily they'll come to you in real-life situations.

TECHNICAL STUFF

## Weird science: Can oxytocin make you an instant outie?

Imagine a magic potion that turns you into an extrovert — at least long enough to get you through a public speech or a holiday party. It sounds like science fiction, doesn't it? But scientists are actually testing a nasal spray that may do just that.

Recently, researchers gave 100 men and women either a placebo or *oxytocin,* a hormone released by the body during childbirth and during social bonding. Ninety minutes later, they asked the people to rate how they felt. The researchers found that people who got oxytocin felt more extroverted and open than those who received the placebo.

But nothing is ever simple! Another experiment found that sniffing oxytocin made people more prone to envy and *schadenfreude* (that gloating feeling people sometimes experience when someone else is suffering). So it looks like becoming an "instant outie" may have some unintended consequences.

### Starting small

If you decide to take up running, it's smart to start off with a quarter-mile and work your way up to a marathon. Similarly, you want to give yourself time to build your pretend-outie muscles before you try them out in a challenging, high-profile setting.

So pick some easy venues at first. Try striking up conversations with grocery store clerks, neighbors, or your kids' teachers. As you get more comfortable playing the outie, pick bigger stages to perform on.

## Recognizing the pros and cons of being a pretend extrovert

Putting on an extroverted act now and then may help you in your career or in social situations. But is it good for your own emotional health? According to research, it depends.

One recent study, which involved college students, found that acting extroverted made participants — both innies and outies — feel better. In fact, the researchers concluded that every single person in their study felt happier when acting in extroverted ways. However, another study came to a somewhat different conclusion. It suggested that although pasting a big extroverted smile on your face could make you happier, there's also a chance that it can take a toll on your well-being.

In this study, researchers asked bus drivers to smile at passengers even if the drivers didn't feel like it. They found that the drivers who offered forced smiles felt emotionally wrung out by the end of the day and tended to withdraw from other people. The effect was even stronger for women than for men. (But there's good news, too. The same researchers found that if the bus drivers produced real smiles, by recalling fun memories or thinking about their lives in a happier way, they improved their mood.)

What's the take-home message? Acting like an extrovert at times may make you feel happier, but there's also a chance it will make you feel worse. So give it a try, and pay attention to the results. Then decide what works best for *you*.

# Can You (and Should You) Become a Real Extrovert?

It's one thing to talk about playing the role of outie temporarily when it suits your purposes. But now, I want to focus on a very different idea: the idea that an innie can (and perhaps should) become an extrovert for real.

This is a thorny topic to say the least! On one side, you have the "be true to yourself" crowd. They feel strongly that trying to turn innies into outies is similar to trying to turn left-handers into right-handers. Instead, they argue, innies should work to make the world less prejudiced against innies and more appreciative of introverts' special talents.

On the other hand, you have the "fake it 'til you make it" gang. They say that in a world geared toward extroverts, it may make sense to change yourself if you're having trouble fitting in. Their idea is that if you start out faking extroversion and keep practicing, pretty soon you may discover that you're an outie for real — and maybe you'll like it. And they point to scientific studies showing that faking it can eventually make a new behavior feel like second nature.

I'm not taking sides on this issue because there's no right or wrong. Every innie is different, and that means that what's right for one person may not be right at all for you.

So instead, I look at what the science says, and what I've found from my own experience and that of my friends and clients. And after that, I discuss why you may naturally become more of an innie or an outie — without even trying — as you age.

# *Can you truly change your stripes?*

One thing scientists are discovering is that the adult brain is much more "plastic" than they once thought. This means that new experiences can actually change the structure of people's brains as well as how they feel and behave.

But does this apply to personality as well? It's a good question. Ask psychologists if changing your core personality is possible, and you'll probably get a variety of answers. Typically, these answers center around one question: Is introversion an ingrained trait or a changeable state?

Here are two of the most popular theories:

- ✔ **The rubber band theory:** Stretch a rubber band, and you can make it longer and longer, but let go, and it snaps right back. According to many psychologists, the same is true for innies who try to become outies. They can stretch their personalities to some degree, but they'll always "snap back" to their innate innie-ness. In other words, introversion is a trait — not a state.

- ✔ **The situational theory:** According to this theory, you can change your personality — at least to some degree — if you're really motivated. In other words, introverts may be able to put their innie tendencies "on hold" to accomplish a goal that's very important to them. According to this theory, introversion is a state — not a trait.

Based on my own personal and professional experience, innies can move toward the extrovert side, but only if they're pulled, not pushed. What I mean is that to change from an innie to an outie, you need to have a strong reason to do it. Other people can't push you to change, but you may be able to do it yourself — to a small or large degree — if there's some reward in it for you.

For example, I was very introverted as a child. But in my early teens, I developed a love of the performing arts — an area in which outie behaviors can help a lot. Also, as I mention earlier in this chapter, I needed to hone my outie skills to become a successful psychologist. That was my "pull."

It wasn't easy at all at first (and, in fact, many times I wanted to quit). But the more I practiced, the easier it got. These days, I'm more of an *ambivert* — one of those people who's pretty much in the middle of the innie-outie scale — although I still get strong tugs from my introvert side.

On the other hand, I know plenty of people like my innie friend Sarah. Her passion is writing, and she spends her days happily tucked away in a home office with a mug of hot tea and only a dog to keep her company. She doesn't have any desire whatsoever to become more of an outie, because her innie nature meshes perfectly with her personal and professional goals.

Our stories show that whether you want to become more of an outie or not, it has to be your decision. Don't listen to the people who say, "You need to come out of your shell" or "Why can't you be more outgoing like your brother?" If being an innie works beautifully for you, don't change a thing! But if you feel a pull to be more extroverted, that's fine as well.

Here are a couple of important steps to take if you're deciding whether you want to be more outie:

1. **Understand yourself.**

   Reading this book will help you realize whether you're truly an introvert.

2. **Completely accept yourself as you are.**

   After you do that, you can decide whether you want to try edging toward the outie side.

When people take these two steps first — understanding themselves, and completely accepting themselves — many realize that they're innies through-and-through, and they're happy to be that way. Some, on the other hand, decide that they're innies who want to cultivate a more outie personality. And happily, both groups do just fine.

 If you decide you want to become more of an outie, pay attention to your feelings and respect them. If you find that it's surprisingly easy to adopt extroverted behaviors, then you're probably a bit of an ambivert (see Chapter 1) and can be happy either as an innie or as an outie. But if you feel drained and exhausted by the pressure of acting outie, it makes more sense to embrace your inner innie and stop trying to be something you aren't.

## Will you get more innie or outie as you age?

A lot of things change as people get older — including waistlines and hairlines! And one thing that may evolve a bit as you age is your personality.

A few years ago, scientists studied adults between the ages of 21 and 60. When they focused on innie and outie behavior, they found that as people got older, women became a little less extroverted, but men didn't. A different group of scientists looked at how people changed over a 15-year period. This team found that both men and women tended to become less extroverted from their 30s on.

This result shows that people aren't just products of their genes and biology. Clearly, they're also molded by their everyday experiences and by the people around them.

So don't be surprised if you're more innie at some stages of your life than at others. Just go with the flow, and remember that either way, you're just fine!

# Part II

# Triumphing in an Extrovert's Work World

## *Five Ways to Be Effective in Meetings*

✔ Keep in mind that as an introvert, you're a better listener than talker. Be confident in your ideas even if you're not willing to blurt them out haphazardly. It's perfectly okay to think through what you want to say.

✔ Ask whether you can get an agenda ahead of time (or at least get a heads-up about what the meeting will cover). Then think quietly about the meeting topics and write down your ideas. Doing so will give you a good head start. And because you're probably a deeper thinker than many of the outies in your office, you may come up with interesting angles that they won't consider.

✔ When it's time to discuss a new topic in a meeting, go first. This instinct doesn't come naturally to innies, but you'll likely find that it's easier to start a discussion than it is to jump into the middle of one.

✔ Memorize a few key phrases that you can use if you experience an innie brain freeze. If someone asks you a question in a meeting and your mind goes blank, you can say something like "That's an interesting question. Can I do a little research and get back to you?" or "I have some thoughts on that, but I'd like to think them through a bit more. Can we get together later and talk about it?"

✔ If you simply can't get a word in edgewise in an outie-dominated meeting, make your points later in an e-mail.

For additional workplace advice for introverts, visit www.dummies.com/extras/successasanintrovert.

# In this part . . .

- ✔ Discover what you need to do to thrive in a noisy, distraction-filled workplace.

- ✔ Make use of your innie strengths in the office and when finding your career niche.

- ✔ Master leadership skills, team development, and public speaking.

- ✔ Find out how to shine the light on your successes within your current job or as you interview for a new one.

- ✔ Build your success as an entrepreneur by playing on your innie strengths and using your outie connections to your advantage.

# Chapter 4

# Playing to Your Strengths: How to Shine in the Workplace

## In This Chapter

▶ Navigating the hazards of the extroverted workplace

▶ Making your office space suit your personality

▶ Asserting yourself confidently at work

▶ Finding the career that works best for you, innie or not

*1*n my job, I meet thousands of introverts with successful careers, from Wall Street wizards, to FBI agents, to Broadway actors. What do these innies have in common? They're all talented, enthusiastic people who love their jobs. And they've all become fabulously successful by learning to thrive in an outie work world.

That world, as you probably know, isn't always easy for innies to navigate. In this chapter, I talk a little about the extra challenges you face when you're working in an extroverted workplace.

But never fear, because you can make your outie office innie-friendly! In this chapter, I share the tricks that my introverted clients use to succeed in the workplace. First, I look at ways to dampen your stress and keep your innie batteries charged in a noisy office. After that, I tell you how to stand out in the crowd and get the recognition you richly deserve. And finally, I delve into a different topic and look at whether some jobs are better than others for innies.

# The Facts of Office Life

A famous line from an advertisement for a sci-fi movie goes, "In space, no one can hear you scream." But here's an even scarier line for today's open offices: "In the office, everyone can hear you talk, sneeze, cough, or laugh — or scream."

For innies, the lack of privacy in cubicle farms can be a real headache. When Jane is arguing loudly with a coworker and Bob is telling everyone about his enlarged prostate, focusing on rows of figures or lines of code can be difficult. And it's annoying to know that Jane, Bob, and everyone else around you can hear every noise *you* make as well.

But that's not the only challenge you face in an outie-friendly office. Here are some others:

- **The emphasis on teamwork:** Innies are independent thinkers who like to work alone. However, today's office revolves around teams. If you work in a typical office, you probably bounce from conference calls to team meetings all day long, with little time to ponder your projects on your own.

   And other dangers of teamwork exist if you're an innie. Because you're likely to be conscientious, you may find yourself taking up the slack for underachieving coworkers (and getting burned out in the process). Or you may get steamrolled by aggressive team members who mistake your quiet nature for a lack of confidence.

- **The multitasking demands:** If you're like most innies, you probably like to focus deeply on a single project. Try to juggle six or seven deadlines, and you may blow a fuse. But in today's highly competitive world, most bosses expect you to multitask with ease. And adding to the stress, you're likely to be dealing with nearly impossible deadlines.

- **The need to promote yourself:** As an introvert, you're not too big on bragging about yourself. But if you don't speak up, you may be overlooked in a sea of noisy extroverts.

- **The constant interruptions:** If you work in a typical office, you're likely to get distracted at least once or twice an hour by someone collecting for a birthday party, popping in to ask a question about the new software, or seeking your advice on a project. As a result, your own tasks may get derailed.

All these challenges can make it difficult to get ahead as a workplace innie, and they can also leave you feeling frazzled at the end of the day. Fortunately, you can make your workplace healthier, happier, and more in tune with your innie nature — and that's what I talk about in the rest of this chapter.

## How healthy is your cube farm?

Guess what: If you hate open-plan offices, science is on your side. As it turns out, these designs appear to be bad for people — both innies and outies alike. A few years ago, researchers took a close look at open offices and found that they lower productivity, raise workers' stress levels, cause turnover rates to rise, increase the spread of germs, and even raise people's blood pressure. In addition, the scientists said that open offices make people feel insecure and can lead to more accidents and conflicts.

Unfortunately, because they're far cheaper for employers, cubicles are probably here to stay — whether you like them or not. But the researchers who did this study suggest that smart employers who want a healthier, more productive workforce may consider bringing back the old-fashioned office.

# Thriving in a Noisy Workplace

The bustle of an open office can drain your batteries, leaving you tense, tired, and with a headache. When you feel that way, it's time to escape — at least for a few minutes. Of course, that's easier said than done when you're trapped in a cubicle jungle. But if you're clever, you can always find a way to take a time-out. The following sections provide a few good ideas for workplace time-outs.

## Making a break for it

When you feel your stress levels climbing, a quick change of scenery can do you a world of good. Two or three times a day, get out of the office and take a quick walk — or if you're in a building with several floors, think of an excuse to dash upstairs or downstairs.

When you take your walks, wear headphones so you have an excuse to avoid talking with passers-by. (And if any outies reading this book think that hiding behind headphones is rude, it's not! It's a survival tactic for overwhelmed innies trying to restore their inner balance.)

Here are a couple of other ways to take a micro-vacation from your noisy coworkers:

- ✓ Leave the building on your lunch break. If a park is nearby, pack a lunch and soak up a little sunshine while you eat. If not, find a cozy restaurant or read a book while you eat in your car.

- ✓ Offer to fetch bagels for a meeting, pick up documents from another firm, or run other errands. Doing these tasks will get you out of the building for at least a few minutes. If you're lucky, you can volunteer for daily or weekly errands that provide you with regular breaks.

## Creating an innie oasis in your cubicle

Years ago, a friend of mine worked in an office where everyone had cubicles except the people in the IT department. Somehow, the IT gang wangled permission to hole up in a large office at one corner of the building. They called it the cave, and they didn't allow anyone in — literally! If you had a problem, you could call them or e-mail them, but you couldn't set foot in their office.

If you're an innie, this setup probably sounds like heaven. However, unless you're very lucky, you're more likely to have a cubicle than your own private cave. The good news is that even in a high-density cubicle farm, you can create an illusion of privacy.

Here are some of the best ways to put a little distance between you and your office mates:

- ✓ Get noise-canceling headphones, listen to music, or use earplugs to help drown out the office noise. Check with your boss first to make sure your company doesn't have a policy forbidding headphones or earplugs.

- ✓ Consider using a white noise machine. You can easily find a small model that won't take up too much space in your cubicle.

- ✓ Create fake "walls." Stack books up on the side of your desk that faces your cubicle door, or put some big pictures there.

- ✓ Get a privacy screen for your cubicle. (Be sure to get permission first.) If your company won't provide one, you can buy one online. It'll probably cost you more than $100, but you may find that it's well worth the investment.

- ✓ Add some greenery. Houseplants can block other people's view of you, and they'll also buffer the noise a little.

- ✓ If you can't see your cubicle entryway from where you sit, position a small mirror on your desk so you can see people coming.

- ✓ When you need uninterrupted thinking time, hang a little sign outside your cubicle that says something like "No interruptions until 2:00, please. Thanks!"

When you're planning your office design, don't make things too cozy for the people who pop in to visit. A candy dish on your desk sends the message, "Hi. I'm so glad to see you." A pile of books on your visitor's chair, on the other hand, says, "I'd rather be alone." So send smart messages when you're doing your interior decorating.

## Scheduling blocks of "alone" time

Do you have some flexibility in your day? If so, arrange your schedule so you have a two- or three-hour block of time in which you can focus quietly on your biggest projects. If clients or coworkers want to schedule face time with you during this period, ask whether they're okay with a different time. And let your manager know that you want to keep this time as free from interruptions as possible.

Also, try spending the first 30 minutes of the day handling all the little messy details that can distract you from those big projects. Often, these hours are golden because the office extroverts are so busy catching up with each other that they'll leave you alone! So answer e-mails, make phone calls, and clear tiny tasks off your to-do list. Doing so will free up the brain cells you need to focus on the big stuff.

## Getting physical

If you're an introvert surrounded by a crowd of noisy coworkers, your stress level can climb until you feel like you're ready to snap. One of the quickest ways to relieve that stress, at least for a little while, is to burn off your stress hormones with a little quick exercise.

But how about those times when you can't escape? Even if you're stuck in your cubicle, you can do some stress-busting exercises. Here are some simple activities that are easy to do in your cube without attracting attention:

- ✔ Sitting at your desk, lift one foot an inch or so off the floor. Now stretch out your leg until it's straight in front of you. Keep it there for a few seconds, and then bend your knee while keeping your foot off the floor for a few more seconds. Put your foot back on the floor, and repeat with the other leg.

- ✔ If your chair has sturdy arms, put your hands on the chair arms and lift your fanny an inch or so off the chair seat. Hold for a few seconds, and then sit back into the chair.

- ✔ Stretch both arms over your head and alternate raising one hand higher than the other.

## Juggling kids and a home office

My friend is a magazine photographer who travels around the world on assignments. When she returns home, she has to spend hours sorting through her photos and writing proposals for new projects. When her children were young, it was hard for them to understand that mommy needed quiet time to work. So she and her husband told them, "When mommy is in the office, think of her as invisible. Even if you can see her, she's *invisible.*"

Of course, they also explained that the children could always come to mommy in a true emergency. Needless to say, it took a little time for the kids to understand that battles over toys or cookies weren't emergencies, but before long, my friend was able to work for long stretches while she was happily "invisible" in her office.

## *Telecommuting*

More and more companies are open to the idea of having employees work from home at least one or two days a week. If yours is one of them, consider taking advantage of this option. It's a great way to recharge after days in the office.

If you do telecommute, be sure to stay in frequent contact with your colleagues back in the office. E-mail often, keep everyone up-to-date on your status, and speak up frequently on conference calls. And even if your manager doesn't require daily progress updates, send them on the days you work from home. You don't want to be "out of sight, out of mind."

Also, follow these guidelines for successful telecommuting:

- ✓ Answer e-mails, texts, and instant messages quickly so people know you're hard at work.

- ✓ Let your manager and coworkers know when you'll be at lunch or out of your home office for any other reason.

- ✓ Set boundaries. Quit at the same time you do when you're working in the office. (And in either setting, work overtime only when it's necessary; otherwise, you're likely to burn out quickly.)

- ✓ Create a designated work space and make sure any family members or roommates know that you shouldn't be disturbed when you're working.

# Establishing Yourself at Work

Even if you're a top-notch employee and you beat every target and deadline, your efforts may be ignored if you're too modest to speak up. And if you're a quiet innie, it can also be tricky to get your ideas across in meetings, to handle difficult coworkers, or to make connections with the colleagues you want to know. In this section, I look at ways to stand out and make yourself heard without stepping too far outside your innie comfort zone.

## Shining a light on your successes

One complaint I hear from innies all the time is that they do the most work and get the least credit. And you know what? Often, it's true! Outies don't hesitate to draw attention to their accomplishments, while innies have a lot of trouble saying, "Look what I did."

Luckily, you can draw attention to your achievements without going against your innie grain. Here are some of my favorite ways to do so:

✔ At the end of a successful project, send an e-mail thanking everyone who helped you, and copy it to your boss. In your e-mail, outline all the highlights of the project. You'll find it much easier to express your appreciation to your team than to brag on yourself — and your boss will be impressed both by your success and by your courtesy in thanking your team.

✔ When you've done a great job on a project, ask yourself: "Could other people in the company benefit from hearing about this project? Did I come up with a more efficient process or try a new software program that proved to be really helpful?" If so, send a note to your boss and offer to share your info with your colleagues.

✔ Offer to write a report on your project for your company's newsletter or blog.

Also, be assertive when it comes to getting credit for joint projects. For example, if you help a colleague write a PowerPoint presentation for a speech she's giving, make sure the title slide lists both of your names.

# Flexing your quiet power at meetings

Does that little ping of a meeting reminder hitting your computer make your heart sink? If so, join the crowd — the crowd of innies, that is.

Why do innies hate meetings so much? Because they're listeners, not talkers. They have plenty of great ideas, but they don't just blurt them out. They'd rather refine them before they share them. So they tend to say as little as possible in meetings or speak so quietly that their ideas get overlooked.

And here are other annoying things you may experience as an innie:

✔ You have a brilliant idea, but you need two or three minutes to think it through. As you're sketching out notes, someone else pipes up with the same idea.

✔ Ten minutes after a meeting is over, you think of a great idea to contribute — but it's too late, and you spend the next hour kicking yourself for missing a golden opportunity.

Meetings will never be fun for innies (and they're not always that much fun for outies, either), but they're never going to go away. So the best thing you can do is to figure out how to make them work for you. Follow these tips:

✔ Ask whether you can get an agenda ahead of time (or at least get a heads-up about what the meeting will cover). Then think quietly about the meeting topics and write down your ideas. Doing so will give you a good head start. And because you're probably a deeper thinker than many of the outies in your office, you may come up with interesting angles they won't consider.

✔ When it's time to discuss a new topic in a meeting, go first. I know this instinct doesn't come naturally to innies, but you'll likely find that it's easier to start a discussion than it is to jump into the middle of one.

✔ Memorize a few key phrases that you can use if you experience an innie brain freeze. If someone asks you a question in a meeting and your mind goes blank, you can say something like this:

- "That's an interesting question. Can I do a little research and get back to you by e-mail?"

- "I have some thoughts on that, but I'd like to think them through a bit more. Can we get together later and talk about it?"

If you simply can't get a word in edgewise in an outie-dominated meeting, make your points later in an e-mail. For example, say, "Carl's new logo concept is outstanding, and I think we can make it pop even more if we use these new packaging colors." Keep your e-mails on point, and express yourself concisely and confidently. (For tips on making office e-mails effective, see the nearby sidebar "Avoiding e-mail miscues.")

## Avoiding e-mail miscues

If you're a good writer, as many innies are, you may prefer e-mails to face-to-face meetings. If so, make sure you use this communication tool effectively. Here are some pitfalls to avoid:

✔ **Being too wordy:** If you send long e-mails, people are likely to skim them and miss key points. So keep your e-mails short, or if you do need to send a long message, highlight key points in yellow so they stand out.

✔ **Being overly terse:** People can easily mistake a short answer for a rude or angry one. So if a coworker tells you he's completed a project, don't just write back, "Okay." Instead, say something like, "Okay — and thanks again for your hard work on this."

✔ **Being unclear:** I once sent an e-mail to a client, outlining two solutions to a problem and asking, "Would you prefer the first approach or the second?" And he wrote back, "Yes, do it." It took hours for me to get in touch with him and figure out what he meant by "it." To avoid this kind of confusion, look at your e-mail from the recipient's point of view and make sure it's crystal clear what you're asking, suggesting, or agreeing to.

✔ **Using capital letters to emphasize a point:** This habit is a huge no-no, because it makes you come across as antagonistic and rude. However, emphasizing words with *italic* is okay if you don't overdo it.

✔ **Looking unprofessional:** Unless your workplace is very laid-back, avoid happy faces and LOLs in your e-mails.

✔ **E-mailing hastily in anger:** If you're furious with a colleague, you may be tempted to fire off a scathing e-mail right away. But resist the urge! Instead, close your e-mail program and draft your response on a piece of paper or in your word processing program. Then wait for several hours or even a day and re-read your words when you've cooled down. Odds are, you'll decide to tone down your tirade.

*Warning:* If you *do* decide to reply right away, at least delete the recipient's e-mail address while you're composing your message. Otherwise, you may hit the send button before you've carefully thought out what you want to say.

## Standing up to workplace troublemakers

If you're lucky, most of your coworkers will be great people who are a lot of fun to work with. But occasionally, you may run into some bad eggs. Here's a look at three of the worst workplace troublemakers and how to handle them.

### Bullies

Bullies don't hang out only on playgrounds. You'll also find them in offices, where their in-your-face attitude can ruin your day and keep you from getting your job done.

Avoid these bullies when you can; but when you can't, handle them carefully. Office bullies often have considerable power. Make them angry, and they may try to sabotage you.

Don't fight back if a bully starts yelling at you, but don't give in, either. Instead, use a technique I call *defusing* and follow these steps:

1. **Allow the person to vent.**

   For example, say, "It sounds like you're really upset that I've changed this software code," and then let the person respond. No matter how angry he is, just listen quietly for several minutes until he starts to calm down.

2. **Using the person's name, restate what he said.**

   For example, say, "Mike, if I'm getting this right, you're upset because I changed this code without consulting you."

3. **Suggest an action.**

   Say, "I have a thought about how we can resolve this." Then spell out your ideas.

If you use this approach over and over, a bully will usually start to back down. If he continues to push you around, go to your manager. And if that doesn't work — or if the bully *is* your manager — discuss the issue with your Human Resources department.

### Steamrollers

Steamrollers are those annoying coworkers who talk over people in meetings or even ignore them altogether. While extroverts fight their way back into the conversation, introverts often just sit and fume.

If a steamroller continually hijacks meetings, your manager should intervene. But if that doesn't happen, you need to take matters into your own hands. Here's how: When a steamroller interrupts you or refuses to let you have the floor, simply take out a piece of paper, write down what you want to say, and pass the paper over to him. Typically, this action will force him to stop and pay attention to you. And if you do this time after time, you'll eventually train him to be quiet while you have your say.

### Time-suckers

One difficult coworker you're likely to encounter at some point is the time-sucker. This person continually interrupts your work with foolish questions, petty grievances, or requests for help. As an innie, you tend to be sensitive and you may have trouble saying no to time-suckers. But it's also crucial to keep these people from taking advantage of you.

So when you realize that a coworker is wasting way too much of your time, try these tricks:

- ✔ Draw boundaries. For example, say, "I'd love to talk about this, but the only time I have is tomorrow between 8:00 and 8:15."

- ✔ Make your own demands in return. Say something like this: "I'd be glad to help with your project, Judy. But because I'm really busy, I'll need you to do this financial report for me in return. Is that okay?" Do this once or twice, and your time-sucker will likely stop pestering you. (Being this assertive when you're an introvert can be difficult, so practice your approach on a friend or partner beforehand.)

## Making allies in the workplace

Working with people who like you is fun, and having workplace allies makes it easier for you to do your job efficiently. When you get along well with your coworkers, they're more likely to lend you a hand, listen to your ideas, and help you solve problems.

As an innie, you may find it a little tricky to cozy up to the people in your office. But it's really not all that hard, if you have a plan. The first step is to target a handful of people you want to have as friends and allies, and then draw their attention in these ways:

- ✔ **Give them shout-outs in public.** For example, if your boss praises you at a meeting, say, "Thanks, I appreciate it. And I'd like to thank Jack in turn, because he really made it possible for us to get this project done on time."

- ✔ **Spot their needs and think of ways to help.** Are they overworked? Maybe you can assist with their projects. Are they struggling to figure out a new technology that you have down pat? Then offer your expertise.

- ✔ **Return their e-mails and phone calls immediately.** Doing so will show them that you respect them.

- ✔ **If you collaborate with them on a project, go above and beyond.** Doing more than they expect will make you memorable.

- ✔ **Come up with reasons to meet with them.** For example, ask a coworker whether you can buy her lunch and pick her brain about the new accounting system she's created, or offer to let her pick *your* brain if you notice that she's having trouble with a new software program you've mastered. If all goes well, you'll have a new ally by the time you get to dessert.

## Never underestimate the power of food!

One surprisingly easy way to make allies in the workplace is to ply them with tasty treats. It's amazing how quickly a batch of cookies or a plate of homemade egg rolls can win people over.

One bank auditor I know discovered this secret in a funny way. He was auditing a bank branch, and the people at the bank were very wary of him (as people often are of auditors). On the last day of his audit, he was driving to work when he realized that he was starving. He stopped to buy a single doughnut, but the store was having a big sale so he wound up buying a dozen, figuring that he'd eat the rest later. At the last minute, however, he decided he didn't need the calories — so he took the box into the bank and set it out in the break room.

Initially, everyone was silent when he came in. Then someone said, "What's that?" Thinking fast, he said, "Because it's the last day of the audit, and you've been really helpful, I brought you some doughnuts." People crowded around the box happily, saying, "Wow!" and "Thanks." Suddenly, they stopped acting afraid of him and started talking with him as a person rather than an auditor. As it turned out, it was the first time an auditor had ever done anything nice for them (even if it was more or less by accident!).

Well, word got around, and a little later, when a different auditor called another branch of the bank to schedule an audit, the manager asked, "Will we get doughnuts?" Eventually, the auditing firm made it a tradition for auditors to bring a box of doughnuts on the last day of each audit.

Also, if your company hosts charity events, volunteer to help at them. Volunteering tells people upfront that you're a good person, so you start out ahead of the game.

When you make new allies, keep in touch with them. Stop by their offices occasionally to chat, keep up with their projects, and invite them to lunch once in a while. When you do this, you'll cement the ties you've made.

# Finding Your Niche: Jobs that Appeal to Introverts and Extroverts

In the earlier sections of this chapter, I talk about how to ace the job you have now. However, there's a chance that you're thinking about exploring a new career. If so, you're in good company! These days, most people change career fields at least a couple of times before they hit retirement.

But here's a question: If you're an innie considering a career switch, are some choices better than others? In this section, I offer some answers and talk about picking the career that's right for you.

# Identifying careers that are a natural fit for innies or outies

In my opinion, defining any career as off-limits for introverts is a mistake. In reality, some innies function best when they're pushing the introvert envelope, while others find that they excel when they stay true to their "inner innie." Still, some careers can be a more natural fit for innies than others.

As you skim through the following lists, realize that no career is completely innie- or outie-oriented. In general, however, some jobs allow you to follow your innie desires most of the time, while others force you to play the extrovert's role.

## Jobs for innies

Here's a sampling of careers where introverts can easily put their strengths to work. These careers tend to require thinking deeply, working independently, or meeting with people one on one.

- Accountant or bookkeeper
- Air traffic controller
- Airline pilot
- Auditor
- Carpenter
- Data entry technician
- Dog groomer
- Engineer
- Farmer or rancher
- Graphic designer
- Janitor
- Landscaper
- Librarian
- Mail deliverer
- Market researcher
- Medical biller or coder
- Medical laboratory technician
- Paralegal

- Photographer
- Plant nursery worker
- Plumber
- Scientist
- Software developer
- Tax or trust attorney
- Truck driver
- Writer, editor, or translator

Innies can also make terrific psychologists and psychiatrists because they tend to be sensitive and have great listening skills. For the same reason, many innies thrive in other one-on-one medical settings, like physical or speech therapy. And plenty of introverts find happiness in home health care or hospice work, where they can form strong bonds with a few patients at a time.

### Jobs more suited for outies

Some jobs may be a bit challenging for innies. These jobs typically involve working on teams, meeting a lot of new people, making small talk, or even getting adversarial at times. Here's a quick sampling of jobs that will require you to use some of those pretend-outie skills I outline in Chapter 3:

- Customer service representative
- Defense attorney
- Grocery clerk
- Hair stylist
- Hospital nurse
- Police officer or firefighter
- Politician
- Realtor
- Salesperson
- Sports coach or trainer
- Telemarketer
- Wedding planner

## Innies and outies on stage

One of the most interesting things I've learned in my job is that introverts and extroverts can approach the same job in very different ways. For example, the actors I work with range from extremely outgoing to very introverted. I've found that the outgoing actors draw energy from their fellow performers and their audiences.

The introverts, on the other hand, create such a rich inner world that they may view the other performers almost as props — and they may ignore the audience altogether! Both groups give brilliant performances, even though they approach their roles from completely different angles.

# *Picking the career that fits you best*

When you're choosing a career field, you want to take your introverted nature into account, but you also want to select a career that meshes with your interests and talents. So how do you know which choice is right for you? If you're not sure, here are some good questions to consider:

- ✔ Just how introverted are you? If you're only mildly introverted, you may fit smoothly into an outie career. If you're an innie through-and-through, however, it's going to be a much bigger stretch.

  As you read through this book, try to get a good feel for where you truly fit on the innie-outie scale. Also, figure out which specific innie traits ring true for you. For example do you hate talking in front of groups, or are you comfortable giving speeches? Do you hate commotion, or can you tune it out? Your answers can give you important insights into which career is right for you.

- ✔ How strongly does one career call to you? If you have an amazing talent or a powerful interest, most likely it'll steer you straight into the job that's right for you — even if it doesn't quite suit your personality. I know innie actors who grit their teeth and put up with all the publicity shots and Hollywood parties because acting is in their blood. And there are extroverts who spend hours locked away writing books about the War of 1812 because history turns them on.

- ✔ Are you brave enough to fail? One friend of mine loves her "innie" job, but a few years ago she decided to take a big risk and go to work for a high-pressure company where she could earn more money. She lasted three years — "the longest three years of my life," she says — before she decided she just wasn't cut out for all the stress and drama. So she quit and went back to her old job. Luckily, she was smart enough to see this experience not as a failure but simply as a wise change in direction.

> If you decide to take a chance on an outie career, approach it in the same way. Recognize that it's a gamble, and give yourself a pat on the back for taking the risk, even if it doesn't work out the way you planned.

✔ Do you need a reality check? Too often, people pick a career field because it sounds like a perfect match for their skills and traits, only to discover that the job isn't anything like what they pictured. One way to avoid this problem is to shadow someone in the field you're considering. Doing so can help you discover how well that career really suits your personality.

✔ Are you assertive enough to stand up for yourself? To thrive in an outie job, you may need to tweak that job so it meets your needs. So you need to be willing to speak openly about those needs — not just to your coworkers but possibly to your boss as well. Ask yourself whether you have the courage to do that. If not, an innie-friendly job may be a better choice for you.

As you're evaluating your career choices, also ask yourself which options can offer you the most flexibility. Some jobs you need to do in an office; others allow you to telecommute some or all of the time. And many careers allow you to branch out on your own as an entrepreneur (something I talk about in Chapter 10).

# Chapter 5

# Making Your Mark as a Quiet Leader

*In This Chapter*

▶ Identifying your leadership skills

▶ Spotting the traps that can trip you up

▶ Taking your talents as a leader to the next level

▶ Coping with daily pressures

A typical stereotype in the business world is that the most effective leaders are forceful, fast-talking extroverts. But try telling that to Bill Gates, Warren Buffet, and Charles Schwab — all confirmed introverts!

In reality, introverts often make the very best leaders, especially when they play to their strengths. In this chapter, I talk about introverts' powerful leadership skills and how you can use them to take charge of a team, a department, or a company.

But to be honest, some parts of a leader's role can be pretty tricky for an introvert, so I also take a look at the challenges you may face as a quiet leader. After that, I offer leadership tips that can help you make the most of your skills and overcome any obstacles you encounter. And finally, I provide survival tips that can enable you to stave off stress and project a confident image when you're in a leadership role

## Assessing Your Leadership Strengths

I work every day with successful executives, including leaders of some of America's biggest firms, and one thing I've found is that many of them are either introverts or introverts-in-hiding. In fact, some research suggests that 40 percent of executives are introverts.

What does this tell you? That innies can be natural leaders. These leaders rise not by denying their innie-ness but by letting their introvert strengths shine — and you can do the same thing. But first, you need to recognize the talents that can make you stand out. The following sections can help.

## Your research and decision-making skills

As an innie, one of your greatest assets is your ability to investigate issues deeply. Unlike outies, who sometimes fly into action without weighing all the facts, you're not easily swayed by the loudest voice in the room. Instead, you probably prefer to collect all the facts before making a decision.

And unlike extroverts, who often go on instinct alone, you're likely to be cautious when you make decisions. Even if you have a gut feeling that you should take a particular action, you'll ask yourself: "Why do I feel that way?"

In addition, you're not a "my way or the highway" kind of person. You make decisions based on what's right for your team or your company, not what strokes your ego or puts you in the limelight.

## Your knack for encouraging independence

Innies are independent thinkers, and they encourage the people around them to think for themselves as well. In fact, a recent study found that the ability of introverts to let their charges think outside the box often makes them much better leaders than extroverts.

In the first part of this experiment, the researchers analyzed the personalities of store managers in a national pizza delivery chain. They also determined whether each store's employees were go-getters who spoke up, suggested improvements, and offered their opinions to managers or whether they were employees who just did their basic jobs. (The researchers labeled the first group as "proactive" and the second group as "passive.") And finally, they looked at each store's profits.

What did they find? That stores with passive employees did better with extroverted managers, but stores with proactive employees did better with introverted managers.

To test innie and outie leaders in a different way, the researchers next asked college students to fold shirts. Each group had one leader and four followers. What the students didn't know was that one follower in each group was an actor. In some groups, the actors simply folded shirts along with everybody else. In others, they came up with bright ways to make the folding go faster.

# Breaking the rules — successfully

One of the best meeting facilitators I ever watched was a quiet, introverted young woman I'll call Carol. Her strategy? To lead by letting others lead.

At the front of the room, Carol positioned herself between the flip chart easel and the group — something that's normally considered a cardinal sin in facilitating. She asked the group a few intelligent, provocative questions to get them started and then simply recorded their comments on the flip chart as they talked. Although facilitators typically make a lot of eye contact, Carol looked at her group occasionally but focused primarily on writing down their ideas.

Carol's tactic had the effect of forcing the group to talk to each other, which was just what they needed to do. Her innate talent for creative thinking helped her frame ideas and questions that kept the conversation on track. She took advantage of her quiet, less social nature to stay out of the group's way, acting as a conduit between their ideas and the flip chart.

At the end of a ten-minute session, Carol turned away from the flip chart and back to the group, showing them what she'd written. They were absolutely astounded at the amount of information she'd collected. Her leadership had inspired them to come up with great ideas and solutions, yet she'd been so quiet that they'd almost forgotten she was there!

One reason for Carol's success is that she used what's called *facilitative leadership*. The key to facilitative leadership is to remain completely neutral at the outset of a discussion. When you remain neutral, the people you're speaking with don't feel the need to either support or challenge your opinions. As a result, they feel that it's safe to open up, so you get authentic information from them.

The shirt-folders in the passive groups did a little better with an extroverted leader. But things were very different in the groups where someone said, "I have a better idea; can we try it my way?" In this case, extroverted leaders resisted the new ideas, while the introverts listened. As a result, the proactive groups folded more shirts when an introverted person led them than they did with an outie leader in charge.

What's the message here? Both extroverted and introverted leaders can get the job done. But if you're looking for bright ideas that can keep your company ahead of the game, your best bet may be matching up a team of bright, motivated people with an introverted boss who will let them sparkle.

# Anticipating the Challenges of Leading as an Introvert

In the previous section, I focus on your strong points as a leader. And one of those strong points is that you're willing to look the facts (even unpleasant ones) straight in the eye. So now it's time to explore some of the things that can hold you back as an innie leader. In my experience, here are the issues that introverts-in-charge struggle with most.

- ✔ **People may mistake your introversion for aloofness or arrogance.** Because you're not a big talker and don't always let your emotions show on your face, people may not be able to tell when you're interested and caring.

- ✔ **People may mistake your introversion for a lack of self-confidence.** In an outie office that rewards people for speaking up and making snap decisions, your quiet demeanor and think-before-you-talk habit may make you seem hesitant — and that can translate into less respect and fewer promotions.

- ✔ **You may hit "people burnout."** When your daily schedule includes meetings, interviews, speeches, fundraisers, and other people-packed events, it can be tough to find the quiet moments you need to recharge your batteries. Without that vital "alone" time, you may have trouble focusing, feel stressed, or even develop physical symptoms. (Headaches and indigestion are common complaints.)

- ✔ **Multitasking can take its toll.** Introverts like to focus on one thing at a time, but that's not an option when you're a leader. And you won't just be juggling a lot of tasks; you'll sometimes need to handle multiple crises as well. That can lead to high anxiety, especially if you're also sensitive by nature.

- ✔ **You may miss some of the facts you need to know.** Because they're not into small talk, introverts can sometimes tune out speakers when they think a topic is irrelevant. When that happens, they can miss important information or offend the people they're talking with.

In short, it's not always a snap to lead as an introvert. But talk to extroverts, and you'll discover that they have their own set of challenges. (For example, people sometimes see them as pushy, overbearing, or shallow — even when they aren't.)

So in the end, successful leadership isn't a matter of being an innie or outie. Instead, it's a matter of mastering the leadership skills that let your inner strengths shine. And that's what I talk about next.

# Setting the Stage for Success

People typically think of the folks at the top of the organization chart as born leaders. But here's the truth: Many of the world's most successful CEOs and managers, whether they're introverts or extroverts, had to work hard to develop the skills that got them where they are.

Building the right set of leadership skills — skills I've helped hundreds of introverted and extroverted leaders master — can allow you to overcome any issues that are blocking your career path. In addition, these same skills can make you a great communicator, an outstanding motivator, and an inspiration to your people. Here are the most important steps you can take to become a successful leader.

## Building your transformational skills

Many leaders have a simple formula for getting results: They reward employees for performing well, and they punish them for performing poorly. That's *transactional* leadership, and it certainly has its place. (After all, it's a good bet that your team wouldn't show up and work hard every day if you didn't reward them with paychecks!)

But successful leaders plan for the long run, and that requires another strategy: getting people to buy into your goals and beliefs. This is *transformational* leadership, and it's the type of leadership that can set you apart from the crowd. Transformational leadership goes beyond maintaining the status quo and allows you to create high-performance teams that are brimming with new ideas and energy.

Some studies suggest that extroverts are better than introverts at transformational leadership, probably because outies are more likely to be charismatic and are big on sharing their ideas. But anyone, innie or outie, can master this leadership style. In this section, I outline the key steps.

Doing all these steps, as you can probably guess, is very hard work. In fact, it's much harder than simply doling out tasks and handing out paychecks. But studies show that people led by transformational leaders work harder, behave better, and have more job satisfaction. That's good for your company, and it's good for your own image as a leader.

### Create an inspiring vision and let your people know they're crucial to achieving it

To get your team excited about your vision, start by getting their input. Outline your vision and ask each person on your staff to come up with five ways they can help make that vision a reality. At the same time, come up with your own ideas.

Next, schedule a brainstorming session where you can all share your ideas. (I recommend using the structured brainstorming method I talk about in the section "Acing the art of structured brainstorming," later in this chapter.) At the end of the meeting, agree on specific approaches to achieving your vision.

For instance, if you're working with a hotel's housekeeping staff, your vision may be, "In addition to cleaning, we brighten each guest's day a little." And the specifics you agree on may include fluffing guests' pillows, putting mints on their pillows after cleaning their rooms, leaving extra washcloths, using guests' names when speaking with them, and keeping hallway conversations quiet while guests are sleeping.

### Encourage your people to come up with their own ideas and solutions

Regularly say things like, "How can we make this design even better?" or "Here's my idea, but can you think of a different way to accomplish this?" Reward people for innovation and creativity, and let them take some risks.

### Have clear expectations

Keep your people reaching for higher goals, but make sure your goals are reachable. And spell those goals out clearly! The biggest causes of dissatisfaction in companies are unstated expectations, miscommunicated expectations, and impossible expectations. So let your people know exactly what you want, and don't let your innie perfectionist streak make you push them too hard.

Also, be realistic about the fact that even your top performers won't be quite as passionate about your goals as you are, so don't expect them to be workaholics, even if you're an overachiever yourself. (**Remember:** Some employees work smarter, and smarter is better than harder!)

### Walk the walk

If you want to create a team of high performers, be a role model. Work as hard as your team (or harder), stand up for them, and share the credit for your successes with them.

### Be a mentor

Nurture your team members' skills and find ways to foster their professional development. Also, help them learn from their mistakes and guide them through rough spots. You can find great tips on peer coaching in Chapter 8.

# Reinforcing effectively

Although transformational leadership can take your team to new heights, good old-fashioned rewards also have an important place in your repertoire. And you can reward your people more effectively when you understand a bit about reinforcement. I talk about reinforcement techniques in the following sections.

## Practicing positive and negative reinforcement

The two types of reinforcement you can use as a leader are positive and negative.

*Positive reinforcement* means rewarding people in some way when they do well. Your rewards can include raises, bonuses, or promotions. In addition, you can offer rewards like these:

- **Praising people both publicly and privately for their contributions:** This acknowledgment is something that both innie and outie leaders tend to overlook. But praise should be high on your to-do list, because recognition is often as important to an employee as money. (And it's free!) In addition to offering verbal praise, compliment your high achievers in departmental e-mails or mention them in your company newsletter. Just make sure your praise is specific and relates directly to their work.

- **Offering additional perks and privileges:** For example, if one of your employees knocks herself out getting a project to come in on time, consider returning the favor by giving her an afternoon off to attend her child's soccer game.

- **Offering plum assignments:** Your best employees work hard to make you happy, so make them happy in return by giving them the tasks they like the most. Just be sure you clearly spell out your criteria for earning those assignments — and reward not only your top performers but also other people who work hard and support your team.

The flip side of the reinforcement coin is *negative reinforcement*. People tend to think of this type as punishment, but it's actually not. Although there are several definitions of negative reinforcement, the primary one is "increasing the behavior you want to see by taking away something unpleasant when the person exhibits the desired behavior."

For example, consider Brandon, a high-school freshman who's taking algebra. He slacks off for the first few months, and his teacher calls him in for a talk. "Right now," she says, "you're likely to get a D in this class. I know you don't want that, because you're hoping to get into a good college in a few years." Brandon thinks, "Yikes! I don't want to get a D." So he studies really hard for the next few months, and his teacher gives him a B. That's negative reinforcement, because he avoided getting the D.

But negative reinforcement doesn't apply only to slackers. If you're a middle manager, one of the best ways to offer negative reinforcement is to act as a shield between your team and difficult upper-level managers. Nothing instills greater loyalty in your employees than taking away something unpleasant by protecting them from tongue-lashings from above, and managers who do this are unsung heroes. (One note, however: If you constantly need to play "human shield" to protect the people under you, you'll eventually burn out. So if you're forever defending your team against toxic upper managers, you may need to make other people in your company aware of the problems these bad apples are creating — or you may need to make the difficult decision to leave your job for a healthier environment.)

### Reinforcing (or punishing) like a pro

To use reinforcement effectively, keep this rule in mind: Think like Las Vegas. To understand what I mean, picture yourself in front of a slot machine in a casino. What makes you keep pulling the lever? Uncertainty. You don't know if it'll take 1, 10, or 100 pulls to get a payoff. And unless you have strong will-power, that uncertainty will keep you testing your luck again and again.

Well, the same thing is true for reinforcing your employees. If you reinforce unpredictably (a method that psychologists call *intermittent reinforcement*), you'll keep your employees guessing about when their next reward will come. As a result, they'll work even harder to earn it.

When you punish, on the other hand, you want to punish consistently. For instance, if you dock an employee's check for being tardy, do it every time.

Be sure to reinforce much more often than you punish. Otherwise, your team won't be motivated and your top performers may leave.

## Acing the art of structured brainstorming

In today's business world, it's a good bet that you'll spend much of your time in brainstorming sessions. And as a leader, you'll probably be heading many of these sessions. If so, I recommend doing things a little differently from what most leaders do.

Here's how the classical version of brainstorming works: You assemble your people in a room, describe the issue(s) you want to address, and ask them to say every idea or suggestion that comes into their minds (no matter how silly or crazy they think it is). As they do this, you write down everything they say without criticizing it. The goal is for your team to come up with fresh, creative ideas.

Does this method work? Well, yes and no. And as an introvert, you can probably guess why.

Typically, you'll hear a lot from your extroverts in a brainstorming session, but not from your introverts. In fact, brainstorming sessions can completely overwhelm innies, causing them to shut down. As a result, you're losing much of the input you need. So instead, I recommend an approach called *structured brainstorming*. This is a technique that brings out the best in both your innies and your outies. Here's how to do it:

1. **Give each participant a sheet of paper and ask your group members to jot down their ideas about why a problem exists and how they can solve it.**

   As in standard brainstorming, tell your group to write down even the ideas that seem silly. Tell them that after a few minutes, you'll call on them to share at least one of their ideas.

2. **After everyone is done writing, go around the room and ask people to talk about their ideas.**

   If people say that other participants already mentioned their ideas, ask them which ideas they liked the best.

3. **After everyone has a chance to share at least one idea, open the floor up for discussion so people can expand on their suggestions or add insights about other people's ideas.**

This approach works beautifully because it lets both innies and outies have a voice. By starting with pen and paper, you let the introverts think quietly about their ideas. (And by saying that you'll be asking each person to contribute at least one idea, you prepare your introverts to speak up.) After that, everyone gets to talk. And finally, you allow the extroverts to take center stage and add more comments. As a result, you'll hear from your entire team, not just the talkative ones.

# Boosting your emotional intelligence

Why do some leaders of average skill and intelligence succeed wildly, while other leaders — sometimes with higher IQs and more talent — fall miserably? Often, the successful leaders score high in a skill called *emotional intelligence* (or EI). Here's a look at what EI is and how to cultivate it.

### Understanding EI and why it matters in the workplace

*Emotional intelligence* (EI) is a fancy term for something that's really not all that complicated. Basically, it's the ability to identify, understand, and control your own emotions and the emotions of other people.

EI has a lot of different descriptions, but the one I think is most accurate is called the *Mayer-Salovey-Caruso Emotional Intelligence Test* (or *MSCEIT*). It zeroes in on these four aspects of EI:

✔ Developing awareness of your emotions and the emotions of others

✔ Using emotions effectively in the decision-making process

✔ Understanding emotional chain reactions

✔ Managing your own emotions and the emotions of other people effectively

The better you become at all four of these skills, the higher your emotional intelligence will be. As a result, you'll reap these benefits:

✔ You'll handle conflicts much more successfully.

✔ The people you manage will be more motivated to achieve your goals.

✔ You'll communicate your ideas more clearly.

✔ You'll be a more powerful negotiator.

✔ You'll be more effective at guiding people through stressful times.

✔ You'll be better at identifying your high achievers and nurturing them.

✔ You'll become more skilled at identifying your clients' or customers' needs.

✔ Your turnover will drop.

When you raise your own EI, you may also become better at identifying job candidates who have high EI themselves. That's important, because these people can elevate the performance of your team. One study found that salespeople with high EI generate twice as much revenue as their lower-EI coworkers, and another found that programmers with sky-high EI scores develop software three times faster than their lower-EI peers.

## Do tech and non-tech leaders need different EI skills?

I did my doctoral dissertation on EI, and one interesting thing I discovered is that different leadership roles require different types of emotional intelligence.

My research showed that compared to non-techies, managers in technical professions (which tend to be "innie" by nature) were generally less hands-on, more focused on task-related problems, more transactional ("by doing x, you can expect y"), and more prone to pointing out mistakes. They also tended to be less touchy-feely and offered less support, praise, and motivation.

You'd think their subordinates would complain about this, but that's not what happened. Instead, subordinates who were techies themselves preferred the honesty and directness of this approach. They were happy to take constructive criticism as long as their managers acknowledged their successes as well.

The more extroverted non-techies, however, were very different. This group needed direct positive feedback, atta-boys, and lots of smiles from their managers. They were open to constructive feedback, but they also needed to hear constantly about what they did right.

In short, both innie types and outie types need acknowledgment. But an innie with an introverted boss may be satisfied with a "good job" said sincerely. An extrovert, on the other hand, may think, "Great — but tell me more, please!"

### Raising your own EI

If you're like most people, you're a whiz in some areas of EI and so-so in others. But with a little work, you can take your EI to a higher level. Here are some ways to do it:

- **Get in touch with your own emotions.** Take time to think about how you react to your coworkers or to events in your office, and see what patterns you can spot. How do you react to stress? To conflict? To annoying people? See if you can identify your strengths and weaknesses.

- **Identify your stress triggers.** Think of the last three or four times you flew off the handle. Can you pinpoint why you "lost it" — and can you think of a better response?

- **Know what drives you.** Make a list of your goals and your values. When you understand what matters the most to you and why, you'll be more in touch with your own emotions.

- **Discover how to lean into arguments.** When someone starts complaining or yelling, your natural response — especially if you're an introvert — is to get defensive. But high-EI leaders do something different: They encourage the angry person to keep talking, using phrases like "Can you tell me more about that?" or "You're clearly angry; can you tell me what happened that upset you the most?" Then they listen quietly to the response, and ask more questions. Try it, and you'll be surprised at how quickly you can turn an angry rant into a calm conversation.

✔ **Open your mind to other people's ideas.** People tend to tune out opinions they disagree with, but that's a low-EI strategy that can close your mind to new ideas. Here's an exercise to help you become more willing to listen to different viewpoints: Find a news program or radio show that you actively dislike, and watch (or listen) for at least an hour. As you do, go beyond simply thinking, "That person is so stupid!" or "I totally disagree." Instead, ask yourself: "What common ground can I find with this person?"

✔ **Put yourself in other people's shoes.** If Joe, your office assistant, snaps at you, don't respond instantly with anger. Instead, imagine how he's feeling. Did you unwittingly step on his toes, or belittle him, or overload him with work? Or is he going through personal problems, such as a divorce or an illness? See if you can look beyond your own hurt feelings and get to the root of Joe's behavior.

✔ **Read people's body language.** When you're talking with people — especially if they're upset — watch their faces, their posture, and their gestures. Often, people's body language will send messages that their words won't convey. (For more information on body language, see Chapter 3.)

✔ **Find safe ways to blow off steam.** When you're angry or hurt, resist the urge to say the first thing that comes to mind or to send that e-mail you'll regret. Instead, say, "I'd like to think about this and get back to you later." Find a private place and write down all your feelings on paper, and then shred the paper. When you do that, you'll take the edge off your anger and you'll be better able to discuss the issue rationally.

## *Mastering the art of focused conversation*

As an innie, you're probably much better at one-on-one talks than you are at speaking to a group. So don't just schedule big meetings, but also look for opportunities to meet with your team members individually. When you do, a technique called *focused conversation* can help you get the most out of your time together. Here's a look at this technique and how to do it.

### *Defining focused conversation*

A *focused conversation* is a technique that allows you to explore issues deeply from several different angles. Think of it as digging down from the surface of a topic to its depth. It's a method that works well in both one-on-one chats and facilitated discussions.

A focused conversation gives you a set structure to follow and allows you to gather the most data possible in the shortest amount of time. In addition, it goes beyond mere fact-gathering and allows you to interpret the facts so you can make smart decisions.

### Following the steps of a focused conversation

The classic model for a focused conversation, developed by the Institute of Cultural Affairs to help diverse groups work together effectively, has four steps:

- ✔ **Fact-finding:** This step is where you gather information. For instance, if Dave is working on a marketing campaign, you can ask him how much time it will take him and what kinds of materials he's planning.

- ✔ **Reflecting:** Here, you can get a sense of Dave's feelings about his project. For example, you can ask questions like "What do you see as the biggest challenge in this campaign?" or "Do you feel that this campaign is going to be more successful than the last one?"

- ✔ **Interpreting:** This is a good place for *why* questions. You can ask Dave, "Why do you think the last campaign didn't do well?" or "Why do you think this new slogan appeals so strongly to our focus group?"

- ✔ **Deciding:** At this level, you and Dave make decisions about how to proceed with the project. Here, you can address questions like "What new elements should we add to our campaigns going forward?" or "How can we use social media to reach even bigger markets?"

At the end of your conversation, recap the key points and make sure you agree on what actions to take next.

# Six Survival Tips for Innie Leaders

In addition to adding new leadership skills to your repertoire, you can take a few simple steps to make your life easier in the office. Here are some tricks that work well for innies.

## Delegating more

Although innies are great at letting their staffs work independently, they sometimes have trouble delegating enough tasks to their people. Here are some reasons why:

- ✔ They tend to be perfectionists, and they're not sure other people will do a good enough job on the tasks they hand off.

- ✔ They may think, "It's faster to do it myself."

✔ They may worry about over-burdening their staffs.

✔ They may get so wrapped up in their own thoughts that the idea of delegating doesn't even occur to them.

One of the quickest ways to burn out as an innie leader is to take on too many projects yourself, especially if multitasking is one of your weak points. So when your to-do list starts to get too long, don't hesitate to share your workload.

## Outing yourself as an innie

If you're worried about coming off as stiff or aloof, there's a simple solution: Tell your employees upfront that you're an introvert. And if you're also shy or sensitive, let them know that as well. When they know where you're coming from, they'll be much more understanding, and they'll appreciate your honesty.

For example, tell your team members, "If it looks like I'm not listening to you at times, it's probably because I'm an introvert and don't always show my emotions on my face. But I want you to know that I really *am* listening, and I value your ideas."

At first, it may be hard for you to open up to your staff in this way. If so, try practicing with your friends or family first.

## Guarding your internal energy by scheduling wisely

To avoid the "people burnout" that so often affects introverts, make good use of your time. As soon as your full team arrives in the morning, hold a short meeting — maybe about 15 minutes long — so you can find out what your team members are doing that day and what issues they're experiencing. To make sure the meeting doesn't run over, make it a "stand up" meeting with no chairs and keep it very structured. This meeting will allow you to determine which team members need more input from you, so you can schedule phone time or face-to-face meetings with them.

Also, try to plan your schedule so you don't have back-to-back meetings. If possible, allow at least a couple of hours between meetings so you can have time to recharge.

## Wearing "power clothes"

There's a saying that clothes make the man (or woman), and that's especially true for innies. If you're worried that your introvert nature makes you appear weak or indecisive to some people, let your wardrobe do the talking for you. Invest in well-tailored suits as well as top-of-the line casual clothes. When you reach the top, you can switch to shabby chic, like Bill Gates, but until then, it's best to stick with classic and classy.

In addition to making you look confident and powerful, dressing sharply may help you climb higher on the leadership ladder. One survey of senior executives found that 83 percent think "unkempt attire" makes a woman seem less like a leader, while 75 percent think that it makes a man look less leader-like.

## Creating a battery-recharging retreat

As a leader, you're probably entitled to some extra perks. So see if you can wangle an office in a quiet corner, close to your team but away from the general chaos. (I know — you may be saying, "I wish!" Not all offices have quiet spots, but see if there's some way to carve out a haven for yourself.)

Don't hide out in your office for too long, however. And don't be absent from your workplace for long stretches, either, or other people will step in and fill the void. For example, a higher-level manager at one company retreated by constantly attending conferences, especially meetings at hotels with great golf courses. While he was out golfing, one of his more manipulative team members took over and created her own little empire. And eventually, the manager's absentee style cost him his job.

## Pairing up with an extrovert

The buddy system isn't just for kids. Sometimes, it can work for adults as well, especially when they're introverted leaders facing stressful situations. So if you're giving a high-stakes presentation, attending a company event, or meeting a major client, consider taking along a trusted outie who can do some of the talking for you.

# Chapter 6

# Keeping a Team Happy and Productive

*In This Chapter*

▶ Identifying the five stages of team development

▶ Leading successfully through each stage

*I*n today's business world, it's all about teamwork — and the higher you go in your career, the more often you head up teams.

Getting tapped to head a team is an honor, because it shows that your company sees you as a strong leader. But heading a team can also be a bit of a challenge for you as an introvert. To keep your team on target, you need to project assertiveness — something that can be tricky for a quiet person. You also need to speak up (probably more than you want) to communicate your expectations. In addition, you need to guide your team through conflicts, troubleshoot when they encounter problems, and reward them when your project comes to a close.

In this chapter, I offer advice to help you ace these team-building skills. First, I talk about the five stages that nearly all teams go through. After that, I tell you how to keep your team happy and productive in each one of these stages.

## Understanding the Stages of Team Development

No two teams are exactly alike, but most teams evolve in similar ways. Years ago, psychologist Bruce Tuckman and his colleagues laid out the five typical stages of a team's evolution, which I outline here:

✔ **Forming:** In this stage, everyone's getting to know each other. People aren't sure what their roles are yet, and they want their team members to like them, so they avoid conflicts. They don't quite trust each other yet, so they may hesitate to share their ideas freely. And they're vague about the team's purpose, so they may go off on tangents. As their leader, you want to give them clear directions and set firm ground rules.

✔ **Storming:** This stage is where people start tossing around ideas. Conflicts arise over the issues the team faces, how they're going to work together, and what kind of leadership they expect. To lead them effectively at this stage, you need to offer strong direction and demonstrate that you're a trustworthy leader. In addition, you want to encourage your team to accept and appreciate their differences.

✔ **Norming:** At this point, your team agrees on goals and how to work toward them. As their leader, you can act as a facilitator, asking questions and keeping them all committed.

✔ **Performing:** Not all teams reach this stage, but if you're lucky, this is where your team kicks into high gear. In this stage, team members work well both together and independently, and they're able to solve disagreements smoothly. As a result, you can step back a little and switch to managing tasks and assessing outcomes. You can also look for ways to make your results even better.

✔ **Adjourning:** This is where you finish your task and disband your team. Here, you show your appreciation for your team members' efforts and help them adjust to the fact that the team is breaking up.

As your teams move through these stages — and occasionally bounce back and forth between them — you need to use a variety of techniques to keep them on target. In this chapter, I look at how you can be successful at each stage.

# Taking Charge in the Forming Stage

One of the most crucial stages of a team project is the very beginning because your actions at this time set the tone for everything that follows. As an introverted leader, you want to show your strength right away and take charge assertively. The following sections describe four ways you can start out strong right off the bat.

# Creating a contract with your team

Strong team leaders communicate their expectations clearly in the early stages of a project. The best way to do this is through an approach called *contracting*. When you create a contract with your team, it guarantees that you all start out on the same page, which will translate later on into fewer of those battles you hate as an introverted leader.

One effective approach to creating a contract is called the *Seven Rs*. This approach has been around for years, but I've modified it to make it even more powerful. Here are the seven elements you and your team will address in this approach:

- **Results:** What the team expects to accomplish
- **Road map:** The basic plan the team will follow
- **Roles and responsibilities:** The part each person will play in the project and the expectations and accountability for each role
- **Resources:** What the team will need in terms of time, budget, materials, and support
- **Reporting:** How team members will communicate and review their progress
- **Relationship:** How the team members will mesh with each other
- **Resolving:** How the team will approach and solve problems

Following is a closer look at each of these elements and the questions you need to ask to get a good grasp of your direction.

## Results

At the outset of your project, your team members will have only a hazy idea about the team's purpose. This section of your contract helps them identify the outcome they need to achieve. Here's what you and your team need to clarify at this point:

- What is the objective of the team?
- What is the scope of the project?
- What are the criteria for success?
- How many areas of your organization will the project involve?
- How do your goals align with your organization's policies?

### Road map

To complete this phase of the contract, you and your team chart the way-points on your journey. Spelling out your milestones as specifically as possible will speed up your project by allowing your team members to schedule their work efficiently. To create your road map, ask these questions:

- ✔ What is the team's overall plan?
- ✔ What are the major milestones in this project?
- ✔ What is the projected time frame for reaching each milestone?

### Roles and responsibilities

In this area, friction often arises among team members. By clarifying what you expect each person to do, you keep disagreements to a minimum. To clearly define team members' roles and responsibilities, ask questions like these:

- ✔ What are the key roles of each person?
- ✔ Will some people's roles overlap?
- ✔ Will some people have permanent roles while others play temporary roles?
- ✔ What are the team members counting on each other to do?
- ✔ What are the team members counting on you to do as their leader?

### Resources

Team members who think you're distributing resources unfairly can drive you crazy with whining and complaints. That's why it's crucial to talk openly and honestly about budget restrictions and to find out what each member will really need to complete the project successfully. To get the information you need, ask questions like the following:

- ✔ What is our available budget?
- ✔ How much of this budget will each team member need and why?
- ✔ What information or learning materials will team members need to do their jobs?
- ✔ What equipment will each team member need?
- ✔ Will the team need any help from outside experts?

## Reporting

To make sure your team members work together seamlessly, you need to keep everyone informed and up-to-date. So take time to define the lines of communication for your team by asking the following questions:

- How often will we review our progress?

- What means will we use to review our progress? For instance, will we have face-to-face meetings or send written reports?

- Who will be responsible for recording and distributing the minutes of meetings?

## Relationships

In this stage of your contract, you outline the relationships among your team members. Here are some of the questions you can ask:

- How will your team make decisions?

- How will your team members exchange feedback?

- Which team members will need to work closely with each other? Which will work independently?

## Resolving

No matter how terrific your team is, they'll occasionally feud — so talk in a very positive way about how your team wants to handle conflict. For example, say, "We're bound to have differences of opinion, and we'll need to reach a consensus on how to handle them. If we're open to hearing everyone's point of view, it will help us come up with new and better ideas." Then ask your team to come up with answers to questions like these:

- Who will be in charge of solving problems?

- Based on their past experiences on teams, what approaches to conflict management do they prefer?

Later, in the storming stage, you revisit the topic of conflict resolution and create a Team Support Agreement (see the "Leading in the Storming Stage" section, later in this chapter).

Some details of your contract will change over time, but make it as specific as you can. When you have the details of your contract defined, put it in writing and make sure each team member receives a copy.

By the way, the Seven Rs also work well when you're beginning a collaboration with a new client — so this is a flexible tool you can use for any type of team effort.

# Establishing accountability

Pardon the cliché, but it's true that a team is only as strong as its weakest member. As you probably know from experience, it takes only one irresponsible or uncaring person to bring an entire team to a standstill. And that's why accountability matters.

To create a high-performing team, you need to make sure all your team members are accountable both to themselves and to the team. Establishing this accountability will empower your team because people who are accountable have more confidence, feel better about themselves, perform more independently, and work harder to achieve the team's goals.

The first step in fostering accountability is to understand exactly what it is. My favorite model of accountability comes from business consultants Russell Bishop and Mark Samuel, and it has three aspects: *creating*, *promoting*, and *allowing*. I look at these aspects in detail in the following sections.

### Creating

Creating is the easiest aspect of accountability to understand. It simply means that you take responsibility for the results of your direct actions — good or bad. For instance, if you drop a pencil, you're responsible for it landing on the floor. Similarly, if you rush an accounting task and get your numbers wrong, you're responsible for creating the mistake.

Good leaders and team members hold themselves accountable for any problems they directly create. So take clear responsibility for your own actions, and reward team members who take accountability for theirs.

### Promoting

This concept is a little trickier to understand. Basically, it means that you take accountability for making an already-existing situation better or worse.

For example, imagine that one of your team members is having a bad day and he snaps at you rudely. If you snap back and make him even angrier, you're moving him closer to a full-fledged meltdown. In short, you're promoting a bad outcome. To avoid situations like this, emphasize to your team that they need to take responsibility for their own actions and emotions even if someone else is being negative (and be sure to follow through on this commitment yourself).

Fortunately, promoting works in a positive way as well. For instance, imagine that a team member volunteers to tackle a grueling assignment that the other members want to avoid. If you praise her and offer support as she's struggling through the task, she'll be more motivated to ace the assignment — and that means you're promoting her successful outcome.

### Allowing

Allowing is a dangerous and insidious way in which your team members can avoid accountability. It means that they see someone else going down the wrong path, but they don't speak up. As a result, they allow a bad situation to happen.

For example, I sometimes sit through meetings where everyone is smiling and nodding as if the speaker is a genius. Then, when the meeting ends, I pop into the ladies' room and find a gaggle of employees saying, "That is such a dumb idea" and "This is never going to work."

Interestingly, allowing is a more common behavior for introverts than for extroverts because introverts are quiet souls who don't want to incur the anger of a fellow employee. So they'll often "check out" in meetings and let their coworkers push through bad ideas or even bully other people. Then they'll come up to the team leader afterward to air their complaints.

If you catch this sort of thing happening, find ways to make it safer for your people to speak up. For instance, if you're debating two approaches to solving a software problem, take your final vote by using secret ballots. Or if you're discussing a product design issue, ask participants to write their ideas anonymously on paper and then have the group take a break. While they're gone, write all their suggestions on the whiteboard.

Also, reward people who accept accountability by standing up for what's right even if it's risky. Let them know that you appreciate their willingness to speak up, and defend them against any backlash from the team.

Finally, if some team members continually steamroll over the rest, put them in their place quickly. One way to do this is to take them aside before a meeting and say, "I appreciate all the great ideas you come up with. But I'm also going to call on some of the quieter team members, because I want to hear what they have to say as well. I need you to hold back at times so they can talk — will you be okay with that?" The extroverts I talk to in this way are always cooperative. Often, I make time for them to come up to me after a meeting so they can share the extra thoughts they held in.

By the way, introverts also will come up to me after a meeting, but in their case, it's because they didn't want to speak up in front of the group. When they offer great ideas, I ask if I can call on them to share their ideas at the next meeting.

## Steve the steamroller

When you ask outspoken team members to let other people talk, it may take them time to get the hint. For example, I once let an overly pushy team member named Steve know that I wanted to let other team members speak at an upcoming meeting. He was actually a really nice guy, and he graciously agreed.

At the meeting that day, I said, "I'd like everyone to contribute their ideas." Most people did speak up, but a few didn't. And Steve, true to his word, kept his own comments short. But at the end of the meeting, he just couldn't resist getting the last word. So he piped up, "Sarah didn't offer an idea. And neither did Ted. And Marco didn't, either."

Steamrollers like Steve are so used to bossing other people around that it's difficult for them to break the habit. So be kind and be patient, but be firm as well.

## Projecting quiet confidence

Innies are typically modest, but too much quiet humility can make people think you're not assertive enough. It's important to show your team right away that you're a take-charge person so they'll fall into step behind you.

One good way to do this is to use some pretend-extrovert body language (see Chapter 3 for details). You'll also look more assertive if you stand at the head of the meeting table during your meetings, so bring in a flip chart and explain that you'll be using it to write down ideas and suggestions. This will give you a good reason to stay on your feet, and it'll help your team stay on track.

You can also hook up your computer so you can show information on the screen — or if you're talking to a high-tech team, you can use software that allows people to post their ideas onscreen for everyone to discuss. However, I find that paper is so natural and comfortable and low-tech that it encourages both techies and non-techies to open up more easily. People still really like flip charts, and you don't have to worry about computer glitches!

During your meetings, encourage your team to share their ideas, but don't let them run away with the show. If they get sidetracked, steer them gently but firmly back on track. Don't allow digressions to go on for more than a minute or two.

To get a rambling team member back on point, use a technique called *bridging back:* Pick a word or feeling from the person's comments and use it to circle back to your main point. For example, if John says, "That was an exciting game last night," say, "It sure was. And I'm even more excited about the new action plans you're developing to reduce our overhead. Can you tell the team about them?"

Another way to keep control over your get-togethers is to specify an ending time for each meeting — and stick to it. You may annoy a few people who don't get to make all their points, but most of your team members will appreciate this.

Although you want to come across as assertive, it's perfectly fine to show your innie calm and quietness as well. In fact, one recent study showed that employees prefer a moderate amount of assertiveness in their leaders, not a high level.

## Getting your team members acquainted

Teams often don't accomplish much at first because they're still getting to know each other and figuring out their roles. If you speed that process up, they'll get down to business sooner.

So hold a "getting to know you" session early on. At this meeting, which can be a casual lunch meeting, don't focus on the project itself. Instead, focus on getting your team members to talk about themselves, their backgrounds, and their interests.

# Leading in the Storming Stage

When you reach the storming stage, hold on to your hat! At this point, your once-cooperative team will start acting up in ways that test your mettle.

Earlier in this chapter, I talk about the three types of accountability: *creating, promoting,* and *allowing.* In the storming stage, you see all three types of accountability come into play — and in negative ways. Some people will create problems by engaging in confrontations, power struggles, and clashes over their roles. Others will promote already-tense situations with snarky remarks. And still others will go into passive-aggressive mode, allowing things to fall apart by refusing to comment in meetings or by missing deadlines.

Emotions can run high in this stage, and team members who once cooperated happily may be at each other's throats. So don't be surprised if your once-quiet meetings turn into free-for-alls. Team members may care more about their own hidden agendas than about results, and your project may bog down.

As a quiet introvert, you may find it stressful to steer your team through this tempest, but it's crucial to keep a firm hand on them, or they'll never move to the next stage. One way to keep them in line is to coach them (for advice on coaching strategies, see Chapter 8). The following sections provide additional ways to address their issues.

# Creating a team support agreement

Storming is the stage in which team members' different values and working styles emerge. For instance, an independent team member may have great ideas but resists following the team's schedule. A team player, on the other hand, may balk at working independently. And some members will focus on what they want to do, not what the team needs them to do.

To get everyone back on the same page, lay down some ground rules in a document called a team support agreement. Your goal here is to get team members to set their individual values and agendas aside so they can work together easily.

The following agreement is a good example of a team support agreement. (This one is adapted from a model my colleague Mark Samuel developed.) But tailor your own agreement to your team's needs, and feel free to make it shorter. Some agreements contain only one or two ground rules, and that's fine!

**Team Support Agreement**

1. We will follow an agreed-upon agenda and keep our energy focused on the stated objective of the meeting.

2. Although we may disagree with other people's ideas, we will respect all contributions as valuable.

3. We will encourage participation and idea generation.

4. We will keep discussions positive and not speculate on "why this idea won't work."

5. We will observe these personal rights of team members:

    a. The right to "pass" by deciding not to comment on a topic.

    b. The right to put comments "on hold" and come back with suggestions later.

    c. The right to take time to evaluate an idea.

    d. The right to revise, restate, or clarify an idea.

    e. The right to insist that dialogue and discussion focus on the topic at hand.

    f. The right to determine causes of problems before being asked to find solutions.

    g. The right to avoid debates, philosophical discussions, or "war stories."

6. We will remain aware of the general level of detail being discussed and keep our comments at that level. If we need to dig deeper into a topic, we will acknowledge this to the group.

7. We will listen attentively to each member's contributions.

8. We will be aware of and sensitive to the level of familiarity of other members and ensure that they understand the issues we are discussing.

9. We will allow only one conversation during the meeting unless the group agrees to break into subgroups.

10. We will expect each member to take responsibility for group productivity.

11. We will summarize each meeting and identify what we accomplished and what could have been improved.

12. We will document all meetings through charts and minutes.

13. When we take actions outside of meetings, we will not make commitments for other team members without checking with them first.

14. We will respect the different skills and working styles of our members.

15. We will focus on empowering rather than criticizing.

16. We will pull together as a unit.

17. We will differentiate between group problems and organizational problems and focus our attention on group issues.

18. When disputes arise between two people, we will bring them to the team leader privately rather than airing them before the entire group.

You and your team can brainstorm together to create your team support agreement by following these steps:

1. **Bring three flip charts into the room. Position one chart on your left, one chart on your right, and the final chart in the center of the room.**

2. **Ask members to list positive behaviors, and write them on the left flip chart.**

3. **Ask members to list negative behaviors, and write them on the right flip chart.**

4. **Ask the team which of the negative behaviors are important enough to work on. Write these behaviors on the center chart.**

5. **Ask questions like these:**

   • Picture our team as 100 percent successful in the areas of participation, communication, and trust. What would we be doing to achieve this success?

   • What do you personally feel is needed for team members to participate more actively?

   • What do you personally feel is needed for team members to communicate with each other better?

   • What do you need to feel a greater sense of trust toward other team members?

Use your team members' answers as a guide for brainstorming the steps of your agreement. As you come up with points you want to add, word them in a positive way. For example, don't say, "We will not ramble on and on in meetings." Instead, say, "We will state our points clearly and briefly."

When you and your team finalize the agreement, have each member sign it. Then give each person a copy.

Initially, people may forget your new rules. Don't get upset when they do; just remind them, and acknowledge them when they do follow the guidelines. Also, review and update your support agreement on a regular basis.

## Analyzing team dynamics

Did you ever have a chemistry set as a kid? If so, you probably discovered that some chemicals mixed well, while others went blooey if you handled them the wrong way.

Well, picture your team as that chemistry set. Get their personalities to mesh, and things will go smoothly. But combine them the wrong way, or allow the more volatile ones to take over, and — blooey! That's why it's a good idea to get a handle on your team's personalities when you're entering the difficult storming stage.

One of the most popular models of personality that I know is called the DISC model, which highlights the following four types of people:

- **Decisive:** These people are confident, impatient, and anxious to get down to work. They can be aggressive when they communicate. They're goal-oriented go-getters, but they can intimidate other team members.

- **Influential:** These team members are friendly, self-possessed, positive, and likeable. They work well with other people, but they can be poor listeners and may fail to keep commitments. They also may get distracted by details, and it's easy to offend them.

- **Stable:** These team members are calm, kind, reliable, and helpful. They like to work in well-defined roles, and they're not aggressive. They're good at sticking to schedules, and they enjoy training other people. On the downside, they can be rigid, stubborn, and controlling — and they can also resist change.

- **Conscientious:** These team members are careful, cautious, and rational. They're proficient and detail-oriented, and they stick to the program. But they can also be indecisive and overanxious, and they don't take criticism well. They have very high expectations for themselves and others, and they tend to be insecure.

# Team dynamics in the animal world

Animals are a lot like people in many ways — and like people, animals appear to have different personalities. According to scientists, that's a very good thing!

For example, one group of researchers studied macaque monkeys. They found that the most effective monkey groups were those containing some monkeys who were highly social and other monkeys who weren't. So although it may be tempting to pack your team with introverts, be sure to add some extroverts as well.

So how do you juggle these diverse personalities? Here's a good way to keep all of them happy and productive:

- **Establish authority with your decisive people.** Use assertive body language and good eye contact when you talk with them, and subtly take control. Encourage them to think imaginatively, and keep them challenged.

- **Give your influencers a lot of praise and attention to boost their sense of self-worth, and be very friendly toward them.** When they speak with you, show them that you're listening by smiling and nodding.

- **Be understanding and patient with your stable personalities.** Keep your voice calm, and use open body language to encourage them to let down their guard.

- **Give your conscientious team members clear directions and specific procedures to follow.** When you talk with them, occasionally use silence to get their attention. Ask a lot of questions to clarify their thoughts, and offer point-by-point directions. Avoid criticism and direct challenges, which can cause them to shut down.

As you analyze your team's dynamics, make sure they're interacting in healthy ways with each other. For example, don't let the decisive people bully other team members, and make sure your detail-oriented conscientious people don't bring other people's work to a halt by missing deadlines.

And of course, get a feel for which of your team members are innies and which are outies. Whenever you can, let each group play to its strengths. For example, let an introvert write up project reports and ask an extrovert to conduct a webinar about a new product.

## Communicating clearly and beware the innie "cone of silence"

As an introvert, you're quiet by nature. However, your team can quickly get off track — especially during the storming stage — if you don't keep your lines of communication open.

Innie team leaders often tend to rely a lot on e-mails, team web pages, and written reports. These tools are all fine, but they don't go far enough. It's easy for people to misinterpret e-mails (see Chapter 4), so regular face-to-face talks are a must. In addition to team meetings, schedule some one-on-ones with your members — and have an open door policy so people can drop in to discuss issues (although it's fine to limit the hours you're available).

Also, when you have information, share it quickly. If it's negative news or something that's very important, share it face-to-face if at all possible; if not, share it by phone. Introverted team leaders sometimes tend to keep too much to themselves, which can lead to misunderstandings and make it harder for team members to do their jobs effectively and bond with each other.

## Troubleshooting effectively

Even the best teams can run into big problems or start falling apart during the storming phase. If this happens, you'll need to take action quickly. In this section, I outline ways to get a derailed team back on track.

### Quashing conflicts quickly

When you toss a bunch of passionate, opinionated people together, conflicts often pop up. And that's especially true during the storming phase, when team members are sorting out their roles and priorities.

One thing to know is that most of the time, these conflicts are a good thing. In fact (believe it or not), teams that are harmonious can be less effective than teams that argue. So although your innie nature may make you cringe when things get heated, don't feel like you need to smooth away every minor disagreement.

If conflicts do escalate, the key is to tackle them quickly. When you let conflicts fester, they don't go away; they get worse. So keep an eye out for these early warning signs:

- ✔ People being rude, short, or hostile to each other
- ✔ Team members forming cliques that exclude other members
- ✔ Team members bad-mouthing other members or undercutting their ideas
- ✔ Once-eager team members becoming apathetic or sullen

When you spot the early signs of conflict, acknowledge the issue openly and positively. Let your team members know that conflicts are a normal part of the team process and that they can lead to new ideas and breakthroughs. Often, your team members will be able to sort out their disagreements with just a few nudges from you.

But what if they don't? When conflicts deepen, they can tear a team apart. So at this point, you need to step in. Luckily, introverted people often make the best mediators after they discover the process. Here are five steps for resolving a conflict successfully.

### 1. Prepare yourself mentally

If you need to resolve a conflict between team members — or you're part of a conflict yourself — the first step you should take toward resolving the issue is to get your own ideas and feelings sorted out. To do this, I recommend using a *dump sheet*. I use this approach often because it's very powerful.

To begin, find a quiet, private place where you won't be interrupted for at least 30 minutes. Bring a big pad of paper and a pen or pencil. Get comfortable, and then start "dumping out" all your thoughts, feelings, beliefs, concerns, worries, anxieties, emotions, hates, and biases. Don't censor anything — even the four-letter words. Don't worry about what you're writing because no one else will see it.

Your dump sheet will kick off a cascade of neurological events, causing you to move from the emotional regions of your brain to the clear-thinking frontal cortex. As a result, you'll find that you're calmer and much better able to come up with creative ideas and solutions to problems. After you complete your dump sheet, the best course of action will nearly always become clear to you. At that point, you'll be ready to bring your feuding members together at the table.

### 2. Clarify the problem

When you sit down with your warring parties, set a positive tone by showing respect, concern, and interest. Focus on opening lines of communication. Solutions can come later.

If you have trouble getting people to open up, ask open-ended questions related to the situation. For example, you can ask, "What do you think the problem is?" Then just sit quietly and wait for a response.

Also, be sure to paraphrase what the other person tells you. Studies show that summarizing another person's comments does more than any other technique to defuse anger and rebuild rapport.

The key here isn't to repeat the other person word-for-word, but to show that you understand what she's saying. So if she says something like "I'm furious because I can't make my deadline thanks to Marty screwing up the data," paraphrase by saying something like, "What I hear you saying is that you're angry because you didn't receive the data from Marty in time."

Here are good phrases to use when you're summarizing or paraphrasing the comments of someone who already knows and trusts you:

- ✔ "What I hear you saying is . . ."

- ✔ "From your point of view . . ."

- ✔ "I'm picking up that you . . ."

- ✔ "It sounds like . . ."

- ✔ "You're feeling . . ."

If the person doesn't trust you yet, be more tentative. This approach is a subtle way of telling the person that you're doing your very best to hear and understand her. Try using phrases like these:

- ✔ "Perhaps you're feeling . . ."

- ✔ "Let me see if I understand . . ."

- ✔ "What I think I hear you saying . . ."

- ✔ "I somehow sense that maybe you feel . . ."

### 3. Seek areas of agreement

When you have all sides of the story, it's time to identify the areas where people agree and disagree. To do this, take a big sheet of paper, draw a line down the middle, and write "Agree" in the first column and "Disagree" in the second. Then make lists on each side.

As you do this task, here's a little psychological trick you can play. In the *Agree* column, write down every possible item people can think of — even the tiny ones. In the *Disagree* column, on the other hand, write only broad issues.

Doing so makes the areas of agreement seem greater and the areas of disagreement seem smaller.

### 4. Get everyone to take responsibility

Most of the time, all parties involved in a conflict contributed to the problem in some way. Often, people will openly acknowledge their role, but sometimes they won't.

If one team member refuses to admit any fault and keeps blaming others, it's important to hold that person accountable. In an assertive and professional tone, outline what you see as this person's contribution to the problem. (Here's where some of that pretend-outie body language I discuss in Chapter 3 can come in handy.)

Also, acknowledge any role *you* played in the situation. Did a team member have too little information to do a task well? Was your deadline unrealistic? Did a team member have the wrong skillset for the task? Did your lines of communication break down? Admitting your own fault will take the other person off the defensive and increase the odds that she'll accept her own responsibility.

### 5. Find solutions

At this stage, it's time to have a brainstorming session. (I recommend the structured brainstorming method outlined in Chapter 5.) Your goal here is to bring everyone involved in the conflict together so they can jointly identify a solution. When they all work together to find this solution, they're much more likely to buy into it.

Sometimes, team members won't come up with a workable solution on their own. If they don't, you'll need to come up with a solution yourself. But even if you do, offer them some options. For example, if they need to rewrite a piece of code, ask them if they'd rather complete the task this week or next week. Having them decide small issues like this together will increase their sense of collaboration.

And if one team member still balks, don't hesitate to show that you mean business. For example, you can make it clear that one option on the table is "no job."

When your team does agree on a solution, thank them and praise them for their hard work. Then write the agreement down and spell out the details clearly. Also, summarize all the events that occurred in your meeting. When you're done, have each party sign off on the agreement to ensure that everyone understands and acknowledges what happened.

### Offering constructive feedback

Even the best team isn't going to be perfect, so don't be surprised if your members sometimes miss deadlines or flub assignments. When these problems arise, you need to handle them effectively and sensitively — especially in the volatile storming stage, when team members are likely to be touchy and defensive. Here's how to do it.

1. If possible, wait a day to discuss the problem to give both of you time to collect your thoughts. However, don't wait more than 48 hours to discuss a serious problem.

2. Before you meet, ask your team member to write down what she feels she did well and what she thinks she could have done better in the situation. Explain that you'll do the same.

3. Make sure you're in an objective or neutral state of mind when you sit down to talk about the error. Even if the mistake caused big problems for you, set your own emotions aside and focus on helping your team member.

4. Ask your team member to share the thoughts she's jotted down. Have her start with what she did well, and then move on to what she could have done better. By letting her talk first, you allow her to admit her mistake herself, making her feel less anxious and defensive. It'll also show you how much accountability she's willing to accept for her error.

5. When your team member finishes talking, offer your feedback.

The best way to provide feedback is to use an approach called *sandwiching*. In this technique, you sandwich the feedback that she'll find unpleasant between positive comments that will make her feel good, like so:

1. **Point out what your team member did well.**

2. **Offer feedback on what went wrong.**

3. **Outline the steps to take next.**

   At this point, be sure to comment on something positive about the situation or about how your team member is handling the meeting. Even saying something as simple as "I appreciate you listening and want to hear your thoughts" can help defuse tension.

If your team member is very upset or defensive, you can also use a technique called *normalizing*. To do this, tell your team member that you fully understand why the mistake occurred. For example, you can say, "We had so much going on that day that I can see why it was easy to overlook that code fix." This approach will show your team member that you have empathy, and she'll relax her guard.

At the end of the meeting, make sure both you and your team member fully understand why her error occurred and how to prevent it from happening again. Also, determine whether your team member needs additional assistance, resources, or mentoring.

# Leading in the Norming Stage

At this stage, your team is ready to come together and create a consensus about what their goals are and how they'll achieve them. This stage is a refreshing change from the storming stage, and it means that you can move from a directive to a supportive role. However, you still need to work hard to keep your team on track and move them to the next level. The following sections provide some ways to do this.

## Focusing on key results

In the norming stage, you want to keep your team moving forward to the performing stage where they can really start to shine. To accomplish this, focus on *key results*. Key results tell you whether your team is making good progress toward achieving their vision.

To analyze your key results, schedule a brainstorming session. In this session, say, "Pretend that you have a magic wand and you can move forward in time to a point when our team's vision is fully realized." Then ask your team to answer questions like these:

- How high would the quality of our results be?
- What would our clients be saying about us?
- How would our team be performing?
- What would our customer service look like?
- What would management be saying about us?

Then ask your team to come up with additional steps they can take to push their performance to the next level and get the results they're envisioning.

## Keeping an eye on your norms and goals

It's a big relief when your team comes together and agrees on norms, but it's important to make sure these norms translate into high productivity and good teamwork. If not, you may need to adjust them.

Also, keep an eye out for *groupthink* — the natural tendency for members of a group to ignore their own doubts or concerns to maintain harmony and avoid conflict within the group. This can be a problem as teams bond in the norming and performing stages. When teams are under the spell of group-think, they can overlook red flags or turn against group members who are brave enough to dissent. So encourage naysayers to question the group's ideas, and listen to their ideas respectfully when they do.

In addition, invite one or more outside experts or knowledgeable colleagues to sit in on your meetings at times. Encourage them to suggest new ideas and challenge the status quo. Because they're outsiders, they'll be more willing to offer fresh viewpoints. They'll also be willing to pipe up and ask questions that your team members may be afraid to ask in case they sound "dumb."

## Building relationships

In the storming phase, your team members frequently feuded. Now, however, they're ready to bond. To help them do this, consider holding one or two team-building events. Just be sure to plan activities that all your team members — both introverts and extroverts — will actually enjoy (see Chapter 17 for details).

Also, be aware that your team may resent it if you add new members at this time. So if you need to bring new people onboard, offer them strong support and make sure your other team members don't shut them out.

As your team begins working together successfully, be sure to give them the pat on the back they deserve. Hold group meetings to celebrate milestones, and thank team members in one-on-one meetings as well. Also, recognize your team members' achievements by giving them more authority and autonomy.

# Leading in the Performing Stage

If your team reaches this stage, congratulations! That means you're doing everything right as their leader. And now you get your reward: You can delegate more responsibility and be less hands-on in managing them.

Of course, you'll still have plenty to do. Your team will need you to make any strategic decisions that are necessary to chart their course, and to make sure they have all the resources they need. In addition, they'll be counting on you to acknowledge their incredible performance — so make sure you offer the reinforcements I outline in Chapter 5. And get plenty of feedback from all your stakeholders to make sure you're meeting or exceeding their expectations.

Finally, be aware that your team is likely to cycle back through storming and norming at some points. Often this happens when the ideas the team had about the project and tasks don't work out in real life, requiring you to tweak the project or its scope. It can also happen if respected team members get replaced by newcomers. So expect to go through the storming-norming-performing cycle several times. If you catch your group backsliding into storming, immediately go back to a more hands-on leadership style.

# Ending on a High Note in the Adjourning Stage

When your project ends, schedule a wrap-up meeting. At this meeting, thank your team and acknowledge their contributions. But don't stop there!

One big difference between great and so-so team leaders is that the great ones aren't satisfied with saying, "Yay, us. We did a terrific job." Instead, they ask, "What could we do better next time?" Of course, you'll do this throughout your project. But now's the time to take an in-depth look at the entire project from start to finish.

As an introverted leader, this is a skill that may come naturally to you. Innies are excellent at thinking deeply about things, and they tend to be self-critical (which is a good thing in this instance!).

So when a project ends, praise all your team members — and then ask them to think about questions like these:

- ✔ Did the team encounter problems that could be avoided in the future?
- ✔ Did the team use processes that turned out to be less than optimal? If so, what processes could they use next time?
- ✔ Did the team need additional (or fewer) members?
- ✔ Did the team have communication issues that could be prevented in the future?

When you take time to evaluate the process, you can avoid making the same mistakes over and over. As a result, you can make each team you lead even stronger than the last one — and that's a quick way to climb the leadership ladder.

# Chapter 7

# Becoming a Confident Public Speaker

*In This Chapter*

▶ Preparing yourself mentally

▶ Practicing to perfection

▶ Winning over your audience

▶ Keeping your energy high

**D**oes the very thought of standing up in front of a crowd terrify you? If so, join the club! Millions of otherwise confident people feel their knees turn to jelly when they think about stepping in front of an audience. Even the extroverts I work with often fear public speaking, and it's scarier still for introverts. (One innie friend told me, "I've given eight speeches in my entire life — and if I die with that total, I'll be happy.")

However, it may surprise you to discover that introverts often make the very best public speakers and seminar leaders. That's because innies are typically very knowledgeable and passionate about their topics, and they know how to put together excellent presentations. What's more, even the most introverted people can overcome their fear of giving speeches. With practice, many innies actually come to enjoy public speaking! (In fact, I'm one of them.)

Now, I understand that you may feel a little overwhelmed at first as you read through these pages. In fact, you may initially say, "No way, Joan. I can't do this. You're forgetting that I'm an introvert." But have faith! I used these same strategies to transform myself from a terrified speaker into a confident presenter. And I've used these strategies to turn hundreds of corporate clients into assertive, charismatic speakers. If you're willing, give them a shot and see what they can do for you. And don't feel like you need to master all these skills at once; just take your time, and do what feels right for you.

To get you started, I begin by offering tips for preparing yourself before you give a speech. Then I provide six tips for giving an electric performance. And finally, I explain how to create a little quiet "breathing room" for yourself during a longer speech or seminar.

# Calming Your Innie Nerves: Preparation Is the Key

I know a handful of people who can give a brilliant speech off-the-cuff. But here's my advice: Don't try this yourself!

For most people, good preparation is the biggest key to becoming a confident, successful speaker. That's true whether you're giving a half-hour keynote or an all-day seminar.

And when I say preparing, I mean preparing both your material *and* yourself. The following sections explore the best ways to lay the foundation for a successful talk.

## Visualizing success

When you hear the word *preparation,* you probably think about writing out your speech and practicing it. But beefing up your confidence and quashing negative thoughts are just as crucial. One of the best ways to do this is through a technique called *visualization.* Virtually all the world's best athletes include this powerful tool in their training programs, and it's a key part of the work I've done with pro sports players.

How powerful is visualization? In one experiment, researchers divided college basketball players into three groups. They asked one group to shoot free throws for one hour each day for a month. They asked the second group to *visualize* shooting and making free throws without actually touching a basketball. And the third group didn't do either activity.

As you can guess, the third group didn't get better at shooting free throws. The group who physically shot free throws, on the other hand, improved their shooting by 24 percent. But here's the shocker: The group that simply visualized shooting free throws improved by 23 percent! In other words, visualization worked just about as well as actually shooting baskets.

Fortunately, what works for athletes works for most people. I use visualization successfully with everyone from CEOs to actors, and it can help you greatly as you're preparing for your speech.

Here are some of the best visualization tricks to try in the days before you give your talk:

- ✔ **Visualize your goal.** Picture yourself at the end of your speech or seminar, happily enjoying the applause of your listeners. And imagine yourself feeling relieved that it's over!

- ✔ **Visualize yourself acing key steps toward your goal.** For example, imagine yourself delivering a flawless opening, getting a laugh when you tell a funny story, and having people come up to you after the speech to ask questions and compliment your performance.

- ✔ **Practice anchoring.** In this visualization method, you identify any negative images in your mind, such as stumbling over your words or forgetting your speech. Then you choose a specific sight, sound, or sensation to replace each negative image.

  For example, tennis champion Rosalyn Fairbank convinced herself that the hostile crowd at the French Open was applauding for her rather than her opponent. (And it worked — she took the French Open Doubles title twice.) Similarly, when you catch yourself visualizing failure, you can replace that image with the sound of your audience applauding you.

 As you do your visualization exercises, picture yourself in the room where you'll be speaking. Better yet, rehearse your speech in the actual room if you have access to it. For example, if you're giving a presentation to a group of managers at your company, practice your speech in the conference room where you'll be talking. On speech day, the sight of the room will trigger your mind to bring up the material you've rehearsed.

People have different mental styles when it comes to visualizing. Some like to fantasize big — for example, some imagine a hundred people coming up to congratulate them after a talk. They find that this image gives them an extra boost of confidence. (And who knows — it could happen!) Others conjure up more modest visions of success, because they feel that they're more realistic. Pick the approach that works best for you.

It's a good idea to schedule your visualization sessions daily. If you're very nervous the day before your talk, do your visualization activities two or three times that day and add coping statements such as, "I know the material more and better than anyone else in the room. I'll do fine." The more opportunities you have to visualize success, the better off you'll be on the day of your talk.

Also, check out the stress-busting and coping strategies I outline in Chapter 11, all of which can make you feel more comfortable getting in front of an audience.

## A medal-winning pivotal point

Olympic diver Michele Mitchell once offered me a great example of a pivotal point. "In a dive," she said, "we tend to look at the whole thing instead of the key part that will make it flow. Find the one point in the dive that you have to execute correctly, and focus on that."

Michele told me she was having huge trouble with one dive until she identified a 1.5-second spot where she needed to turn her hands at a certain angle from the board. Once she nailed that, she could do the entire dive superbly — and she won a silver medal as a result.

## Identifying your pivotal points

When people first start giving speeches, they tend to think that their talks need to be perfect from start to finish. So they fret over every sentence, every move, and every PowerPoint slide. However, I've discovered that if you can nail down a few key elements, or *pivotal points,* of your speech, the rest will fall into place. So when I coach people on public speaking, I ask them to identify pivotal points in their talks.

For example, one of my pivotal points is connecting with my audience at the very beginning of a talk. If I can get them engaged or laughing right away, I know that the rest of my talk is likely to go well.

As you rehearse your speech, look for your own pivotal points. For example, do you find that your speech works better if you start walking around the room as you deliver it? Or do you notice that your words flow smoothly after you break the ice with a great story? If so, make notes about these pivotal points and focus your attention on them. When you zero in on them, you'll automatically feel more confident about your delivery.

## Mastering your material

The more time you spend polishing your presentation, the more calm and collected you'll sound on the big day. Rehearsing your speech also helps you identify weak spots and repair them. So follow the age-old rule: Practice, practice, practice! Here's how to get your presentation down pat.

### Organize your ideas

Initially, your head will be swimming with ideas for your talk. It takes time and effort to tame those ideas and get them to fall into a logical order, so begin working on your speech as soon as you find out you're giving it.

To get a handle on your material, start by identifying exactly what type of talk you'll be giving. Typically, a *keynote speech* is about 30 minutes long. A *workshop* or *seminar,* on the other hand, can last anywhere from half a day to several days. Know your exact time frame and what topics you're expected to cover.

Also, know the context of your talk. If you're giving a speech at a conference, find out what the overall theme of the conference is so you can tailor your talk accordingly and refer to this theme in your own speech. If you're offering a workshop or seminar, make sure you know what the organizers want you to cover.

Next, identify the type of presentation you'll be giving. Most likely, it will fall into one of these three categories:

- ✔ **Informative:** This type of talk centers around sharing your knowledge. A good example is a speech about your company's current financial status. Here, your priority is to make your talk clear and interesting.

- ✔ **Technical:** This is a "how-to" talk in which you teach people a skill. Your priority in this case is to be clear, accurate, and interesting.

- ✔ **Persuasive:** In this type of talk, you're selling your audience on an idea, a proposed change, or a product or service. Your priority here is to gain buy-in.

At this point, it's also a good idea to create a working title. It may not be what you end up with, but it'll steer you in the right direction. For example, you may start out with "Five Ways to Grow Your Customer Base."

With this information in hand, it's time to start collecting material for your talk. I like to use a manila folder to save notes, clippings, humorous stories, and other material. If you prefer high-tech tools, collect and store your material on any device that works for you.

Also, keep a supply of sticky notes with you so you can write down ideas as they come to you. Don't censor or judge your ideas at this point — just get them down on paper. At the end of the day, add them to your file. If you're coming up short on ideas, go online and look for articles on LinkedIn or other sites.

It's also smart to keep a recording device in your car or a notepad by your bed while you're working on your speech. You may find that some of your best ideas surface while you're driving or during the night.

### Create your dump sheet

When you think you have enough material to start roughing out your speech, create a *dump sheet*. (Journalists coined the phrase *dump sheet* ages ago to describe the process of "dumping out" their ideas on paper.)

Creating a dump sheet serves these purposes:

- ✔ It allows you to identify what you currently know and don't know about your topic.
- ✔ It helps you spot your biases.
- ✔ It shifts you to the frontal lobe of your brain, allowing you to think logically. This will help you overcome your anxiety and identify the practical steps you need to take to make your talk a success.
- ✔ It helps you identify questions your audience may have.

If you have only a week's notice to prepare your speech, do your dump sheet first and then collect the material you need to fill in the gaps.

Use your dump sheet to help you answer questions like these:

- ✔ What do I know about this topic?
- ✔ What do I *not* know about this topic?
- ✔ What additional research do I need to do to fill in the gaps?
- ✔ What do I like most about my material?
- ✔ What should my focus be?
- ✔ What key points do I want to cover?

To create your dump sheet, find a quiet block of time and hide out somewhere with a pen and paper or your laptop. Then write down every single thought that comes to you regarding your topic. Don't censor your ideas at this point. Instead, just use a stream-of-consciousness approach.

### Use index cards

After you've finished your dump sheet, write each of your ideas on an index card, or use storyboarding software or PowerPoint slides to create "virtual" cards. (You can also use sticky notes on a felt board.) Leave some extra space at the top of each card so you can add keywords later.

# Knowing yourself

As you're working on your speech, think about what type of speaker you are. Decide which of these three categories best describes you:

✔ An *educator* who can clearly outline facts and convey information.

✔ A *persuader* who has the power to win over people's hearts and minds.

✔ A *facilitator* who's great at guiding an audience to find answers for themselves.

In a good speech, you'll probably play all three of these roles at some point. But if you identify the role you like best, you'll know how to make the most of your strengths. For example, I like to facilitate. So at my talks, I often break my audience into groups and have them come up with solutions (with a little help from me).

If you're using either real or virtual index cards, here's what to do next:

1. **Go through your cards, and at the top of each one, add a few keywords to describe the material on the card.**

   As you do this, think about the top three to five key points you identified from your dump sheet.

2. **Organize your cards so that cards with similar keywords are together.**

   Arrange your cards until they start to fall into a logical order. (Don't worry if you have some blank spots at first.)

3. **Add cards to define your "openers" and "closers."**

   These spots are good places for humor, so think about things you can say to make your audience laugh. Try to come up with more than one idea.

4. **Keep revising your cards to cover new ideas or refine existing ones. Then pick the best material from each subheading.**

   Now you can start adding, subtracting, and rewording your cards and looking for ways to bridge your topics together. Here's where you can begin mapping out your PowerPoint presentation as well. (Don't start too early on this stage, though, or you'll have to re-do a lot of your work.)

5. **When you're happy with your material, create a final set of cards.**

   Don't write your entire speech on the cards; just write keywords to remind you of what you want to say.

As you're working on your talk, allow time for your ideas to *incubate*. Incubation is the time during the creative process when you aren't consciously thinking about your speech. When you let your ideas incubate, you're likely to find that elements of your speech that are giving you trouble fall right into place. That's because while you're busy making an omelet or watching a football game, your ideas — like chicks in their shells in a real-life incubator — are growing and evolving. I've solved many a thorny speech problem just by *not* thinking about it!

## Focusing on your priorities

Every speech is different, but successful speakers all focus on a few essentials. As you plan your talk, consider the answers to these questions:

- ✔ **Who is your audience?** Think about the backgrounds and experiences of your audience, and make sure your material is relevant. (For example, a joke about something that happened in the 1960s may fall flat with a younger audience.) Also, think about how familiar your listeners are likely to be with your topic. Use language they'll understand, but make sure you're not talking down to them. You may even want to survey some members of your audience ahead of time to find out what they're expecting to learn from you.

- ✔ **What is a good title for your speech?** Earlier, you came up with a working title for your talk. Now, it's time to finalize that title. Your title should accurately reflect your material — and if you're presenting at a conference, it should tie in with the conference theme. It should also be catchy, especially if you're competing for an audience with other presenters during break-out sessions. To see whether your title works well, try it out on your partner or friends.

- ✔ **What are your key points?** You should have one core message that you emphasize at the beginning, refer to throughout your talk, and circle back to at the end. Make sure you don't go off on too many side paths that don't relate to this core message. A good talk will focus on a handful of key points, not on a dozen.

- ✔ **How long is your talk?** Time yourself as you practice your speech. If the conference presenters have given you a strict time limit, plan a speech that runs five or ten minutes short to make sure you'll finish in time. If you're afraid you'll finish up too early, on the other hand, add an extra five or ten minutes of optional material to your talk.

- ✔ **How will you grab your audience at the start of your talk?** It's important to start your presentation off with a bang. For example, open with a compelling story, a touch of humor, or a surprising statistic (see the later section "Grabbing their attention with stories and humor"). One good way to get ideas is to watch TED talks online and see how the speakers start out their presentations.

✔ **How detailed should you be?** You want to prove your points, but avoid the urge to drown your listeners in a flood of statistics. If you want to offer a lot of facts and numbers, one solution is to keep your presentation simple and offer handouts with more detailed information.

✔ **How can you make technical information easy to understand?** See whether you can present this material in several ways (for example, both verbally and with a slide), and make sure you summarize it before moving on to your next point.

✔ **How can you get your audience to visualize the scenarios you're painting?** One good way to help your audience visualize is to use "imagine" phrasing. For example, if you're talking about identity theft protection, say, "Imagine that you go online to check your bank account today, and . . . it's empty."

✔ **How can you make sure you're offering the best and most up-to-date information possible?** One way to know whether your material is state-of-the-art — and to find great ideas to cover in your talk — is to search for "best practices" on the Internet. Be sure to put the phrase "best practices" in quotes and then list your topic, like so:

```
"best practices" on inventory control
```

✔ **How can you get buy-in?** If you're giving a persuasive talk, you'll succeed only if you get your audience to agree with you. I talk more about how to do this in the "Persuading with power" section, later in this chapter. For now, here are questions to address:

- Why should people be interested in what you have to say?

- What problem can you solve for them?

- What do you want them to do, and how can they do it?

- What are the benefits to them, their companies, or their families if they do what you're asking?

- Are there any costs or risks involved? If so, how do the benefits outweigh the risks?

- What action should they take right away, and why?

✔ **How can you use visual aids to add spice to your talk?** Visual aids are a must for any long talk, because they grab your audience's attention and make it easier for them to grasp key points. However, it's easy to lose your audience with a boring or too-wordy PowerPoint. If you aren't an expert at producing PowerPoint presentations or other visual aids, enlist the help of a friend or coworker who's skilled in this area.

✔ **How can you end your talk strongly?** Think of a way to finish your speech on a high note. For example, if I'm speaking on personal growth, I may close by saying, "You've all heard the famous quote, 'To be, or not to be: that is the question.' Today, I've given you some great ideas for how 'to be' and how to like that being inside you." You can also end with a call to action or, if you have a strong rapport with your audience, a humorous remark. No matter which approach you choose, be sure to make it clear that your talk is done. (At the end of a workshop, I often say, "Thank you! Now get out of here and go have some fun!")

# Getting the details down pat

A lot more goes into giving a talk than just, well, talking! Even the best speech can go awry if your audiovisual equipment isn't in place, your room is set up wrong, or the air conditioner malfunctions.

To help prevent surprises like these, which are especially devastating for introverts, make careful arrangements ahead of time. Here are some of the details you'll want to check out.

### Preparing for a talk in your office

If you'll be speaking in your workplace, the very first thing you'll want to do is something many people forget: Reserve the room. I can't tell you how often people miss this little but all-important detail.

Also, make sure you have all the audiovisual equipment you need. If you're not an expert at using this equipment, get lessons from your more tech-savvy colleagues — and make sure at least one of them can be on hand for your presentation.

Finally, decide how you want to set up the room for your meeting. If more than 20 people will be attending, set up chairs on the right and left sides with an aisle in between them. This setup will allow people to get in and out of the room easily — and if you're feeling confident enough, you can walk up and down the aisle as you're speaking.

### Preparing for a speech at a facility

If you're giving a talk at an outside location, be sure to work out all the details with the facility or the talk's sponsors ahead of time. For example, if you're giving a keynote speech, ask the following questions:

- Who can you contact at the facility if problems arise during your talk?
- Where can you park when you arrive at the facility?
- How many people are expected to attend your speech?
- Who will introduce you?
- Who else is speaking at the event, and when?

This last bit of information is especially important because it allows you to refer to other people's talks, which is a great way to create goodwill. For example, I recently spoke at a conference about the psychological profiles of business leaders who commit fraud. Before the conference, I discovered that one of the other speakers was going to talk about the connection between fraud and pornography, which was a topic I planned to touch on very briefly. So in my own speech, I mentioned my thoughts and then said, "I notice there's going to be a session on this later today that's likely to be very interesting." The other speaker appreciated the plug, which helped him draw a big crowd.

Also, specify what type of microphone you want, and what kind of podium (if any) you prefer. In addition, make sure you know how to operate any equipment you'll be using. And guarantee that either you or the event site will have backup equipment in case anything goes wrong.

If you're giving a longer seminar or workshop, you need to make additional arrangements. For example, work with the facility to determine how you want the room set up, what refreshments they should serve, and when you want to take breaks. You may have special lighting requests as well if, for example, you find it easier to speak when the lighting is lower.

One excellent way to make sure you cover all the bases is to send out an event planning form to the facility or the meeting sponsors. You can find examples online by searching for "event planning checklist."

Finally, make plenty of copies of your handouts as you finalize them. Pack them in your briefcase or car at least a day ahead of time so you won't make the classic mistake of leaving them at home. You can also ship your handouts ahead to the facility. And bring a hard copy, thumb drive, CD, or laptop to make sure you can make new copies fast if you need to. (If you give enough speeches, you eventually will — trust me!)

## *Practicing your technique*

When you speak, you want to come across as clear, strong, and convincing. To do that, you need to be comfortable with your material.

About a week ahead of time, start rehearsing your speech out loud. Here's a seven-day plan for building up to the big day. (Feel free to adapt it so it suits your needs.)

✔ **Day One:** Say your speech out loud for the first time. It will sound different out loud than it does on paper, so make adjustments. If you can, record your speech as you practice it. As you're talking, you'll spontaneously come up with good lead-ins, transitions, and phrasings. You can transfer these ideas from your recording to your speech notes.

✔ **Day Two:** Focus on the big picture. Familiarize yourself with your main points and the stories you want to tell. Also, look for spots where you have weak transitions, dreary wording, or a lack of "punch." See whether you can enliven these spots with proverbs, one-liners, quotes, and stories.

✔ **Day Three:** Work on adding flair. Imagine that you're a politician, and try adding forcefulness, enthusiasm, or even flamboyance. To improve the way you come across, work on the following skills:

- **Breathing correctly:** Breathing is the most important skill to master as a speaker, because it allows you to sound assertive and to project your voice well. To practice correct breathing, place one hand at the top of your stomach, just below the ribs, so you can feel your diaphragm. Now breathe in through your nose, imagining the air filling your stomach and flowing toward your back. Your diaphragm should expand out. When you breathe out, your diaphragm should move back in. Your shoulders should not move when you're breathing.

  By the way, this skill will serve you well not only in public speaking but also in everyday life. I used to frequently get sore throats and ear infections, and I even developed nodes on my vocal cords as a teenager. All of these cleared up as soon as I mastered the correct breathing technique.

- **Adjusting the volume knob:** Nothing says "boring" like a monotone voice, so change things up occasionally. Get a little louder when you're making a key point, or get very quiet when you want to catch people's attention.

- **Moving around:** The more you move, the more your voice will move, which helps keep your listeners' attention.

- **Pausing before or after a key point:** A brief silence will wake up your audience and ensure that they latch on to your message.

- **Leaning in toward your audience when you make an important point:** This trick projects confidence and helps you connect with your listeners.

- **Projecting:** Sometimes introverts tend to mumble. To avoid this problem, practice standing up straight and projecting your voice. The secret is to pretend that there are extra rows behind the last row and project your voice to the imaginary row.

- **Pivoting:** Introverts often make the mistake of talking to the screen behind them rather than to their audience. To avoid this error, master the art of pivoting back to your audience even when you're pointing to the screen. Better yet, have your presentation appear both on the screen behind you and on a laptop in front of you. This way, you won't need to look as frequently at the screen behind you.

---

## Dressing for success

Introverts often prefer clothes that camouflage — gray suits, subtle ties, discreet jewelry. But a chic dress or a bold tie may help you come across as a more influential speaker.

When you're planning your clothes for a speech, here's a good rule: Look at the most successful people in your company, division, or profession. Identify the most stylish people, and match that level.

---

✔ **Day Four:** Rehearse with your props and audiovisual equipment. Mark your cards to show where you'll use your audiovisual materials. Practice walking to the podium, and work on your gestures.

✔ **Day Five:** Do a dress rehearsal. Wear the clothes you plan to wear the day of the event, and use all your props. Do a complete run-through without stopping.

✔ **Day Six:** Give your speech in front of a few friends. Have them ask questions at the end. Think about any final tweaks you can make.

✔ **Day Seven:** Use the "whisper and speed-through" approach. The day of your talk, whisper the first few minutes of your speech to yourself and then run through the rest of the speech in double-time. Then say "Hey" a few times at full volume to limber up your voice. After that, do a big stretch — like a lion. Now you're ready to face your audience!

Although all this practice is important, it's also crucial to schedule some time to relax. Distracting yourself with a book, a TV show, or some time with friends or family will help you lower your stress level.

# Grabbing Your Audience: Six Ways to Win Them Over

People know that giving a speech is a challenge, and they admire folks who are brave enough to do it. So even before you start your talk, your listeners will be ready to love you. Here's how to make sure you keep them on your side when you start talking.

## Making your listeners feel comfortable and connected

When you step out in front of an audience, they expect a lot from you. They want to be informed, entertained, persuaded, or even challenged. But do you know what they want most of all? They want to know that you're comfortable — because that will make them comfortable as well.

So let your listeners see that you're relaxed and enthusiastic. In fact, act like you're having fun. Keep in mind that emotions are contagious! This is the perfect time to use some of that pretend-extrovert body language I talk about in Chapter 3. Lean toward your audience, use wide gestures, and smile with your entire face. (By the way, if you find it difficult to get extroverted body language down pat — and many introverts do — you may find it helpful to hire a skills coach. I talk more about coaches in Chapter 10.)

Also, make it clear that you believe in what you're saying. If you're passionate about your topic, let it show in your voice and your body language.

And remember that all-important pivot I talk about earlier in this chapter. When you're pointing to a slide behind you, pivot your body at least partly toward your listeners. That way, you'll stay connected with them instead of looking like you're talking to the wall.

Here are some other good ways to connect successfully with your listeners:

- ✔ **Make eye contact.** If you're speaking to a small audience, make meaningful eye contact at least once with each audience member. And try to make eye contact with at least three of them before you speak.

  If your audience is larger, or if making direct eye contact is extremely hard for you, use the "third eye" technique. When you look at people, direct your eyes to their foreheads, right between their eyebrows. To your listeners, it will appear as if you're looking directly into their eyes.

- ✔ **Show concern for your audience's comfort.** For example, if you think the room may be a little warm, ask them: "Is it too hot in here for you?" If so, ask the staff to turn down the thermostat.

- ✔ **Be sincere with your audience.** For example, you can compliment them sincerely by saying something like, "It's fun to talk about this topic with people who know so much about it."

- ✔ **Move closer to your listeners.** The less distance there is between you and them, the more strongly they'll connect with you. For example, if you're speaking on a stage, move to the very front of the stage.

- ✔ **Let your audience know what to expect.** For example, inform them upfront about how and when you'll handle questions, and when you'll offer breaks.

✔ **If you're talking in front of a large group, repeat each question you get.** By doing so, you can ensure that everyone in the audience (especially the people in the back of the room) can hear it and that you heard it correctly yourself.

✔ **When you're responding to questions, satisfy the people who ask them but also consider your entire audience.** Avoid going off on tangents that may interest only a few people in the room. And give everyone a chance to ask questions before letting someone ask a second question.

✔ **If you can't answer a question, say, "I don't know, but I can find out for you."** Doing so lets the audience member know that you care.

✔ **Finish on time!** Stop when you've said all you *need* to say — not all you *could* say.

And here's another tip: Stay in the moment. Don't just go through your speech exactly as you practiced it. Instead, observe your audience's reactions to your talk. Watch to see whether they're interested, amused, offended, confused, or just plain falling asleep. If they're still onboard with you, keep doing what you're doing. But if you're losing them, adjust your talk. For example, if they look confused, stop and ask for questions. If they're starting to doze, take a quick break.

Also, take mental notes about the problem areas in your speech so you can rework it later. If you find it hard to improve on your material or presentation, this is another area where a skills coach can help out.

---

# Handling mistakes with grace

Early in my speaking career, I worried a great deal about making mistakes. But one eye-opening speech changed my whole perspective on this issue.

I went to see Terry Cole-Whittaker, an author and minister. She was speaking to a thousand or more people, and her talk was being taped live. Terry was standing at the center of the stage, with a podium to one side. Suddenly, just in the middle of making a point, she forgot what she wanted to say.

Was she embarrassed? Not a bit. She simply held up her index finger to the audience, said, "Hold on a sec," and went to the podium to flip through her notes. As she did, she said to herself, "Covered this, covered that — aha!" With that, she walked right back to the center of the stage and continued her talk.

As I looked around, I saw the audience acting as if nothing had happened. Because Terry was comfortable and wasn't self-conscious, her listeners took her little goof right in stride.

Her example came in handy for me some time later when my contact lens suddenly started causing me eye pain in the middle of a speech. I simply stopped, held up my index finger, said "One moment," and walked to the podium to remove the lens. Then I turned to the audience and said, "Contact attack!" I got a big laugh and even a little round of applause.

Finally, resist the urge to apologize for any minor mistakes you make. This can actually make your audience uncomfortable. And it's unnecessary, because although you'll notice every error you make, your audience will miss most of them. So if you flub a sentence, just correct yourself and move right along. If you make a huge mistake, however, take a few seconds to say you're sorry, and then get right back to your material.

## Grabbing their attention with stories and humor

Dry facts and statistics can prove your points, but a great story makes your message unforgettable. And stories serve another important purpose: They help break the ice between you and your audience.

Because stories are so powerful, every world-class speaker sprinkles them throughout a talk. The trick, of course, is to pick the right stories and deliver them well. Here are some guidelines:

- **Keep your stories short at first, so listeners don't get lost in the details.** When you get more comfortable telling stories, you can try out longer ones.

- **Focus on stories that reinforce your key points.** Otherwise, you may distract your listeners.

- **Tell stories about yourself.** A story or two about your own foibles and failures can make you seem humble and help win over your audience. But tell stories like these only if you're confident that you can come across as an assertive presenter. Otherwise, they may make you seem weak.

- **Tell stories that play on people's emotions.** For example, one of my talks is about how people can master their minds and emotions to become outstanding leaders. In this talk, I tell stories about excellent leaders, but I also tell stories about parents dealing with children and teens, relating these stories to leadership behavior. These stories resonate emotionally with everyone in my audience (and they often get laughs from parents who can relate!).

- **At the end of a story, tie it back to the point you want to make.** For example, say, "So the moral of the story is . . ."

Connecting with your audience is crucial when you're telling a story, because storytelling is a little like having a personal conversation. So come out from behind the podium, look your audience members in the eye, and use some of the conversational gestures I outline in Chapter 4. Also, find spots where you can insert a little humor — especially at the beginning of your talk.

Although humor is a great way to bond with your audience, do use it carefully. Here are some cautions:

✔ **Make sure everyone will understand your humor.** For example, one friend of mine told a funny story involving a Raggedy Ann doll. The only problem was that several dozen audience members were from other countries, and they had no idea what she was talking about.

✔ **Within the body of your talk, stick to humorous stories or jokes that relate to your topic.** Although off-topic humor may get a laugh, it ultimately detracts from your message. (However, it's fine to use an off-topic joke or story to lighten the mood when you're getting back down to business after a break. I especially like to use humor — either on-topic or off-topic — to get people in the right frame of mind if I'm giving a keynote speech after a luncheon.)

✔ **Consider your stories or jokes from every angle to make sure they won't offend anyone.** And avoid any jokes that are even remotely off-color — even if your friends think they're hilarious. I'm often amazed by the inappropriate jokes speakers tell at meetings! My advice: If you're not sure a joke is inoffensive, don't say it.

✔ **Avoid puns and groaners.** One bad joke may be okay, but two or more could turn your audience off permanently.

One of the best ways to find humorous stories is to talk to the people you meet each day. For example, my friend Jeanne Robertson, a professional speaker and humorist, makes a habit of asking taxi drivers questions like "Who was the strangest passenger you ever had?" and "What's the most bizarre experience you remember in your career?" You can ask similar questions to grocery store clerks, teachers, and anyone else you meet.

And here's a trade secret I'm giving away: One of the best sources for funny stories is the good old *Reader's Digest.* You can also pick up humorous stories or jokes from news programs, late-night shows, and newspapers. I've even gotten laughs with "stupid burglar" stories I heard on TV. So look around you — you'll find plenty of laughs.

## Persuading with power

A persuasive speech is one of the trickiest talks to give. That's because you need to win over a roomful of people who may be apathetic, unsure, or even hostile.

The biggest mistake speakers make in this kind of talk is to use a hard sell. If you twist your listeners' arms, they're likely to resist. And if you try to persuade through fear, your words won't have a lasting effect.

Instead, smart persuaders focus on two skills: *matching* and *pacing*. I take a look at these skills next, and then show you how to use both in a persuasive speech.

### Understanding matching and pacing

Matching and pacing are two of the most powerful tools in a speaker's repertoire. In fact, they can make the difference between a masterful speech and one that flops.

*Matching* is based on the principle that to get people to change, you need to start by seeing things from their point of view. For example, imagine that I think a flower is pink, and Tom thinks it's orange. I can hammer Tom all day long with facts and opinions, but the odds are he'll just spout his own facts and opinions back at me. And eventually, he'll simply shut down.

If I'm smart, I'll use matching instead. I'll put myself in Tom's shoes, and do my best to understand why he thinks the flower is orange. This doesn't mean that I need to agree with him. But it means that I need to look at the flower from Tom's perspective.

When I do this, I won't risk coming across as a judgmental person who's thinking, "I need to enlighten Tom about his delusion." Instead, I'll come across as an ally who's interested in his ideas and opinions.

Similarly, if you're trying to persuade an entire audience to make a change, you need to know where they're starting out. For example, if you're hoping to get a roomful of people to consider a new phone system, ask yourself questions like these:

- ✔ What do these people like about their current phone system?
- ✔ Could they have good reasons for resisting a change?
- ✔ Are they likely to be thinking about the benefits but also the extra costs to them if they get a new system?

With this information in hand, you can show your listeners that you grasp their reality. And once you do that, you can begin moving them gradually to your position — a trick called *pacing*.

### Identifying the five stages of a persuasive talk

To gain your listeners' attention, trust, and buy-in, you need to win them over in stages. Here are five steps for doing so.

### 1. Create awareness

In your introduction, you want to use *matching* to show your audience that you understand their situation. In addition, you want to clearly describe the issue you're focusing on and explain it in a way that grabs your listeners' attention. And finally, you want to persuade them that you're an expert who's worthy of their attention.

For example, are you trying to sell your audience on a new and more secure type of banking software? If so, include these elements in your opening:

- ✔ To get your audience to grasp the risk they're facing, offer an example of a hacker bringing down a bank's entire system. (And to really bring your point home, you can tell a story about a theft that occurred at a bank very similar to theirs.) After that, offer statistics about the cost of online theft.

- ✔ To show that you understand your audience's concerns, mention one or two reasons they may hesitate to buy your new system. For example, acknowledge that budgets are tight, and they may not want to spend the money. (That's *matching*.) Then reassure them by saying that you'll address this concern in your talk.

- ✔ To show your audience why they should listen to you, establish your credibility. You're expecting people to change, and that makes them nervous — so show them that you're someone they can trust to steer them wisely. To do this, lay out your credentials and tell real-life stories about your experience with banking systems.

If you succeed in this step, your audience will think, "I want to hear this" and "This person knows what he's talking about." And that's the first stage of persuasion.

### 2. Outline the issue

In your first main point, dive more deeply into the issue you want your listeners to address. Give them solid facts about how the issue affects them now and how it's likely to affect them, their families, or their company in the future.

When you do this, avoid making strong assumptions such as "If you don't upgrade your system, you're going to be attacked within the year." Instead, say something more tentative like "I have grave concerns that your current system is leaving you open to an attack in the near future, and here's why."

Also, keep letting your listeners see that you understand and empathize with their situation. For example, say things like "It's frustrating when that happens, isn't it?" or "When this issue occurs, it knocks your entire project off the rails, doesn't it?"

At the end of this stage, you want your audience to think, "He understands our position, and we understand his. And he's not just giving us the hard sell. We can see why he believes this issue is so important for us."

### 3. Describe the solution with pacing

In your second main point, tell your listeners exactly how they can address their issue. Here's where you'll get into *pacing* — that is, moving your audience from their point of view to yours.

Start by describing all possible solutions, and then narrow your focus to the best solution (which, of course, is the one you're recommending). As you do this, be honest. Outline the pros and cons of each solution, including the one you recommend. Doing so will win your listeners' trust.

Your goal at this stage is to create a collaborative attitude. When you do, your audience will be thinking, "Of all the possibilities, this is the best."

### 4. Get your listeners to visualize success

In your third main point, get your audience to actively picture themselves solving their problem. Doing so will make the solution feel real to them.

For instance, say things like the following:

- ✔ "Imagine that you're using this technology on your nursing floors right now. Picture what the nurses are doing. Can you envision how the technology may make their jobs easier while also saving you time and manpower? Will it give you better readouts that improve patient care?"

- ✔ "Imagine that our firm takes over all these tedious bookkeeping tasks for you. In addition, we make sure your financial reports comply with every federal and state law, so you don't need to lie awake nights worrying about making dangerous mistakes. And we do all of this for a price that's well within your budget."

Also, get your audience in on the game. Open the floor for comments, and have your listeners suggest ways in which they can visualize themselves using your product or service. At this stage, you can actually turn your talk into a brainstorming session — and your audience may come up with great ideas that you never even thought of!

Finally, if possible, physically demonstrate a product, service, or skill. This activity is a very powerful way to win your audience over.

Master this step, and your audience will say, "I see how we can address this problem or issue, and this is the way to do it." Now you're nearly done — but there's one final step you need to take to get full buy-in.

### 5. Lay out action steps

As you approach the end of your talk, spell out the actions your listeners can take to accomplish the goal you've recommended. Break these actions into small, easy-to-do steps. Ask whether your listeners have any questions about these actions, and make sure you clarify any misunderstandings.

Succeed in this step, and your audience will say, "I want to do this" and "How can I participate?" And then you can say "hurray," because you've accomplished your mission!

## Changing things up to keep your listeners' attention

Your audience has a short attention span, and they'll soon start snoozing if you lecture them for too long at a workshop or seminar. Here's the general rule: Don't go more than 30 minutes without doing something to break the routine.

You can offer a lot of different activities to give your listeners a change of pace. For example, ask your audience to do problem-solving activities or have several listeners role-play a situation. Depending on what your topic is, you may even be able to pass objects around the room for your audience to inspect.

Also, find ways to play to the three different types of learners:

- **Auditory learners:** These people like lectures and question-and-answer sessions.
- **Visual learners:** These people prefer handouts, PowerPoints, and slide shows.
- **Kinesthetic learners:** These learners like action, so get them involved by asking them to fill out forms or even move around the room.

## Handling hecklers with ease

If you're lucky, all your audience members will be kind and sympathetic. But there's always a chance that you'll encounter some rude or obnoxious people. An extrovert can generally shake these people off easily, but if you're an introvert, a heckler can derail your entire speech.

I know this from first-hand experience, because it happened to me when I was just starting out in my career. I was talking to about 200 people at a convention, and I'd just listed four keys to a good marriage: good chemistry, trust, mutual respect, and true friendship.

That doesn't sound very controversial, does it? So I was startled when a woman in the middle of the room jumped out of her seat and yelled, "How do you know that?"

I froze, stunned by her belligerence. Somehow, I stumbled through a response and finished my talk, but I never regained my poise.

Afterward, I met up with a friend of mine who'd attended the talk and said, "Give me the bad news." She replied, "You were doing great until that woman yelled at you, but after that you never smiled again." As a result, I'd lost my audience for good.

 That's when I learned the biggest trick for handling hecklers: No matter what, just keep smiling. I've tested this over and over in real life, and it works like a charm. So these days, if an audience member disagrees strongly with me, I do what I call "talking to my face." I say, "Face — just keep smiling." This shows the audience that I'm in control. It also relaxes me, so I can calmly paraphrase the person's remarks and address them.

Another effective trick is to make strong eye contact if you're heckled. Doing so shows your audience (and your heckler) that you're assertive.

When someone heckles you, repeat the question so the entire audience hears it. And make sure you understand exactly what the person is objecting to, so you can address the criticism clearly. You may discover that you simply didn't communicate your point effectively. If so, you can apologize and restate your information.

Also, see if you can reframe the person's question to make it more positive. For instance, if the person says, "You're completely wrong about that," respond calmly by saying, "It's interesting that you feel strongly about that point. Many people do, so let me take a moment to outline the evidence that led me to my conclusions." In addition, seek out areas where the two of you agree. This will make the person more open to listening to you.

If a heckler doesn't seem satisfied by your response, and the rest of your audience wants to move on, you can offer to talk with the person further after your speech. Or, on very rare occasions, it might be wise to simply say, "Let's agree to disagree." If you choose this last approach, be specific about the point you disagree on.

One thing to remember if you're heckled is that the audience will typically turn against the heckler and want to protect you. So if you just keep your cool, your listeners will have an even deeper rapport with you after a heckling than they did before.

## Being yourself

Now that you're equipped with the rules for grabbing your audience, here's one more secret: Feel free to break these rules if it works for you.

Why? Because one rule trumps all the others: *Stay true to yourself.* You'll be more relaxed and authoritative when you're not pretending to be someone you aren't, and your audience will reward you for your authenticity.

As an example, I recently attended a talk by a well-known author. I could tell from the outset that he was an introvert. Before his speech, as he sat off to the side of the stage with several other people, he turned on his cellphone, completely tuning out both the audience and the people next to him. In fact, he didn't put his phone away until after another speaker introduced him. Then he got up and proceeded to give one of the most brilliant speeches I've ever heard. He didn't make as much eye contact as most speakers, and he focused more on his presentation than on his listeners, but the audience ate it up with a spoon.

So follow the basic rules for public speaking, but put your own personal stamp on them. Just make sure you're still reaching your listeners and getting your message across.

# Catching Your Breath and Briefly Taking the Spotlight Off Yourself

If you're an introvert, talking for a long time to a roomful of people can drain your batteries. The best way to regain your energy is to step out of the picture for a few minutes. In this section, I offer three good ways to do this.

## Asking your audience for input

If you're giving a workshop or seminar, identify spots where you can ask your audience to contribute their own opinions. If you're lucky, you'll kick off an interesting discussion and you can relax for a few minutes while they carry the ball.

One excellent technique is to throw a provocative question out to your entire audience. For example, I start one of my presentations by telling the audience the details of a horrific crime committed by a young woman — a case that's relevant to the topic I'm discussing. And then I say, "So why do you think she did it?" Within seconds, my audience is happily bouncing ideas off each other and offering good (or wild) guesses. It's a real crowd-pleaser, and it focuses their attention on each other, not on me. Because I'm naturally more introverted and facilitative, this makes me feel more comfortable and allows me to ease into my speech.

Another technique is to direct a question at a single member of your audience. For example, ask, "Can anyone here tell me how your company currently handles product recalls?" Then pick on that extrovert in the front row who's waving frantically, and let him take the floor for a while. If you have a large audience, stop the person occasionally and let him know that you want to paraphrase what he's saying so the whole audience can stay with him.

And here's a good trick: Redirect a single audience member's question to the entire group. For instance, say, "That's a great question! What do the rest of you think about that?" It's a fun way to energize your audience, and it lets you step into the background for a moment.

## Offering handouts

No matter what your topic is, it's a good bet that you can come up with some handouts to offer your listeners. Doing so is a great idea because you're not just providing a handy source of information; in addition, these handouts can provide a quick time-out for you.

At my talks, I often seat people in groups around tables and give them handouts that allow them to work together while I take a few minutes to relax. For instance, I like to offer case studies they can discuss.

Make sure your handouts are attractive and error-free, but don't spend too much money on them if they're for a conference breakout session. (Many people will toss them out right after the meeting.) Do put your name and contact info on each page, so the people who keep the handouts can contact you if they want to. Also, copyright any original material you're using, and be sure to ask permission and give credit if you use someone else's material.

Some speakers put their handout material online at their websites so people can access it later. But do this only if you don't mind having other people "borrow" it and pass it off as their own.

# *Scheduling battery-recharging breaks*

Breaks can quickly restore your audience's energy after a long spell of sitting. And if you're an innie, they're lifesavers for you as well! So if you're giving a workshop or seminar, schedule quick breaks frequently.

It's standard to offer one 15-minute break in the morning and one 15-minute break in the afternoon. I sometimes offer two breaks in the morning and two in the afternoon, and I always provide a break when food arrives. In addition, I like to offer a "stand up and stretch" break every hour or so. (And I always tell my listeners to feel free to get up and leave at any time if they need to dash to the restroom.) I also know speakers who break on the hour every hour.

If you're hoping to escape the room for a few minutes during a break, be prepared with a polite excuse that will help you avoid any audience members who want to stay and chat. For instance, you can say, "I need to dash out and make a phone call right now, but I'd love to talk after my speech." And check with the facility beforehand to see whether it has a private area where you can hide out and regroup during longer breaks.

# Chapter 8

# Managing Up

## In This Chapter

▶ Strengthening your relationship with your boss

▶ Adding value by going beyond your job description

▶ Avoiding common mistakes when you're managing up

*I*f you're an introvert, you may find it difficult to get the recognition you deserve in the workplace. There's a chance that your boss overlooks you even when you're doing a stellar job, because the office extroverts tend to steal the spotlight.

So what's the solution? A technique called *managing up.* This method is a great way to show your quiet power, and it fits right in with your introverted nature.

Managing up enables you to make a strong impression on your manager and put yourself on the fast track to a raise or promotion. In addition, it empowers you to gain the trust and respect of others, so they'll be more willing to hear what you have to say.

Managing up has two key elements: Getting in sync with your manager, and redefining your role to make yourself more valuable. In this chapter, I tell you the secrets for doing both. And because managing up has its pitfalls, I also spell out the mistakes to avoid. Last but not least, I tell you how to make managing up a habit.

# The First Step in Managing Up: Knowing Your Manager

When you manage up, you have two goals: to get ahead, *and* to help your boss get ahead. When you accomplish both these goals, you can transform yourself from a useful employee into an indispensable one. You'll go beyond simply being a person with handy skills and experience and become an asset your boss can't live without.

To succeed at this win-win game, you need to start by building a stronger relationship with your manager. And to do this, you need to get in tune with her working style, identify her personal agenda, and earn her trust. In this section, I explain how to achieve all three of these goals.

## Responding to your manager's style

Picture your relationship with your boss as a dance. If you're following your manager's lead smoothly, you'll make a great impression. But if you're doing the samba when your boss wants to waltz, you'll get tripped up quickly.

So one of the most important keys to managing up is to study your boss's style and fall into step with it. To do so successfully, you have to zero in on your boss's likes, dislikes, strengths, weaknesses, and relationships with others. For example, see whether you can answer these questions:

- Is your manager an introvert or an extrovert?
- Is your manager a hands-on leader, or does she prefer to delegate?
- Does your manager like to get information in person, over the phone, or via e-mail or instant messaging? How often does she want people to report to her?
- Is your manager interested in learning about her team's personal lives, or is she all business?
- Does your manager thrive on chaos, or does she get overwhelmed easily?
- Does your manager want people to be assertive and outspoken, or does she prefer quiet humility?
- What kind of sense of humor does your manager have?
- Is your manager experienced and secure, or is she new and a little nervous?
- Does your manager like risk-takers, or does she prefer people who follow the rules?

### *Understanding your manager's personality*

You should make an attempt to analyze your boss's personality. In Chapter 6, I introduce the DISC model of personality. DISC divides people into four categories: *decisive, influential, stable,* and *conscientious.* (These categories can sometimes overlap.) Here's how these dimensions play out when it comes to managers:

✔ **Decisive bosses** tend to focus on the big picture. They're forceful, goal-oriented leaders who are a terrific asset if their values mesh well with the company's. On the downside, they can be intimidating. In addition, they often make decisions on their own and forget to notify other people before acting on those decisions. They also tend to be black-and-white thinkers.

✔ **Influential bosses** tend to focus on the big picture. These likeable managers are natural motivators who offer a lot of positive and general feedback, like "atta boy" and "keep it up — this is great work." They like to get advice from a wide range of people instead of relying on a few opinions. They're upbeat and positive, but they can be poor listeners who often interrupt with their own ideas (although they'll listen to your feedback). Also, they tend to take on too many commitments and don't always follow through on them. Their management and organization skills may be lacking, and they have a tendency to put people they like ahead of top performers.

✔ **Stable bosses** have their people's backs. They're also protective of the company and its finances. They're good about guarding their people against flak from others (including upper management) and generous about giving their people credit for their efforts. They like to depend on a small group of trusted advisors and bounce ideas off of them. They give quiet positive feedback, often in indirect ways. On the negative side, they can be stubborn and rigid, and they may have trouble being assertive. And of the four types of managers, this group struggles the most to communicate what they expect.

✔ **Conscientious leaders** are task-oriented. They love to dig into the details of a project, and they're especially keen on knowing how a team plans to go about achieving a task. They're into quiet feedback, and they're good about giving credit to their staffs. But they may have poor listening skills and interrupt people. They can also be determined to get their own way, and some of them fail to take criticism well. They tend to have a perfectionist streak, and they may micromanage. In addition, they may go on and on about detailed and technical ideas without asking for feedback, checking to see whether you understand them, or letting you get a word in edgewise.

### *Matching your skills to your boss's style and personality*

After you identify your boss's style and personality, decide how your own skills can mesh with her needs. Here are some examples:

- ✔ If your boss is a conscientious, detail-oriented leader, offer a lot of information in your reports and update her frequently. But if she's a decisive, big-picture person, focus on the key points and trim down the details. (But no matter what style your boss prefers, always make sure she gets crucial information quickly. No manager wants to be blindsided and have to say, "Er, sorry, I wasn't aware of that problem.")

  By the way, one good way to please either type of boss is to write a detailed report and highlight the key points. A big-picture boss will simply read what you've highlighted, while a detail-oriented boss will tend to read it all but focus primarily on the highlighted points.

- ✔ If your boss is an introvert, give her the facts she needs without spending a lot of time on small talk (unless she initiates it). But if she's an extrovert, put on your pretend-extrovert act at times and schmooze with her.

Also, adjust your pace to suit your manager's needs. Some managers can absorb tons of information quickly and efficiently. Others easily get overwhelmed, and they'll do better if you slow down and deliver your facts in small, easy-to-digest chunks after giving them a heads-up about what you'll be covering.

You can learn a lot just from watching your boss in action, but it's also important to ask her upfront about her preferences. For example, say, "Would you like to get these reports in person or via e-mail?" A good rule to follow is: When in doubt, ask! In addition, schedule regular meetings so you can update your boss on your work and make sure you're meeting her expectations.

Always keep this concept in mind: Your goal isn't to change your boss; it's to change *yourself,* so she and the other people above you will respect and trust you and be interested in what you have to say.

## *Identifying your manager's goals*

Managers work hard to achieve their company's goals, but they also have their own agendas. When you know what your manager's most important goals are, you can focus on helping her achieve them — and that's an excellent way to gain her respect.

# Talking tactfully with your boss

When you're building a relationship with your manager, it's vital to communicate in ways that build bonds rather than strain them. Here are some good ways to get your message across tactfully when you need to address problems.

✔ Focus on one specific situation or behavior that truly concerns you. For example, it may be an area in which you're getting a lot of push-back from other departments.

✔ Acknowledge any extenuating circumstances, and describe the situation in neutral or sympathetic language. For instance, say, "I know you've been extremely busy with the reorganization. At the same time, the deadline for handing in performance appraisals is coming up."

✔ Share your concern. The best way to begin is by using the phrase "I am concerned . . . ," which is non-judgmental. (You can also say "I'm worried," but go with "concerned" if you can.) For example, say, "I am concerned that we may not get the appraisals done in time unless we start right away."

✔ Never share a problem without having suggestions for a solution! Ask your boss, "What can I do to get the ball rolling?" Or say, "What if I get the ball rolling by getting the forms to everyone and asking them to fill them out and get them back to you by Friday?"

✔ Ask permission to take action. Do this even if your meeting is informal and especially if you're discussing a sensitive matter. When you ask permission, use tentative language. For example, say, "Would you be comfortable with that?" Keep your tone of voice soft and your body language sympathetic. If you gesture, keep your hands open and your palms up with your fingers together. Forceful gestures, such as pointing at your boss (or anyone else in the room), can make her angry or defensive.

To get in touch with what's important to your manager, determine what she values the most. Think in terms of what I call the *Six Ps of Motivation*: *pleasure, power, prestige, productivity, profit,* and *problem solving.* Rank these values in the order you think your boss would rank them. (It may take you a couple of years to get to know her well enough to do this.) At the same time, rank them for yourself and your company to help you see how well your goals, your boss's goals, and your company's goals align.

Also, focus on specific questions like these:

✔ Is your boss hoping to earn a promotion?

✔ Does she want to expand her staff or her authority?

✔ Does she need more funding?

✔ Which projects does she feel are the most important?

✔ What kind of pressure is she under?

✔ What are her personal values and beliefs?

✔ Is she concerned with balancing her work and her home life?

## Keep an eye on your boss's friends and enemies

To promote your manager's agenda, you need to know who her strongest allies are. In addition, you want to know whether she has enemies within the company or at least people who may undermine her efforts.

When you spot your boss's friends and foes, here's how to handle each group:

✔ Keep the allies in the loop about your boss's projects and needs, and call on them for help if you need to. Go out of your way to help them with their projects as well, so you can strengthen their ties with your boss. Get your boss's permission first, of course.

✔ Be extra-careful in your dealings with the people who aren't on your boss's side.

Double-check to make sure you don't commit any errors or oversights that would give them ammunition to use against your manager. If you have any questions about what they need, ask for clarification — and if they're angry, defuse their ire by listening to them carefully. But be careful never to suggest that your boss or department was wrong, unless that's clearly the case. (If it is, apologize and do everything you can to correct the situation.) In addition, find ways to help these people, after making sure your boss is okay with this. If you're lucky, you may be able to convert them to allies.

When you have a handle on your boss's agenda, you'll know where to focus your own energy. For example, if she's concerned about increasing productivity, look for ways to speed up your team's or department's processes. And if she's heavily invested in a particular project, devote a lot of time to it even if it's not at the top of your own priority list.

## *Earning your manager's trust*

Managers have a lot of different styles and personalities, but they're all alike in one way: They need to trust you.

This idea sounds pretty simple, but it's not. After all, managers are people, and people come with a lot of baggage. Some people are naturally unable to trust other people. Others are slow to trust, possibly suspicious because they've been burned in the past.

So don't automatically assume that your manager trusts you. Instead, actively demonstrate that you're worthy of trust. Here are some good ways to do so:

✔ Defend your manager if other people criticize her. To do this, first listen carefully to what the critics are saying and then paraphrase their message, for example, "If I'm hearing you correctly, you're concerned that you aren't getting enough feedback from Cheryl." Next, offer a different perspective on the problem. For example, you can say, "I'm sorry you're having that experience. I do know that Cheryl has been overwhelmed for the last few months with several other initiatives that were scheduled for this time frame as well, and her sister is also getting married next month. So she's been pushed to the wall. I'll pass this information on to her, but in the meantime, is there a way to get the info you need without depending on Cheryl; or do you have other ideas about how we can make things work better?"

✔ Avoid gossiping or spreading rumors, and stay out of office politics unless your boss has specifically asked you to keep an ear out for certain information. If that isn't the case, it's probably best not to share gossip (ever heard of "shooting the messenger"?). Good bosses don't get upset at people who pass on bad news — are you listening out there, managers? — and will actually thank the people who clued them in. But unless you know for sure that your boss is one of these wise people, keep your lips zipped.

✔ If you have a disagreement with your boss, keep it to yourself. Don't complain to your coworkers.

✔ Admit your mistakes upfront instead of trying to cover them up. Then do everything you can to correct those mistakes.

✔ Follow through on everything you promise to do; if you can't follow through, inform your manager quickly.

✔ Pass on crucial information to your manager as quickly and as accurately as possible.

Also, stay strong when things fall apart. Your boss needs to know that she can trust you to keep your wits about you when crises occur. So in troubled times, don't panic or whine. Instead, stick your chin up and ask, "What can I do to help?"

At those times when your boss is wrong about something, fight the urge to just keep quiet. Sometimes it's difficult for introverts to point out the flaws in a manager's reasoning, but it can earn you respect. Most managers don't fully trust "yes" men, so share your concerns politely and professionally.

Of course, there's always a chance that your boss won't respond well to your honesty. If she doesn't, ask yourself whether you want to stay with this manager. Good managers encourage different viewpoints, and if your boss doesn't do this, you may find it hard to build an honest and mutually beneficial relationship.

# The Second Step in Managing Up: Expanding Your Role

In a highly competitive world, you can't always catch people's attention simply by doing your job well, especially if you're a quiet introvert who doesn't like to blow your own horn.

What's the solution? Make yourself memorable or even essential. To do so, you need to look beyond your job description and ask, "How can I stretch my role and make myself more valuable?" In this section, I help you answer this question and provide some good ways to accomplish this step.

## Spotting avenues for growth

Do your job competently day after day, and you'll get by, but you may not get ahead. So if you're aiming for a higher spot on the organizational chart, you want to keep updating and expanding your skills.

One good way is to take advantage of any training your company encourages or any training that can improve your job skills. Also attend workshops and conferences in your area, and think about updating your skills by taking online courses or classes at a local college. When you master new skills, be sure to tell your boss about them.

And don't just focus on mastering new skills that fall within your current job description. Instead, make a list of any skills that could make you a greater asset to your company. For instance:

- Would learning a foreign language make you more valuable to your manager and your firm or further your career?
- Would taking a course on business writing help you communicate with your boss and coworkers more effectively?
- Would joining a public speaking club help you express yourself better?

In addition, think about joining professional organizations. These can help you stay current in your field and allow you to make connections that may benefit both you and your manager. Joining these organizations also demonstrates to your manager that you're willing to invest your own time and effort in bettering yourself.

# Becoming a problem solver

All day long, people come to your manager with problems. To set yourself apart, come to her with solutions.

As an introvert, you're likely to have excellent research and problem-solving skills. So when an issue arises at work, take these steps before telling your boss (unless the matter is urgent):

- ✔ Collect as much information as you can about the problem. Why did it arise? Who is involved? How will the problem affect your manager, your department, or the firm?
- ✔ Are there steps you can take on your own to solve the problem or at least reduce the damage?
- ✔ Are there coworkers who can help you solve the problem?

When you have answers, tell your boss about the problem and sketch out your ideas for solving it. Do this frequently, and you'll become her go-to person when crises come up.

# Stepping outside your comfort zone

Introverts often hesitate when it comes to taking risks. That can be a good thing if it protects you from making big mistakes. But it can be a bad thing if it keeps you stuck in place.

To manage up successfully, you need to push your limits by taking on new tasks and responsibilities. This can be very hard for you if you're a perfectionist, as many introverts are. But after you have a strong track record, you'll be much more confident about trying new things. And with each additional skill you master, you'll become more valuable to your manager and your company.

So don't just wait for your boss to expand your responsibilities. Instead, actively seek out challenging projects that will help you stretch your wings.

# Volunteering as a peer coach

Your manager wants to build a strong team, and here's a place where you can be a big help. When new employees come onboard or existing employees need help, ask your boss if she'd like you to help them get off on the right foot by coaching them.

Coaching is a big job, and it's not as easy as it sounds. For one thing, it requires skill in giving constructive feedback. (For tips on doing this, see Chapter 6.) You'll also need a lot of patience and a good attitude. And you'll need good organizational skills as well, because you'll need to do your own job while training your peer to do hers.

But if you understand the basic principles, you can become a very skilled coach — and that will make you, the employee you coach, *and* your boss look good. Here are good guidelines for coaching in a winning way.

### Setting coaching goals

As a coach, you'll work with your peer to create good goals. The best approach is to use what's called the *SMART* goal-setting method. To find out about this method, see Chapter 9. As you create your SMART goals, ask these questions:

- ✔ What skills does the person need to achieve this goal?
- ✔ What information and knowledge does she need?
- ✔ What help, assistance, or collaboration will she need from her coach? From others?
- ✔ What resources will she need?
- ✔ What can block her progress?

When you have a good handle on these goals, it's time to prioritize them. Ask yourself:

- ✔ Which is the most important goal we need to work on?
- ✔ In what order should we work on our goals?

Next, break the goals down into a monthly and weekly timetable. (It's best not to work on more than three goals at a time.) Spell out the skills and behaviors your peer needs to master to reach each goal.

Also, let your manager and coworkers know about the goals you're working on. That way, everyone can support both of you. And encourage your peer to post her goals where she'll see them daily.

As you write out goals, state each one in a positive way. For example, avoid saying "Joshua will stop writing incomplete reports." Instead, write a SMART goal like this: "Joshua will write and submit five reports following the guidelines as outlined in the internal business writing class."

In each meeting with your peer, focus on which goals you're working on and which ones your peer has mastered. A clear understanding of your peer's progress will keep both of you on the right track.

## *Cultivating a non-judgmental approach*

When you first start coaching a peer, it's tempting to judge the person. For example, you may think, "Jerry seems lazy," or "Brenda is very moody." But judging is a quick way to alienate your peer, especially if you voice your opinions out loud.

Instead, focus on activities, behaviors, events, and results. When you do so, you'll remain neutral or positive. You'll also do a better job of pinpointing areas in which your peer can improve.

To see the difference between judgmental and non-judgmental statements, compare these sentences:

> "Jack, you've been very uncooperative lately."

> "Jack, yesterday I noticed you didn't get the attendance list to the department by the deadline. When can you get it over there?"

The first statement will make Jack angry and defensive. The second, on the other hand, will tell him that he needs to improve a specific behavior: turning in the attendance list on time. As a result, he's likely to come through next time.

Another good approach is to ask your peer to interpret her own behavior. For example, ask these questions:

✔ "Is this behavior helpful or hurtful?"

✔ "How do you think other people would interpret this behavior?"

Asking your peer to interpret her own behavior is an excellent method because it allows you to remain totally neutral. As a result, you can maintain a positive relationship while helping your peer spot negative behaviors and correct them.

## *Embracing your roles as a peer coach*

As a coach, you'll wear four different hats. You'll educate, motivate, collaborate, and delegate. Here's a little more about each role.

### *Educating*

You'll put on your educator's hat if an employee needs to learn new information, do something she's never done before, or improve her existing skills. As an educator, you'll create a safe environment that allows your peer to ask questions and try out new skills. You'll also assess what she knows, set realistic goals, and offer detailed step-by-step instructions.

Here are the types of things you can say to an employee in this stage:

- ✔ "What would you like to learn in our time together?"
- ✔ "How do you learn best? Do you prefer pictures, verbal instruction, repetition, or hands-on practice?"
- ✔ "Tell me what you already know about this skill."
- ✔ "Can you show me how you learned to do this task?"
- ✔ "Have you done similar tasks in the past?"
- ✔ "Here is what we're going to do, step by step. I'll stop and ask you frequently if you have questions, so I can coach you more effectively."
- ✔ "Here are the results we expect at the end of this task."
- ✔ "Are you ready to move ahead, or am I going too quickly?"

When you're educating, let your peer shadow you or perform tasks in a way that allows her to learn without creating damage. That way she can build her confidence before you turn her loose in the real world.

### Motivating

You'll switch to your motivator's hat if your peer is apathetic and needs a gentle push. Here, you'll listen patiently and encourage questions. You'll also explain the value of tasks, emphasize the benefits of doing them well, acknowledge any difficulties the person is having, and applaud progress.

Here are some good questions to ask an employee when you're trying to motivate her:

- ✔ "What parts of this assignment do you like?"
- ✔ "What about this assignment is frustrating for you? Where do you feel stuck?"
- ✔ "How can I, as your coach and your coworker, support you?"
- ✔ "Do you have any personal goals that you believe fit into this project?"
- ✔ "How will you reward yourself when you achieve your goal at the end of this assignment?"
- ✔ "What do you think is the best solution to this problem?"
- ✔ "What will you be able to do as a result of accomplishing this goal?"
- ✔ "Let's discuss what's working well and also areas to improve upon, and come up with a plan of action."

The best motivators know that every peer has an unspoken question: "What's in it for me?" So give your peer a lot of positive reinforcement (see Chapter 5 for more on this). When she succeeds, let her know you're delighted. And if she fails, praise her for trying. Make it safe for her to talk about where she's successful and where she needs more help — and then give her that help.

Also, make sure the person you're coaching works with you to decide the following:

- ✔ What behavior needs to change
- ✔ Why the change is necessary
- ✔ How the change will occur

The toughest peer-coaching tasks often involve long-term employees who say, "That's the way I've always done it." If this happens, acknowledge their viewpoint and then review the task with them to make sure you're both on the same page. Also, *thank them* (even before you start the review) for their willingness to demonstrate how they perform the task. They may be right and truly know more than you thought! Or they may be wrong and realize it as you step through the task together.

If it turns out that these peers do know their stuff, you can move pretty quickly to the next stage. But never move straight to the final stage (delegating) unless both you and your boss are convinced that these employees are ready to go solo. Otherwise, you may be setting them up for failure.

### Collaborating

You'll become a collaborator when your peer starts getting comfortable in her role. Now it's time to let her stretch her wings! So push her to try new things and to address new challenges. Also, let her work with you as an equal when you're solving problems and making decisions.

In this phase, you can ask your peer questions like these:

- ✔ "What are you learning from this project? How are you applying the methods you've learned?"
- ✔ "What additional skills would you like to hone now that you understand your job?"
- ✔ "What are some of the ways we can streamline this project?"
- ✔ "Why do you think the team is struggling on defining the scope of the project?"
- ✔ "Are we forgetting any important details? If so, what?"
- ✔ "What do you have in mind for handling that difficult client?"

Be sure you continue to praise your peer each time she tries a new skill or reaches a new milestone. In particular, reward her if she keeps setting the bar higher for herself.

### Delegating

You'll take on the role of a delegator when you see that your peer is ready to fly on her own. At this point, you won't need to monitor her tasks. Instead, you'll encourage her to evaluate her own skills and output. Here are the kinds of questions you can ask your peer at this stage:

- ✔ "Did you accomplish the goals of the task as well as the personal goals you set for yourself?"

- ✔ "Were you satisfied with your results? Are they measurable and noticeable?"

- ✔ "How do you feel about your performance? What were three positive things you did?"

- ✔ "What have you learned?"

- ✔ "How do you know the task was accomplished successfully? What signs or indicators let you know this?"

- ✔ "Can you complete all facets of this task?"

- ✔ "What support do you need from me or others to continue to be successful in this and related projects?"

- ✔ "Are you able to teach all or a portion of this task to others?"

When you reach this stage, you can cut down to a few face-to-face meetings each month. Be sure to announce this milestone clearly so your peer knows she's ready to go out on her own. For example, say, "Congratulations! Although I'll be checking in with you a few times over the next few months, you've officially graduated from working with me. Lunch is on you!"

When your peer is ready to soar on her own, be sure to let your manager know. And if you enjoyed your coaching experience, let your boss know that you're willing to take another coworker under your wing.

# Avoiding Pitfalls When You're Managing Up

Managing up is a powerful tool that can help you move quickly up the career ladder. But just like any tool, this one comes with a few warning labels! That's because if you do it wrong, you'll risk offending other people instead of impressing them.

So when you plan your managing-up strategy, be careful to keep these rules in mind:

- ✔ Before stretching yourself beyond your job description, make sure this plan is fine with your manager. In fact, consider showing her this chapter. It can be a great way to start a conversation that will lead to a better relationship between you.

- ✔ Avoid stepping on other people's toes. Ask for additional tasks and responsibilities, but make sure you aren't stealing assignments from other coworkers.

- ✔ Don't bite off more than you can chew. When you volunteer for additional projects or offer to take over some of the tasks on your manager's to-do list, make sure you have the time to follow through. Good intentions won't make up for dropping the ball.

- ✔ Avoid placing your own goals ahead of the company's. Look for ways to go beyond your job description, but don't ignore that description! Make sure you handle all your core tasks before you seek out new responsibilities.

- ✔ Protect your boss, but don't cover for her. All managers make mistakes at times, and they need you to stick by them when they do. But your loyalty shouldn't extend to covering up if your manager is committing unethical or dishonest acts. Hiding a higher-up's misbehavior can eventually bring both of you down, so if you become aware that your boss is breaking the law or clearly hurting the company or certain employees, do the right thing and report her. Just be sure to document everything first.

# Making a Habit of Managing Up

It's easy for good intentions to fall by the wayside when you're busy with day-to-day chores and challenges. But to move up in your job, you need to put your managing-up skills to work for you every day.

To make sure you stick to your plan, add at least one managing-up item to your to-do list each day. This task can be anything from mentoring a new employee to asking your boss about project priorities.

And keep track of your results. At the end of each month, make a note of the progress you've made. Analyze your results, and identify the actions that best show how you're expanding your role and increasing your value. Add these items to your personal portfolio. Doing so can help you remember your achievements at performance reviews and in future job interviews, and it will also give you the personal satisfaction of seeing in black-and-white that you're making a difference in your company and in your life.

# Chapter 9

# Moving On: Acing a Job Interview the Introvert Way

## In This Chapter

▶ Assessing your interview strengths and challenges

▶ Getting yourself ready for interview day

▶ Succeeding in phone and face-to-face interviews

▶ Determining whether a company is right for you

▶ Moving forward from rejection or job offer

▶ Examining your career goals

*T*hink of all the things that drive you crazy as an introvert: Meeting a lot of strangers, being the center of attention, multitasking, small talk, high-pressure situations, and having to "sell" yourself. Now, roll them all together, and what do you have? A typical job interview!

Job interviews aren't fun for most people, but they can be extra challenging for introverts because they push a lot of innie buttons. However, it may surprise you to discover that innies have some big advantages when it comes to impressing interviewers.

In this chapter, I describe how to play to your strengths in a job interview while avoiding the pitfalls that can trip you up. I also offer suggestions for sizing up a potential employer. In addition, I describe the best ways to handle either a turndown or a job offer.

After that, I turn to a new topic: laying out your path to long-term career success. When you put a step-by-step plan for advancement in place, you'll move up more quickly in the work world and you'll break through the barriers that can keep you from realizing your full potential.

# Identifying Your Strengths and Challenges

If you're an introvert, it's all too easy to focus on the reasons job interviews are tough for you. But in reality, you have strong assets that can help you stand out in the crowd. Here are some of the most important ones:

- **You don't go overboard on the charm.** Extroverts often focus on getting interviewers to like them personally. However, too much smiling, joking, or bantering can be annoying. Your quiet brand of charm, on the other hand, can be refreshing.

- **You don't "over-answer."** Extroverts tend to go on and on when they're answering a question. You're more likely to offer a succinct answer and let your interviewers keep things moving along.

- **You don't jump in too quickly.** Sometimes outies are so eager to get in their two cents' worth that they don't even let an interviewer finish a question! You, on the other hand, are likely to wait patiently until the other person is done talking, which means you can offer thoughtful answers that are right on point.

- **You're talented at doing research.** As a result, you're likely to go into an interview well prepared to talk about the company's products, needs, and goals.

All these reasons make you a powerful candidate for any job, but it's also helpful to understand potential weak points, such as the following:

- **You're prone to negative self-talk.** Instead of focusing on interview questions, you may be listening to that inner voice saying, "This is a disaster. I look nervous and my voice is shaky. And I didn't answer that last question well." If negative self-talk is a problem for you, see my advice in Chapter 11 for handling it.

- **The job interview calls for an entirely different skill set than actually *doing* the job.** For example, imagine that you're applying for a job as a truck driver — an ideal job for an introvert. To do this job well, you need to be a good driver (duh!), keep to schedules, work well on your own, handle paperwork efficiently, keep your dispatcher updated, and have some mechanical know-how.

  But when you interview for this job, your interviewers may look for a very different set of skills. For instance, they may expect you to carry the conversational ball, think fast on your feet, and persuasively promote yourself. All of these, of course, are extroverted skills.

To be sure your strong assets outweigh your weak ones in an interview, be sure to practice your pretend-outie skills (see Chapter 3), and do your homework before you walk into the interview room.

# Prepping for an Interview

The more prep work you do before an interview, the easier it'll be for you to relax and speak confidently in your interview. In addition, good preparation will help you determine whether a company is right for you. The following sections explain some of the best areas to focus on.

## Doing your detective work

Interviewers will be impressed if you're knowledgeable about their company and its needs. And that's where your innie research skills can shine.

Before you go to your interview, do some Internet data-mining. Start at the company's website, but don't stop there. In addition, dig up any other info you can find, including newspaper or magazine articles. See how much information you can uncover in these areas:

- What products or services the company offers
- What projects it's currently working on and where your skills fit in
- How the company is doing financially
- What the company culture is like
- Who the company's biggest competitors are
- What charities the company supports
- How this industry as a whole is doing right now and what its prospects are for the future

With these facts in hand, you'll know how to present yourself as a perfect match for a job. In addition, you'll be able to plan and practice some smart questions to ask on the big day.

Also, see whether you can network with current or past employees of the company. Ask about the company's culture and whether it's a good place to work. If the people you talk with are no longer with the company, ask them why.

## Creating a powerful portfolio

If you're an introvert, one of the best ways to wow people in an interview is to let your achievements speak for you, and the best way to do that is to create a killer portfolio. For an introvert, a portfolio serves two purposes: It showcases your strong points, and it takes you out of the limelight for a few minutes.

For example, imagine you're vying for a software job and one interviewer asks you to describe your biggest accomplishments. You can struggle to find the right answer as a roomful of people stare at you, or you can flip to the right spot in your portfolio and say, "Here's a write-up in the *Times* about the medical software I helped develop." As your interviewers turn their attention to your portfolio, you'll have a few seconds to de-stress before their next question.

Better yet, a portfolio can help you overcome your innie urge to be humble (a trait that's not all that helpful when you're trying to score a job). Photos of your work, stellar performance reviews, and letters of recommendation from professors can do your bragging for you. And if you pair your hard-copy portfolio with an online portfolio that your interviewers can access after the interview, you'll make yourself even more memorable.

Here are some of the most important items to include in your portfolio:

- ✔ Your résumé

- ✔ Samples of your work

- ✔ Samples of relevant schoolwork, if you're applying for your first job

- ✔ Any newspaper or magazine articles about your work

- ✔ Performance reviews from previous jobs

- ✔ Letters from former managers or professors

- ✔ Copies of any job-related awards you've won

- ✔ A description of your skills and the experience that makes you perfect for the job

- ✔ Information about any certifications or special training you have

You may also want to include information on any volunteer work you do, if it's relevant to the job. For example, if you're applying for your first job as a nurse, list any experience you have as a hospital volunteer.

## Rehearsing with a friend who won't go easy on you

I'm a great fan of holding a dress rehearsal before any big event — whether it's a wedding, a stage play, or a job interview. When you rehearse before an event, you become more confident and figure out how to protect yourself against hazards that may trip you up.

So before an interview, ask a friend to play the part of your interviewer and run through some questions with you. Consider dressing in the outfit you're planning to wear, so you can really get into the part. If you encounter a question that's hard to answer, have your friend keep asking it until you come up with an answer that sounds good.

As you're practicing, be aware that most interviewers these days use an approach called *behavioral interviewing*. Basically, they ask you how you handled situations in the past so they can make a good guess as to how you'd handle them in the future.

The problem for introverts in this kind of interview is that they often underplay their strengths and overplay their weaknesses. (It's that humble streak again!) So zero in on common behavioral interview topics or questions while focusing on coming across as confident, assured, and capable.

You can find long lists of behavioral interview questions and prompts online. Here are some favorites of interviewers:

- ✔ Describe a time when you needed to resolve a conflict at work.

- ✔ Tell me about a time when you thought your manager was wrong, and describe how you handled the situation.

- ✔ Give me an example of a time when you needed to persuade a team to do something your way.

- ✔ Tell me about a time when you used your problem-solving skills to handle an issue at work.

- ✔ Describe a time when you had too much to do and had to prioritize your tasks.

- ✔ Tell me about the hardest decision you ever had to make at work.

- ✔ Give me an example of a time in your career when you made a mistake and needed to correct it.

- ✔ Tell me about a time when you turned around a bad relationship with a client.

As you're practicing, tell your friend not to throw you too many softballs. It's not the simple questions that are likely to trip you up in a job interview; it's the tricky or antagonistic questions that may cause you to stumble. So tell your friend to be tough on you. Practicing the harder questions serves two purposes: It helps you get your answers down pat, and it makes you feel more confident about succeeding in a stressful interview setting.

In particular, have your fake interviewer ask questions like these:

- ✔ Can you describe a project that you failed at?
- ✔ Can you tell me about a time when you missed a deadline?
- ✔ Why have you been out of work so long?
- ✔ What is your biggest weakness?
- ✔ Why should we hire you?
- ✔ If your previous boss was here, what negative things would he or she say about you?

Also, ask your friend to make sure you're offering concrete examples of your assets and experiences, not just making vague comments. And tell her to offer feedback if you're getting too technical and need to translate your remarks into plain English.

## Writing down your key points

It's perfectly fine to take a "crib sheet" to your interview. On a few notecards, write down the key points you want to make and the questions you want to ask.

Don't get too dependent on your notes, however, because you don't want to sound too rehearsed. When you're practicing what you plan to say, glance at your notes but then immediately take your eyes off them and talk naturally.

## Making a wish list

Before your interview, jot down all the things you'd prefer in a job. For example, maybe you want to telecommute one day a week or you want to work in a quiet area.

After you list your preferences, go back through your list and star each item that you feel is a deal breaker. For example, if you're a diabetic, you may need to take your lunch break at a specific time each day. And if you're a high achiever, you don't want to get stuck in a job with no room for advancement.

In your notes for your interview, include questions about your deal breakers. The answers you get will help you decide whether this place is right for you.

# Scoring in a Phone Interview

In the old days, phone interviews were often just a formality. But these days, the competition for jobs is fierce, and you may get a tough grilling in your initial conversation.

To make a good impression in this interview, be ready to answer both technical questions and questions designed to see whether you're a good fit for the company's culture. Prepare yourself by writing down the key reasons you're right for the job. Also, review all the notes you made when you researched the company so you can ask smart questions about its products or services.

During your conversation, speak in an upbeat tone and use language that's geared toward your interviewer's level of understanding. For example, it's okay to use some technical terms if you're talking with a high-tech peer — as long as you're *sure* you're not talking over the person's head — but use simpler words if you're talking with someone from human resources.

If you're a quiet introvert, practice the tips for projecting that I outline in Chapter 7. Also, try to "paint pictures" as you're describing your skills and experience. For example, imagine that you're describing a situation in which you saved the day for your previous company by coming up with a quick software patch. Don't just say, "I came up with a patch that solved the problem." Instead, describe how frantic things were before you fixed the glitch and how relieved and happy your clients were when you got them back up to speed.

It's important to come across as confident during your interview. So if a long job search and a string of rejections have left you feeling less than perky, try exercising for half an hour before your interview. Doing so can clear your mind and make you sound strong and invigorated over the phone.

During your interview, avoid the urge to dazzle your interviewer with a long string of your accomplishments. Instead, do your best to sound authentic and down-to-earth while you point out your key assets and achievements. If you sound genuine, you'll create a rapport with your interviewer.

And don't worry if you flub a question! A fumbled answer can derail an introvert's train of thought, but it shouldn't. In reality, nearly every job candidate falters on one or two questions. If you remember this fact and stay confident instead of folding after a slip, your interviewer will be impressed.

At the end of your phone interview, it may be difficult to tell how well it went. Extroverts tend to think, "That went pretty well!" while introverts typically think, "I messed that up." To find out for sure, say politely to your interviewer, "I'd like a summary of your thoughts. It sounds like we may be a good fit for each other. Can I come in for a face-to-face interview?" Her answer will give you a good idea as to how successful the interview was.

# Performing on the Big Day

When interview day rolls around, it's normal to feel butterflies in your stomach. In this section, I offer some tips for easing your pre-interview stress and making a good impression when you're in the hot seat.

## Getting ready for your interview

On the morning of your interview, get yourself in the right frame of mind before you leave the house. Try the following:

- Arrange some "alone time" or quiet time with your family so you can charge your batteries. A little mindful meditation (see Chapter 2) can help relax you and clear your mind. Do a few stretching exercises, and roll your shoulders to work out the tension.

- Spot any negative self-talk ("I know I'm going to screw this up") and nip it in the bud by forcefully thinking "Stop." Then picture yourself getting through your interview calmly and confidently — or make a mental list of all the reasons this company will be lucky to get you onboard. In Chapters 7 and 11, I provide more tips for visualizing success and squelching negative self-talk.

When you arrive at your interview site, turn off your cellphone and put it away. Hardly anything turns off interviewers faster than job candidates who read texts or answer calls during their interviews.

## Looking assertive at interview time

At your interview, put some pretend-extrovert body language to work for you. Shake hands confidently, and lean forward a little in your chair as if you're eager to hear your interviewers' words. And no matter how nervous you are, smile frequently. (For more on body language, see Chapter 3.)

Also, watch your interviewers' body language. If they're animated, be animated yourself. If they're calm, be calm. If they lean in a lot, do so yourself. (Otherwise, they may think you're not motivated.) But if they lean back more, lean back yourself — but also lean forward at times to show your interest.

These days, most companies use team interviews. If that's the case in your interview, be sure to talk to everyone in the room even if one person is asking most of the questions. Also, remember that it's not about what *you* need; it's about what *they* need. Keep looking for ways to show how your skills and experience mesh with the company's goals.

## Interview survival kit

Has this ever happened to you? You're in the middle of an important conversation when you get a tickle in your throat or get surprised by a sudden sneeze.

If you're a carefree outie, this embarrassing moment won't be a big deal. But if you're an introvert, it can throw you completely for a loop. So can discovering that you have spinach stuck between your teeth after your interviewers take you out to lunch or finding that the wind has turned your carefully styled hair into a bird's nest.

To help combat these scenarios on your interview day, make sure you have these items in your purse or wallet:

- ✔ A couple of cough drops
- ✔ Some tissues
- ✔ A comb
- ✔ A few toothpicks and some breath mints if your interview includes lunch

When it's your turn to talk, ask questions that make you sound like a go-getter. For example, ask, "What is the first issue you need the person in this position to handle?"

And don't panic if your interviewer asks a question and you can't come up with an answer right away. It's okay to say "I'm not sure" or "Give me a moment to think." If you draw a complete blank on a question, that's all right, too. Just be honest and say, "I'm having a brain freeze." This will make you seem humble and down-to-earth, and it'll give you a minute to come up with an answer. You want to respond to each question, but keeping your poise is more important than answering instantly.

At the end of your interview, show your appreciation. Say something like, "I'm very grateful to have the opportunity to meet with you. Thank you for your time." When you get home, write a short note thanking your interviewers and adding that you'll be glad to answer any additional questions they may have. Hand-write your note and send it by regular mail instead of sending an e-mail. Doing so will show that you put some thought and effort into it.

If you're applying for a techie job, sending an e-mail right after your interview is okay, but it's still important to follow up with a hand-written note, especially if you're applying for a management position.

# Assessing Fit: Are the Job and the Workplace Right for You?

When you interview for a job, your potential employers are taking a close look at you to see whether you're right for them. And you should be asking yourself a similar question: Are *they* right for *me?* Following are ways to find the answer.

## Asking the right questions

You can pick up a lot of clues by asking smart questions. So as you're interviewing, do a little digging and see what you can find out about the company. To do this politely, say, "I would like to ask you a few questions to make sure we're a good fit." Then ask things like these:

- Can you tell me about your corporate culture?
- Can you describe your management style?
- Do you offer training so employees can improve their skills?
- Do you promote from within?
- How do you measure performance?
- Are employees sometimes expected to work overtime? If so, how often?
- Do you allow telecommuting or flex time?
- What do you like best about working here? What do you like least?
- How long did the last person in this position work here?
- Does your company participate in any charitable events?
- Do you have a casual environment, or is it suit-and-tie?

Also, pay attention to your interviewers' behavior. Do they seem open and honest, and do they sincerely seem to like the company and their fellow employees — or are they terse, abrupt, or even rude?

Finally, clarify who you'll be working for if you get the job and what your exact title and role will be.

## Gathering clues on a tour

Your interviewers will probably invite you to tour the company. If not, ask whether they can show you around. As they do, assess their corporate culture. Pay particular attention to these things:

- How happy do the people in the office appear to be?
- How busy do they appear to be?
- Are the furnishings and equipment modern, and will you have the tools you need to do your job?
- How much privacy do employees have? Are they stacked like sardines in cubicles, or is there a little breathing room?

## Weighing the pros and cons

After your interview, you should have some feel for what the company is like. While your thoughts are still fresh in your mind, make a quick list of the things you liked and disliked about it. Then ask yourself questions like these:

- Is this a company where I can probably advance?
- Would I be happy here five years from now?
- Are these the kind of people I want to work with?
- Does the company's product or service seem valuable?
- Is the company culture too strict or too laid-back for my tastes?

If you aren't happy with your answers, think twice about accepting an offer (unless you're desperate). Otherwise, you may wind up seeking a new job shortly after you land this one.

# Handling a "No"

Nobody likes getting turned down after a job interview, and it's especially upsetting for introverts. While outies can often bounce back fairly fast, innies may brood over a rejection and wonder, "What's wrong with me?"

But in reality, nothing is wrong with you. Job hunting is hard, and getting a "no" (or even a string of them) is a pretty universal experience. So avoid negative self-talk. (For tips on doing this, see Chapter 11.) Realize that interviewers have a number of reasons to say no. Maybe they filled the position from within. Maybe another candidate had more experience or a skill set that was a little bit closer to what they needed. Maybe you looked too much like the hiring manager's ex-wife. Or maybe the team just flipped a coin and you lost.

You'll probably never know, so don't dwell on it. Instead, take these steps:

- ✔ If possible, ask the person who interviewed you why you didn't get the job. Be gracious, and don't argue or get defensive. Your goal here is to get tips you can use to be more successful next time around.

- ✔ Make a quick note of any things that you think went wrong in the interview and think of ways to handle these situations better in your next interview. Then practice your interview skills again with a friend.

- ✔ Give yourself an A for effort. Instead of beating up on yourself, acknowledge that you prepared well, did your best, and deserve a pat on the back.

- ✔ Move on.

If you continually find yourself getting close to an offer — for example, if you're always coming in number two — consider getting an interview coach. Working with a coach is also a good idea if you find it difficult to get past the very first stages of the interview process. Sometimes people who are extremely extroverted or introverted just need a little help refining their interview style.

Finally, don't fall into the trap of believing that the interviewers rejected you because of your age, gender, or ethnicity. Occasionally, this may be true. But it's not likely to be the case in every interview, and thinking this way can give you a chip on your shoulder that's likely to turn off future interviewers.

# Responding to a "Yes"

At last — all your hard work is paying off, and you have a job offer! But don't grab your pen and sign on that dotted line just yet.

As a humble introvert, you may hesitate to negotiate for a better deal. But what's the worst that can happen? Your new employers may say no, but they'll respect your assertiveness. And there's a good chance that they'll say yes. If they do, you may walk away with anything from a bigger paycheck to a more convenient schedule.

So don't agree to an offer right away. Instead, analyze it and see what else you can ask for — and then ask for it. I show you how to do so in the following sections.

## Negotiating salary

In some cases, salaries are set in stone. But if that's not the case for your new job, ask yourself whether your employers-to-be are offering you a fair deal.

To decide, find out what the average salary is in your area for the job you'll be doing. You can find this info at sites such as the Bureau of Labor Statistics (www.bls.gov) or salary.com. If your employer isn't offering a comparable amount, you can use this research to ask for more.

Also, ask yourself whether the employer should pay you more than the going rate for the work you'll be doing. For instance, consider these questions:

✔ Do you have advanced training in your field?

✔ Do you have a great deal of experience in your field?

✔ Does your track record include major accomplishments that set you apart from the average employee?

If you have valid reasons you're worth more than a typical person in your position, calculate how much you think you should get. Also, decide whether you're willing to compromise on a number somewhere between what they're offering and what you want.

Then call the person who made the job offer and say something like this: "Thank you so much for your job offer. I'm looking forward to working with you, and I know I will be a big asset. However, I was anticipating an offer closer to $70,000 because I have more expertise and experience than most people in this position. Would your company be willing to offer that amount?"

It's a good idea to rehearse your request out loud several times before you say it for real. Make sure you sound confident — but *ask,* don't demand.

If it's appropriate, also ask about bonuses or stock options. And no matter what replies you get to your questions, be polite and positive.

## *Talking about vacations, schedules, and benefits*

When you get a job offer, it's tempting to focus on the bottom line: money. But there's more to life than work!

So see whether there's any wiggle room when it comes to taking time off. Sometimes it's easier for a company to offer two or three extra vacation days than it is for them to offer a higher salary. If you can't get extra paid vacation days, see whether they'll say yes to unpaid days off. Those days out of the office can help you keep your innie batteries charged.

Also, ask whether you can work flexible hours or telecommute on some days. These options can make life much easier for an introvert who likes a little private time.

Sometimes, you can also negotiate benefits and perks, especially if the company can't meet the salary you want. For instance, consider these questions:

- If you're relocating, will the company agree to pay your moving expenses?
- Can they offer you training to improve your skills?
- Can they give you a better job title?
- Can they cover your tuition if you want to get an advanced degree in your field?

## Setting a start date

Here's an interesting thing about companies. They'll ask whether you can start right away, but they may think less of you if you say yes. That's because they'll wonder why you're so willing to leave your former employer in the lurch.

So if you're currently employed, say that you'll need to give two weeks' notice. And if you want a little extra time, don't hesitate to ask for another week. As a new employee, you may not get much time off right away, so if you can afford it, take a little mini-vacation upfront.

# Planning Your Path to Career Success

When your job search pays off and you score a good position, congratulations! But don't get too comfy, because you want to keep growing and moving up in your career. That takes planning and hard work — and luckily, introverts are good at both. If you're serious about advancing in your career, you need to take the necessary steps to keep moving forward. I show you how in the following sections.

## Setting smart goals

When you're charting your career path, you need to set two types of goals. First, focus on setting long-term goals. After that, you can create the short-term goals that will get you where you want to go. Here's a look at both kinds of goals and how to create them.

### Long-term goals

Think of your long-term goals as "big picture" goals. These goals define where you want to be in 5, 10, or even 15 years. To create your goals, think about these questions:

- ✔ What do you enjoy doing?
- ✔ What are you good at?
- ✔ How much money will you need to make to support the lifestyle you want?
- ✔ Do you want to work for a company or eventually own your own business?
- ✔ Is a good balance of work and personal life important to you?

Also, consider what will work in the long run for your introverted nature. (See Chapter 3 for tips on determining how to mesh your innie nature with your career choices.)

### Short-term goals

Now that you know your destination, it's time to chart your trip. Here, you come up with the goals that will move you closer, step-by-step, to your ideal career. For example, you may need to get more education or training in your field, overcome personal challenges, or beef up your computer skills.

The most effective goals are called *SMART goals.* Here's what the five letters in this acronym stand for:

- ✔ **Specific:** Be very specific when charting your goals, and avoid vague goals that don't lead to clear-cut actions. For instance, don't say something like, "I want to get more education." Instead, say, "I will get my master's degree from Syracuse University within five years."
- ✔ **Measurable:** Create goals that allow you to assess your progress. For example, avoid goals like "I will get better at public speaking." Instead, set a goal like "I will join a public speaking club and attend at least six meetings this year" or "I will give five public speeches each year for the next two years."
- ✔ **Actionable:** You want your goals to be challenging, but they also need to be doable. So make sure they're realistic, or you'll simply get frustrated. Ask yourself whether you really have the time, money, skills, or resources to accomplish each goal. If not, scale it down.
- ✔ **Relevant:** Make sure your short-term goals are really key to accomplishing your long-term mission. For example, if you want to be a professional musician, cross out goals like "I want to climb Mount Rainier."
- ✔ **Timely:** Write goals with specific milestones and deadlines. Doing so will help you stick to them.

When you have your long-term and short-term goals firmly in mind, type them up and post them somewhere where you'll see them often. That way, they'll stay at the front of your mind.

Finally, keep your goals flexible. After all, life is full of surprises! You may find yourself getting married or divorced, having a child, changing career interests, or moving — and life changes like these may require you to tinker with the goals you've set. So stay on track with your goals, but don't feel like they're cast in stone.

## Gaining the job skills you need

Maybe you already have enough training to advance to your dream career. But if you don't, make a list of all the skills you need. Then decide which skills you need to master first. Also, consider which of these settings will help you gain the skills you need in the shortest possible time and at the least expense:

- A traditional college or university
- A vocational training program
- Online courses

Before you jump in to getting a new degree or training, think carefully about how you're going to juggle your job training with your home life and your current job. One problem that can occur if you're trying to go to school and work at the same time is burnout. So if you decide to get additional training or education, plan on a realistic time frame that will let you achieve your skills without stressing you out too much.

# Chapter 10

# Succeeding as an Entrepreneur

. . . . . . . . . . . . . . . . . . . . . . . . . . . . . . . . . . . . . . . . . . . . .

*In This Chapter*

▶ Getting off to a great start

▶ Marketing effectively

▶ Finding and keeping loyal customers

▶ Dealing with customers and rejection

▶ Adding the best people to your team

. . . . . . . . . . . . . . . . . . . . . . . . . . . . . . . . . . . . . . . . . . . . .

*I*f you're an introvert, becoming your own boss has a huge upside. When you work for yourself, you can escape the crowded office, you're in charge of your own schedule, and you can work for long stretches without interruption. And here's the best part of all: no office meetings unless *you* want to call them!

But for every advantage, there's a challenge as well. First, you need to create a strong business plan and develop the necessary skills and discipline to follow through on it. You also need to find customers and keep them — and to do that, you probably need to spend some serious face time with them. In addition, you need to figure out how to handle rejection, which can be very tough for introverts. And if your business takes off, you may need to hire and manage a staff as well.

Fortunately, as I explain in this chapter, the right business plan and marketing strategies can help you bring in business while playing to your introverted strengths. In addition, you can find out how to shake off rejection and to turn some potential brush-offs into buy-ins. I also provide some tips in this chapter to help you assemble a great team that can complement your innie talents and send your profits through the roof.

# Starting Off on the Right Foot

Running your own business is exciting, but it takes a huge amount of work. To succeed, you need to begin with a good business plan, master some basic skills, and muster the energy to see your plan through. In this section, I offer a little innie-oriented advice for succeeding at all three goals.

## Creating your business plan

As an introvert, you're likely to have a big advantage over many extroverts when it comes to laying out a business plan. Outies often jump headfirst into a venture without knowing what they're getting into, while you're likely to do a lot of research and deep thinking. However, introverts are prone to one big error when they're creating a business plan. They're great at coming up with a product or service they think is valuable, but they sometimes forget to ask themselves whether *other* people will think it's valuable.

To avoid making this mistake, determine who your target audience is. Then survey friends and family members who are part of this target audience to see whether your product or service interests them. In Chapter 8, I talk about the *Six Ps of motivation* — pleasure, power, prestige, productivity, profit, and problem-solving — and they apply here as well. Find out whether your product or service provides any of these rewards. If so, find out how much people are willing to pay for it.

Also, as you're refining your marketing plan, decide whether you want to refine your target market. For example, one introverted insurance sales-woman I know discovered that working with middle-aged people and seniors was much easier for her than working with high-pressure CEOs. As a result, she decided to adjust her business plan so she could focus on selling long-term care policies.

## Strengthening your entrepreneurial skills

To compete in the business world, you need more than just a great product or service. You also need terrific marketing skills, a good grasp of finance, and at least some basic computer skills.

So before you even hand out your first business cards, analyze your strengths and weaknesses when it comes to these skills. If you don't have all the knowledge you need, sign up for courses at your local school or online. Also, consider hiring a coach who can help you hone your business skills. (I talk more about coaches later in this chapter.)

# *Overcoming the urge to procrastinate*

Some parts of running your own business are fun. However, some aren't. And it's all too easy to avoid those not-so-fun parts. But here's the problem: If you're an introvert, the jobs you hate the most are likely the very ones that are crucial to your success, such as calling potential clients and scheduling meetings with current customers. Long ago, I discovered a great method for overcoming the urge to procrastinate on chores like these. The credit for this method goes to Ashok Davar, a noted artist and writer, who described it to me many years ago.

Davar explained that to stop procrastinating, he had to approach his work in baby steps. First, he'd simply walk to his office door and look in. After that, he'd wander back to the kitchen and get a pot of coffee going. As it brewed, he'd tell himself, "I'll just go back into my office for a minute and make sure my work tools are all set up." When his coffee finished brewing, he'd say, "I'll just pour a cup and set it on my desk." He'd continue in this way, taking one baby step at a time, until he eventually found himself ready to dive into the day's work.

Also, if Davar found himself stuck on a certain part of a book, he'd set it aside and think of ideas for a different part. Eventually, he'd circle back to the first part.

You can use techniques like these to overcome your own resistance to getting started on a project. Here are some ideas:

- ✔ Create a morning ritual to ease yourself into the day. For example, spend your first 10 or 15 minutes in the office playing some of your favorite music and enjoying a cup of coffee. As you're doing this, think about the parts of your job that you *do* like, such as the fact that you're not in traffic heading for an office.

- ✔ If you find it hard to get down to work at the end of your ritual, take baby steps. For example, say, "I'm just going to open the file that I'm working on today." After you do that, get another cup of coffee or surf the Net for a few minutes, and then say, "I'm just going to review the first paragraph of the file." Think of each step as a pebble of progress.

  When you collect enough of these pebbles, you'll hit "critical mass" and your resistance to diving into work will vanish. (In fact, if you're an introvert, you may find it hard to *stop* working once you hit this point, so be sure to pace yourself.)

- ✔ If you're avoiding a project because you've hit a roadblock, find a different part of the project to work on. After you make progress on the new task, circle back to the one that was giving you trouble. When you're in the groove, you'll find the tough task easier to tackle.

## Are you an "intrapreneur"?

These days, many firms give key employees the authority to create their own products or offer their own services under the company's umbrella — a status that's called *intrapreneurship*. For example, financial advisors, attorneys, realtors, and banks' customer service representatives are often intrapreneurs. If you're in a position like this, read on! Many of the tips in this chapter will work well for you.

Practice these tricks every day, and you'll find that after about 21 days, they become habit. When they do, it'll get easier and easier to tackle the tough tasks on your to-do list.

# Marketing Yourself

To succeed as a business owner, you need to make a name for yourself, and that means getting in front of the public. Fortunately, doing so is now easier than ever for an introvert.

Why? Because the Internet is leveling the playing field. Although face-to-face networking is still important (and I offer tips for succeeding at it in Chapter 17), most real networking and marketing happens on the Net these days. Introverts love Internet marketing and are very good at it, while extroverts — even though they do it — don't enjoy it as much.

In this section, I describe one of the smartest ways to market yourself as an introvert: by branding yourself as an expert on the Internet (as well as in other ways). In addition, I offer four more tips for making a splash with potential clients.

## Building your reputation as an expert

Introverts often find promoting themselves or their products difficult because bragging doesn't come naturally to them. However, they frequently enjoy (and excel at) educating people, which is why I recommend establishing yourself as an expert in your profession. When you do this, you'll be actively helping other people, and at the same time, you'll be doing what I call "marketing without marketing."

The Internet is a particularly good tool for branding yourself as an expert. Here are some excellent approaches:

- ✔ **Post helpful articles on your website.** For example, if you own a plumbing company, post articles describing how to unplug a drain or do other simple plumbing repairs. If you're an attorney, offer articles on estate planning. And if you're a realtor, provide information on staging a house for sale.

- ✔ **Create a blog or write guest posts for other bloggers.** A blog is a terrific way to create a reputation for yourself. If you add new posts regularly, you'll keep people coming back over and over. But one caution: Stick to topics that relate directly to your business, and avoid the urge to stray into politics or other touchy topics that can turn off some potential clients.

  Don't have time to keep up a blog of your own? Then scour the Internet for excellent blogs that fall within your area of expertise, and offer to contribute material to these blogs for free.

- ✔ **Create a presence on LinkedIn and other social media sites.** Introverts frequently have an advantage on these sites because they're often good at expressing themselves in writing, and they don't make the mistake of coming on too strong. For great tips on getting the most from social media, check out *Social Media Marketing For Dummies,* by Shiv Singh and Stephanie Diamond (Wiley).

- ✔ **Record videos demonstrating a skill or technique.** For example, if you're a daycare manager, post YouTube videos showing parents how to handle tantrums or sibling rivalry.

In addition, here are three off-line ways to create a reputation as an expert:

- ✔ **Volunteer to write articles for your newspaper.** Many communities have small local newspapers, and these papers are always looking for new writers. Writing for your newspaper is a great marketing opportunity, especially if you can score a regular column.

- ✔ **Offer to speak to area groups on topics of interest to them.** This one is a bit of a stretch for introverts, but it can really pay off. For tips on giving good presentations, see Chapter 7. If standing up on a stage by yourself is too intimidating at first, offer to participate in sit-down panel discussions.

- ✔ **Write a book.** These days, self-publishing is easy and cheap. So if you have strong writing skills, consider sharing your expertise in a regular book or an e-book. But be careful because a badly produced book may tarnish your reputation rather than enhance it. If you decide to try your hand as an author, hire a professional editor and proofreader to polish your book.

No matter which avenues you choose for establishing yourself as an expert, be sure to present your information in plain, easy-to-understand English. And don't focus on making a marketing pitch. Instead, focus solely on addressing the needs of your audience.

## Teaming up with other entrepreneurs (especially outies)

One great way to market yourself is to pair up with another business owner and host joint events. Doing so can cut your costs and help you reach new markets. If you partner with an extrovert, you can make your differences work for you; you can do the behind-the-scenes work while your partner handles the meeting-and-greeting jobs.

For example, if you're a dress designer, consider teaming up with an extroverted restaurant owner to host a fashion show at his restaurant. You can provide the clothes and the script for the show, while the restaurant owner handles the runway chatter. The restaurant will pull in extra customers, you'll find new fans for your fashions, and both you and your fellow entrepreneur will improve your bottom lines.

If you choose this approach, look for someone who shares your values and has complementary goals and passions so you can work together for a long time to come.

## Asking extroverts to help you make contacts

Your outgoing friends and relatives can often come in handy, and that's especially true when it comes to networking. Outies have a lot of friends, so they're likely to know people who want exactly what you're selling.

Also, extroverts aren't the least bit shy about making introductions. So let them lay the groundwork for you by making initial contacts and telling people how fabulous you are. When they do this, thank them even if their efforts don't pan out. If possible, thank them online or in front of other people so they get even more recognition. And if they have their own businesses, promote their products or services in return. Doing so will make them want to keep spreading the word for you.

# Integrating Internet and face-to-face marketing

One mistake that introverted entrepreneurs tend to make is to rely solely on Internet marketing. For some small businesses, that's sufficient. But if you're really trying to make a big splash, there's often no substitute for meeting people in person.

So let people contact you via e-mail or your website, but then do your best to turn each online connection into a real-life meeting. E-mail the person and ask for permission to follow up with a phone call. When you talk together, end your conversation by saying something like, "I'm glad that you like what I've told you about my program. Do you want to get together on Thursday to get started, or would Friday be better for you?" (This is a powerful approach called an *assumptive close,* because you're assuming that the person is interested.)

If the person agrees to meet with you, you're good to go. And if he says "I'm not sure," don't let him off the hook. Instead, say, "That's fine. I'd still like to follow up next week and see whether you have any questions. Would you prefer an e-mail or a call?" Often, this extra nudge will get clients to open up about their concerns so you can move them closer to buy-in.

If you're very introverted and absolutely can't bring yourself to do face-to-face marketing, it's still possible to be a success. However, you'll need to go out of your way to impress potential clients. (For example, one printer surprises online customers by providing free proofreading for their newsletters.) And be patient, because it'll take you longer to build a large customer base if you're not meeting prospects in person.

# Polishing your online presence

To patronize your business, people need to find it first. These days, they'll usually start by searching the Internet. If you don't have a strong online presence, consider hiring a search engine optimization (SEO) expert who can help you move up in search engine results. Also, make sure your site looks professional and works flawlessly. (I talk more about this later in the section "Hiring the right person to make your website sparkle.")

In addition, keep an eye on what people are saying about you on the Internet. Comments from consumers can make or break a business. So take complaints seriously, especially if they keep cropping up. And if someone writes a blog post that's critical of your product or service, see whether you can contact the blogger personally to address his complaints. Companies do this sort of thing all the time these days, and it's a great way to turn a scathing criticism into a rave review.

# Creating Long-Term Loyalty

Persuading people to try your products or services is just the initial step in creating a healthy business. To succeed in the long run, you need to keep those customers coming back. How? By proving that your customer service is remarkable, your company is ethical, and you value and respect your clientele. In this section, I offer good ways to do this.

## Being available

Have you called a company recently to get help with a problem? If so, there's a good chance you wound up pulling your hair out. Customer service is so bad these days that you can stand out from the crowd simply by responding quickly to phone calls and e-mails. Of course, providing outstanding customer service can be tricky when you're a solo entrepreneur. So even if you have a skimpy budget, make it a priority to hire an assistant who can handle this task when you can't.

 If your business draws customers from around the country, try to provide customer service that's convenient for people in any time zone. And if you have clients worldwide, see whether you can find a way to offer 24-hour customer service.

## Influencing in the right way

As an introvert, you may get so wrapped up in your own ideas and passions that other people see you as inflexible. But to keep your customers loyal, you need to show a clear willingness to listen to them and acknowledge their ideas. People can sense when you're focusing solely on pushing your own agenda, and they'll resist rather than buy in.

So when you work with customers, don't insist on getting your own way. Instead, be *influential*. For example, don't ignore a client's concerns about the cost of a home renovation, and don't say something like "you get what you pay for." Instead, say something like this: "I respect your concerns. Let's talk about them so I can clearly understand them, and then we can come up with a good solution together." (For more pointers on being influential, see Chapter 7.)

# Building deeper relationships with your clients

One reason many entrepreneurs fail is that they take their customers for granted. In contrast, successful business owners are always asking their clients, "How can we do better?"

Luckily, introverts can excel in this area because they're often good at deep, thoughtful, one-on-one conversations with clients. The following sections provide a couple ways to build deeper relationships.

## Solicit feedback

Contact your most valued clients and say something like this: "We're always looking for ways to improve our service to you. We really want your feedback; is there anything that we can do better, even if we're already doing things pretty well?" Make your questions friendly and open-ended to encourage people to speak their minds.

When you receive feedback, respond positively. For example, say, "This feedback is great! This type of information is exactly what we want to hear." Then ask for specifics. For example, say, "What about our customer service? Can we improve it in any way?"

If you hear negative comments, address the issues. Then let the clients know that you acted on their concerns, and thank them sincerely for bringing the issues to your attention.

After that, impress your clients even more by saying, "Can you think of any other ways in which we can improve our service to you?" This is a good time to dive deeper into specifics, such as your order forms or your loyalty program.

## Work on your customer service

Show your long-term customers that you care about them as people. When you meet with your clients personally, make notes in your Customer Service Management (CSM) software about each client's interests, hobbies, and family. Then, when you get together again, say something like "How's your daughter's soccer team doing?" or "Did you enjoy your trip to Sweden?" Although small talk probably isn't your favorite thing, comments like these can show a client that she's not just another sale.

In addition, go the extra mile to make dissatisfied customers happy, even if it costs you money upfront. And if you have employees working under you, train them to be courteous and to take your customers' needs seriously. A good employee can create amazing customer loyalty. (And customers will start to contact that employee directly, saving you time and effort.)

If you find that some of your employees are truly stellar at customer service, be sure to acknowledge the great job they're doing. Tell them specifically what they're doing right, and you'll encourage more of this behavior.

## Giving back to your community

One of the most powerful ways to influence your customers positively is to volunteer at local charity events. Doing so tells people that you're a generous person who cares about your neighborhood — and that's great PR for your business.

If helping out in person doesn't suit your introverted nature, plenty of other options exist. For example, consider volunteering your help in these ways:

- ✔ Paying the printing costs for an event
- ✔ Providing food or beverages
- ✔ Providing prizes for events
- ✔ Providing T-shirts or caps

And even if you're humble, as many introverts are, don't hesitate to ask event hosts to mention your company's name on their programs or websites. Charities are always happy to do so. Also, mention the event in your own mailers or on your website. When you do, here are some good guidelines:

- ✔ Don't brag about yourself. Just mention briefly upfront that your company helped sponsor the event.
- ✔ Focus on the great things other people did at the event. For example, headline your story, "Disabled Veteran Shines in 10K Run."
- ✔ Explain why you chose this charity, and talk about the good it does. If you have a personal tie to the charity, mention that as well.

## Thanking your clients in small ways

Most marketers use e-mail or snail mail to tell customers about their services or products. But you can also use these approaches to say a quiet "thank you" to the people who patronize your business.

For example, do you ever buy items at online auction sites? If you do, you'll notice that some sellers include handwritten notes thanking you for your purchase. This little act takes only a few seconds, but it may make you more likely to buy from them in the future.

Similarly, sending your clients cards on their birthdays or holidays can make you memorable. (If you run a business for pets, you can even ask owners to enter their pets' birthdays and send Fido and Fluffy cards as well!) And here's another way to enhance your reputation: Include a little gift with large orders, such as some free stickers when someone orders a toy. It costs only a few pennies, and it's likely to make customers come back again and again.

Loyalty programs that reward repeat customers are another excellent way to thank them for coming back. And think about providing some type of special service for your clients. For example, one accountant hosts a "shredding day" and invites his clients to bring their boxes of old files for safe, free shredding.

## Avoiding marketing approaches that irritate clients

Sometimes companies pick the wrong marketing approach and actually wind up "anti-marketing" — that is, transforming happy customers into dissatisfied ones. For example, some entrepreneurs send marketing messages by fax because faxing is easy and costs next to nothing. But this is a huge mistake. Faxing wastes people's paper and toner, and it gives you a cheap, fly-by-night image. As a result, recipients are likely to actively dislike you — and that's hardly the result you want from a marketing campaign!

If you truly feel that you need to fax marketing info to clients, include a checkbox marked "unsubscribe" and provide a number so they can fax the form back to you. But it's far, far better to use regular mail or e-mail.

And speaking of e-mail, make sure you don't overdo it. Advertise your big sales and announce major news, but don't fill up people's inboxes with daily messages. Also, consider using Twitter to send occasional messages to customers without being too overbearing.

Finally, send messages to customers' smartphones only if people ask to receive them. Unsolicited phone messages can turn off your clients quickly.

# Coping When Prospects Don't Pan Out

No matter how fantastic your marketing skills are and how terrific your product or service is, you won't get a "yes" from every prospect you approach. That's why one of the biggest keys to doing wildly well as an entrepreneur is to react wisely when things *don't* go well. In this section, I offer tips for handling two big headaches: prospects who suddenly drop out of sight, and prospects who outright reject you (ouch!).

## *Dealing with disappearing acts*

It's an all-too-familiar scenario for an entrepreneur: You approach a client, he sounds very interested, and then — poof! — he vanishes. Just when you thought you had him hooked, he stops answering your e-mails or returning your calls.

This situation is where introverts in particular often drop the ball because they think that silence means rejection. But frequently, people who are interested in a product or service fail to respond simply because they're too busy or don't have time to get back to you quickly. And other times, prospective clients may need to wait for more information from a manager or family member before they make a move. Also, although a connection may be all-important to you, it may not be your prospect's highest priority.

That's why I use what I call *the Rule of Seven*. When a prospect pulls a vanishing act, I attempt to contact the person up to seven more times — and you'd be amazed how often I wind up with a positive response. Sometimes it takes a year or even longer to earn that "yes," but it's well worth the wait and the extra effort.

The Rule of Seven approach allows you to keep in touch with prospects and remind them that you'll be there when the time is right for them. It also encourages them to tell you if the timing will *never* be right, which is hard to hear but better than wasting your efforts.

So don't give up too quickly when a once-hot prospect fails to answer a follow-up call. Instead, wait two or three days and then e-mail or call with a message like this: "Hi! Just following up. I know how busy people get, so I'll assume you're still interested unless I hear otherwise. Would you like me to contact you by phone?"

If you still get no reply, wait a few more days and send an e-mail with the subject "second attempt" and a similar friendly message. After that, contact the person three to five more times, spreading your messages farther apart each time. If you get no response after the seventh attempt, add the person to your mailing list so he still won't forget about you. And if he does reply but says he's not sure if he wants to hire you, tell him that's fine and ask when you can contact him again.

In short, be as determined as the proverbial dog with a bone. You'll be surprised at how often your persistence pays off.

## Handling rejection

Rejection is a fact of life for any entrepreneur, but introverts in particular tend to ruminate over it. They may spend days or weeks wondering, "What did I do wrong?" or "Am I really cut out to run my own company?"

If you find yourself asking these questions, try a different approach. First, do the exercises for turning off negative self-talk that I describe in Chapter 11. Then do the following:

✔ Ask the prospect who said "no" whether he's willing to tell you why he rejected your offer. Make your request gently, for example, say, "I hear that you're not interested. May I ask why?" People won't always answer this question truthfully, but when they do, their responses can be helpful.

For instance, you may find that the person was turned off by some aspect of your plan, product, or service that you can change. In this case, a few tweaks can improve your odds of success with your next prospect. Often, however, you'll discover that a rejection has nothing to do with you personally. For example, a company may decide not to buy your product because it's undergoing budget cuts or restructuring.

✔ Fight the urge to respond to a rejection by underselling yourself the next time. A lot of introverts trip themselves up in this way and wind up earning far too little for their hard work. However, do some extra research to make sure your prices and your offerings are comparable to those of your competitors. If your prices are higher than what your rivals charge, you'll need to adjust them or find a way to show clients that you're worth the extra money.

✔ If you get enough rejections to threaten your business, consider hiring a coach who can help you refine your marketing strategy. (I talk more about coaches later in the section "Considering a business coach.") You can also contact the Small Business Administration for free help.

# Building Your Dream Team

Some entrepreneurs work entirely on their own, but many have part-time or full-time staffs. In addition, many hire business coaches to help them elevate their performance. If you're thinking of adding to your staff or calling on a coach, you can make your life much easier and increase your profits by making the right hiring choices. In this section, I tell you how.

## Interviewing wisely when you're hiring staff

In Chapter 9, I talk about an interviewing approach called *behavioral interviewing*. In this approach, you ask job candidates how they handled situations in the past so you can get clues about how they're likely to handle similar situations in the future. This is the most popular interviewing technique these days, and it's an excellent approach to use.

To decide which questions you want to ask your candidates, think carefully about the strengths you're looking for. For example, are you looking for someone with great customer skills? Then focus on questions like these:

- Can you tell me about a time when you calmed down a very angry customer?
- Can you describe a time when you disagreed with your manager about how to deal with a dissatisfied client?

And if you're looking for someone who can handle a highly stressful job that requires a lot of multitasking, ask questions like these:

- Can you tell me about a time when you had to juggle multiple projects?
- Can you describe a time when things got very stressful at work and tell me how you handled the pressure?

If possible, do face-to-face interviews even if you're filling a telecommuting or out-of-state position. And if you need an employee with a specific skill set, find ways to test the person's skills during the interview. For example, I ask candidates to type a summary of a book chapter in my presence. This "test" allows me to evaluate their language, spelling, and grammar skills as well as their ability to present information in a concise way. Let your candidates know ahead of time that you'll be testing them, so they'll be prepared.

As you're busy finding out what your candidates have to offer you, remember to describe what you can offer *them*. If you're a cash-strapped entrepreneur, you may not be able to provide a great salary. But see whether you can make up for this by offering flexible hours, extra vacation days, or telecommuting options.

At the end of an interview, ask for references, and be sure to check at least a couple of them. When you call someone who's listed as a reference, call *after* work hours and leave a message like this: "I know that if this person was a good employee, you'll want to at least call me back and leave a quick message." If your candidate was truly a great guy, his reference will nearly always respond, even if it's just to say, "John is fine; he'll do a good job for you. Bye." Some people aren't allowed to say anything at all about former employees, but even if they just call back and say "I'm returning your call as you requested," that's a good sign.

## Before you interview, snoop around

All's fair in love and war — and in hiring! These days, a lot of people put tons of personal information online where anyone can read it. So before you call someone in for an interview, do a little detective work and see what you can find out. Don't be too concerned about a few little indiscretions, especially if a candidate is young, but look for major red flags. Also, check to see whether the information you find online matches the information on the candidate's résumé.

If you don't get a call back, call the reference a second time and say, "I'll understand if I don't hear back from you." If you don't hear back after that call, consider this a big clue that the person you're considering may not be up to snuff.

## *Choosing employees who can complement your skills*

Visit my office, and you'll discover one of the biggest reasons for my success — my staff! They're all amazingly talented, and that's not the only reason they're so valuable; another is that they fill in the gaps in my skill set.

For example, I'm terrible at scheduling. But Pam is a master at it, and she makes sure I never miss a phone call or a client meeting. Jill is a whiz at technology, while I can barely figure out my smartphone. Shannon, unlike me, is brilliant at handling all the details that go into planning talks and workshops. And Camille, who still lets me con her into coming out of retirement occasionally, is one of the best writers I know, so when I can't think of a clever phrase, she can always help out.

Similarly, it makes sense for introverts to add at least a few extroverts to their team because outies are strong in areas where innies have challenges. So if you're hiring, think about looking for people with skills like these:

- ✔ A desire and ability to take care of customers and make small talk

- ✔ Strong sales skills

- ✔ A willingness to attend professional meetings and social functions on behalf of your company

- ✔ A love of travel, if you prefer staying home

If you do hire some extroverts to round out your staff, be sure to give them the information they need to do their jobs efficiently. If you don't communicate your ideas well, you're likely to wind up with employees who don't understand your products, services, or time frames. As a result, they may promise more than you can offer.

## Hiring the right person to make your website sparkle

If you're an entrepreneur, your website is your most important marketing tool. So be especially careful if you're hiring an employee or consultant to create or enhance your online presence. Many people who bill themselves as experts on website design or search engine optimization (SEO) aren't as good as they say they are, so ask to see examples of their work and talk with people who've used them.

In addition to searching on your candidates' names or their companies' names, search by job description. For example, type in "website design" "San Francisco." If your candidates truly excel at their jobs, they're likely to show up on the first page or two of your search results. Website design also requires strong language skills, so make sure the person you hire can create accurate, compelling text and still make the website work flawlessly.

## Considering a business coach

You're probably familiar with sports coaches. These people can help you master new skills, gain confidence, and find ways to beat out your competition. A business coach does the same thing but in the corporate arena rather than on the playing field.

Sports coaches and business coaches also have something else in common: They're essential if you want to take your game to the highest level. In fact, nearly all CEOs and senior-level executives currently have coaches or have used them at some point as they climbed the corporate ladder. Most top leaders rely on coaches throughout their entire careers.

For an entrepreneur, a coach can serve the same purpose as a board of directors in a company. This person can help you develop stronger marketing strategies, hone your leadership skills, and avoid the bad decisions that trip up many business owners.

### Determining what kind of coach you need

Coaches offer a wide range of services. So before you hire one, identify your specific needs by asking yourself which of these goals are important to you:

- ✔ Becoming more persuasive
- ✔ Communicating more clearly
- ✔ Giving public speeches with confidence
- ✔ Building relationships with employees and customers
- ✔ Overcoming anxiety
- ✔ Networking effectively
- ✔ Creating high-performing teams and collaborations
- ✔ Becoming a stronger leader
- ✔ Dealing with organizational change
- ✔ Handling conflicts successfully
- ✔ Negotiating assertively
- ✔ Conducting productive executive strategy sessions
- ✔ Researching your market and creating powerful marketing and public relations campaigns
- ✔ Dealing with the financial aspects of your business
- ✔ Getting a handle on safety and compliance issues

After you identify the kinds of help you need, look for a coach who focuses on these specific areas. For instance:

- ✔ Think about hiring a coach who's a certified public accountant (CPA) if you have trouble figuring out your finances.
- ✔ Look for a marketing or IT coach if you're having difficulty in one of these areas.
- ✔ Hire an organizational or industrial/organizational psychologist if you want someone who can help you address both "people" and organizational issues.

### Finding the right coach

If you decide to hire a coach, look for someone who's licensed and has a master's degree or PhD in business coaching. Most master's programs in business or organizational psychology include coursework and internships related to business, so this degree guarantees that you're getting someone with lots of experience. And if you hire a licensed coach, you'll be able to contact the licensing agency if you're dissatisfied with this person.

And look for a coach who uses a *cognitive behavioral* approach. This means that in addition to teaching you practical skills, he can help you overcome negative thoughts and behaviors that are holding you back.

It's also important to hire a coach who's highly trained in doing assessments. A coach who starts working with you without doing any assessments is a lot like a doctor who starts treating you without doing any lab tests! So be highly skeptical of "off the shelf" coaching programs that don't look at your individual strengths and needs.

By the way, many coaches are certified but not licensed. Certification is fine, but it's not enough because some certificates take as little as 20 to 40 hours to earn. So it's best to be picky, and insist on a licensed professional. If you do want to consider someone who only has a certification, ask how long the certification program lasted, what skills it covered, and what the person is and isn't trained to do.

If you're looking for help in sales, branding and marketing, or business expansion, be cautious about hiring a coach whose only experience is as a clinical psychologist. It's much better to hire a licensed professional who understands business and has experience working with entrepreneurs at your level. Also, find out whether a coach has a good understanding of your specific strengths and challenges as an introvert. A good coach will tailor her training to your personality.

When you interview candidates, be sure to ask for references. Call these references, and ask lots of questions about how satisfied they are with the services they received.

Talk upfront with candidates about fees, and find out exactly what you'll get for your money. And spend plenty of time interviewing a prospective coach to make sure you're a good fit for each other.

Also, make sure you understand the boundaries of the coach-client relationship. Coaches can help you develop emotional intelligence (see Chapter 5), grow more assertive, become less anxious, and relate to other people more effectively. But they'll refer you to someone else if you need help conquering severe anxiety or depression, or if you're going through major personal crises.

Good coaching takes time, so make a long-term commitment. Plan on working with your coach for at least six months and preferably a year or more. (Successful executives frequently work with coaches on-and-off for many years.) Most likely, the extra business you'll bring in as a result of your improved skills will vastly outweigh what you're paying your coach!

# Part III

# Finding Personal Happiness as an "Innie"

## *Five Ways to Improve Communication with an Extroverted Partner*

- When your extrovert is talking, let your interest show on your face and in your voice. Smile, lean in to the conversation, and express enthusiasm with phrases like "No way — he really did that?" or "That's amazing!"

- Cut your outie partner a little slack when it comes to small talk. It's important to him, so pretend like you're interested even when you aren't!

- If your partner is itching to share his news but you need a little time to charge your battery before a long conversation, be honest but sensitive. For example, say, "I really want to hear about that, but can you give me a few minutes to clear my head and get dinner started? Then we can sit down with a glass of wine, and you can tell me all about it."

- When you get on a roll about one of your favorite topics, watch your partner's body language. If he looks confused, sketch out some of your ideas on paper for him. If he starts looking bored, on the other hand, consider wrapping it up and switching to a different subject.

- Remember that extroverts tend to be "big picture" people. Unless it's crucial to give your outie partner a lot of details, focus on your major points.

Check out www.dummies.com/extras/successasanintrovert for more tips on how to be happy in an extrovert's world.

# *In this part . . .*

✔ Discover ways to be less critical of yourself, think positively, and visualize your success.

✔ Get control of your thoughts, emotions, stress, and anxiety.

✔ Meet new friends in places you may not have thought of, and find out how to join the dating scene as an introvert.

✔ Develop and nurture healthy relationships (and self-image), whether you're just getting to know one another, handling innie-outie difference, or splitting up after realizing it just isn't going to work.

✔ Use a few innie tricks to help you be a gracious guest at an event when you'd much rather be at home.

✔ Find ways to take the focus off yourself and recharge your batteries when you're the host.

# Chapter 11

# Being Your Personal Best

*In This Chapter*

▶ Becoming kinder to yourself

▶ Saying no to pessimism and catastrophic thinking

▶ Coping successfully with life problems and stress

▶ Welcoming new friends into your life

For me, the greatest reward of being a psychologist is helping people realize their full potential. And that's what this chapter is all about: removing the roadblocks that can stand in the way of the life you want.

Changing your life for the better starts with changing your beliefs and behaviors. Healthy thinking paired with healthy behaviors and choices leads to deepening peace, joy, and satisfaction. And over time, it allows you to create opportunities to build relationships with people you truly like, do work that you enjoy, and make your unique mark in the world.

In this chapter, I offer my best advice for achieving your full personal potential. The techniques in this chapter are ones I use myself and teach my clients, and they're scientifically validated so you can have faith that they're effective.

At the beginning of the chapter, I provide powerful tools for overcoming negative self-talk — a huge problem for introverts (and many extroverts as well). After that, I offer tips for confronting life problems, handling stress, and dealing with the pessimism that often plagues introverts. And finally, I look at ways to enlarge your circle of friends because having a few good buddies is essential to your well-being.

## Being Kind to Yourself

Introverts are remarkable people. The problem is, they don't always realize this! As an innie, you're likely to engage in far more than your share of self-criticism. And if you're a shy introvert, that's doubly true.

This negative self-talk can hold you back from reaching your full potential. It can stop you from making friends ("I'm so boring, who would want to hang out with me?"). It can keep you from climbing the career ladder ("I'm not good enough to apply for a management job"). And it can even stop you from meeting your soul mate ("He's way too amazing to want someone like me").

Where does all this negative self-talk come from? Intentionally or unintentionally, the people we count on for our survival as children — parents, teachers, and others — often send messages that we're bad when we act in ways that are socially unacceptable. Only rarely do we get the right message: that we're good people at heart and that only our behavior has to change. So even as little kids, we start thinking "I'm unacceptable" instead of "my behavior right now is unacceptable." And introverts, because they're so introspective, are especially likely to latch onto thoughts like these.

Over time, negative messages become core beliefs: "I'm unlovable" or "I'm incompetent" or even "I am bad and don't have a right to exist." We develop positive core beliefs as well, but it's those nasty negative ones that really get ingrained. If we don't confront these beliefs, we start living our lives in accordance with them, and as a result, they become self-fulfilling prophecies.

The important thing to know about negative self-talk is that the overwhelming majority of the time, it's both unhelpful and untrue. So when you make life decisions based on your negative thoughts, you'll be basing those decisions on faulty data. And that's a recipe for trouble.

Canning this trash talk can change your life for the better. You'll be more confident when you're not kicking yourself all day, and you'll make smarter decisions as well. So try these tricks for making that voice in your head a kinder one.

## Using the dump-sheet-and-flower technique

Breaking the habit of running yourself down is easier said than done. The key is to acknowledge your *positive* thoughts and behaviors (no matter how large or small). When you do this, it empowers you to either abandon negative thoughts or put them in perspective. And that, in turn, leads to a surge in self-confidence.

Over the years, I've helped thousands of people quash their negative self-talk with a simple two-part approach. The first part is called a *dump sheet* (I offer several versions of this method in this book), and the second part is called the *flower*. In this section, I tell you how to combine these two methods to turn off that negative tape recorder in your head.

## Creating your dump sheet

If you're reading the chapters of this book in order, you're already familiar with a dump sheet. (For a little background on this method, see Chapter 7.) But this time around, you're going to use it for a new purpose: to spot your negative thought patterns.

To begin this activity, find a quiet, private place where you won't be interrupted for at least 30 minutes. (If necessary, lock yourself in the bathroom.) Bring your laptop or a big pad of paper and a pen or pencil.

Get comfortable, and then start spilling out all the feelings, ideas, thoughts, worries, fears, and beliefs that come into your head. They don't have to pertain to anything particular; just throw them out there on paper. For example, your list may contain items like these:

- ✔ I'm not very attractive.
- ✔ I often say embarrassing things.
- ✔ I'm afraid people will realize that I'm not as smart as they think I am.

As you write, don't censor yourself at all. If a thought comes to mind — positive or negative — write it down. And keep writing until you can't think of anything else to put down. This technique allows you to see what the many voices in your head are saying.

By taking these hidden thoughts and exposing them to sunlight, you'll be able to think about them more logically. And that's where the next part of this activity — the *flower* — comes in.

## Drawing your flower

As you write your dump sheet, you're likely to see that certain negative beliefs pop up over and over again, such as "I'm not very interesting," or "I always say something stupid when I'm meeting new people."

Unfortunately, people have a tendency to believe these negative messages even when the evidence shows exactly the opposite. And they often feel helpless to change their negative thoughts. Those thoughts feel so strong and true!

However, you *can* overcome the negative beliefs that are holding you back. It takes hard work to recognize these beliefs and take control over them, but it's well worth the effort. To help you put your own negative thoughts in perspective, use this flower exercise.

First, head back to your quiet spot. Bring some paper, a pen or pencil, and two colors of marking pens — one color you like and one color you don't like. Then follow these steps:

1. **On one sheet of paper, draw a flower. Shape it like a daisy, and give it a round center and four to six petals. Outline the center of the flower in the color you don't like and outline the petals in the color you do like.**

   (If you're not into flowers, feel free to use a different design. For example, some people like to create a stained-glass window design, with colorful panels on the outside and a drab or ugly color at the center.)

2. **Inside the circle at the center of your flower, write a negative core belief or emotion that you've spotted from your dump sheet.**

   For example, you may write, "I'm not confident" or "I can't get ahead."

3. **At this point, set your flower drawing aside and pick up a blank sheet of paper.**

4. **On the new sheet of paper, list four to six positive things — one item for each flower petal you drew — that you know are true about your life.**

   Each positive thing you list should be something that's a provable fact, even if you don't feel it in your gut. For example, think about positive acts that people praised you for, awards you've won, or promotions you've received at work. The things you list can be big or small and may include items like these:

   - At my latest performance review, my manager gave me high marks for my hard work and creativity.

   - My parents didn't have enough money to send me to college, so I worked full time and saved up the money myself.

   - I won a new account last month that no one thought our company could score.

   - I overcame my fear of traveling and went to France five years ago.

   As you're making your list, visualize yourself at each event you're describing so you can relive the feelings you experienced. And don't censor yourself. Don't rush yourself, either; some people write their list in an hour, and others take a week.

When you're done, set your list aside. Now, make another one.

This time, list situations in which you "know in your gut" that you did something good — even if no one else knows about or appreciates what you did. This list can be difficult to create if you're particularly hard on yourself (as many introverts are). That's especially true if others in your life have convinced you that it's not okay to feel good about your own actions, qualities, and innie traits. But this list is important, so stick with it!

Again, the things you list can be big or tiny, and you can draw them from any time in your life. For example, here are some items I put on my own list:

✔ I spent hours as a young child training my parakeet Pretty Boy to feel comfortable around people and to do tricks.

✔ I used to sing in the school choirs and would unconsciously start dancing in the spot where I was standing as I sang. I was embarrassed when people pointed this out, but eventually I grew to appreciate the fact that I could openly express my own joy in this way.

✔ I truly enjoy watching people grow, and I know I can assist them in making their lives better.

You may immediately get a positive vibe when you look at your two lists. If you instantly recognize that an item is true (either because you can prove it or because you instinctively know it), write it on a petal of your flower.

If some of your items don't feel real to you yet, read them over every morning or night for a week or so. When an item on your list starts feeling authentic to you and makes you feel proud or happy or confident, transfer it to a petal of your flower. (You'll have items left over when you fill up your petals, but don't worry — I'll tell you what to do with them later.)

## Revisiting your flower

Now, here's the most crucial part of this exercise. Once a day for the next several weeks, stop what you're doing and focus for a moment on your flower. As you do this, visualize the petals moving to the forefront as the negative belief that's currently at the center moves back, becomes smaller, and eventually gets covered over by the positive.

You don't necessarily have to make the negative thought in the center vanish entirely. The key thing is to put it in perspective, so it doesn't overpower the many positive accomplishments and joys of your life.

At first, your mind may resist this process. Those negative feedback loops you've created are pretty powerful! But keep working at it, and eventually you will anchor the new positive thoughts in your mind.

As you feel this happening, rotate some of your remaining items onto your flower. You can even start a second flower if you want.

If you're skeptical about doing this exercise — and introverts frequently are — try starting small. Think of it as an experiment, and focus on one negative thought and three positive experiences. And realize that it's perfectly okay if it takes time to anchor your positive thoughts in your mind. You may need to "fake it till you make it," but eventually your positive thoughts will become part of your core.

When you do this exercise, I think you'll be delighted at the results. Your dump sheet will kick off a cascade of neurological events, causing you to move from the emotional regions of your brain to the clear-thinking frontal cortex. My clients all over the world tell me that this simple exercise helps them gain control over negative thoughts, put past mistakes in perspective, and view their lives with more objectivity and clarity.

## Reframing your thoughts

As you become increasingly aware of your negative thoughts, you'll have more power to get rid of them. So after you've completed the dump-sheet-and-flower activity I outlined in the previous section, you'll be ready for another technique: *reframing*. In this approach, you replace negative thoughts with positive ones that are more realistic.

Here are some examples of ways to reframe your negative thoughts:

- ✔ If you're at a party and you catch yourself thinking, "I'm feeling anxious," think this instead: "I'm proud of myself for coming here tonight — and I can get my anxiety under control by taking some deep breaths."

- ✔ If you find yourself ruminating over something embarrassing you said at work, tell yourself this: "Everyone does embarrassing things, and it wasn't that big a deal. Most likely, my coworkers hardly even noticed it."

- ✔ If you're thinking, "I'm not good enough to handle this new task," think this instead: "I will ace this project. All I need to do is take it step by step."

- ✔ If you lose a sale and find yourself thinking "I'm a failure," reframe your thoughts and tell yourself, "No one makes every sale. I did a really good job of trying to convince this client to buy in, and I learned enough from this experience to do an even better job with the next client."

## Practicing thought-stopping

Do you ever get partway into a movie and say, "I don't like this movie, and I'm turning it off right now"?

Well, your own mind is full of movies you've created. Some of them are positive, but many of them aren't. And when you catch those movies running through your head, you can hit the "stop" button.

To do this, start paying conscious attention to your thought processes. When you identify a negative movie starting up, say to yourself: "Stop!" or even, "Stop the film!" Then consciously rewrite the movie's script. Rewind it to the beginning, replay it slowly, and change the negative scenes to positive ones.

Each time your brain tries to run the old film again, say "Stop!" and play the new one. Eventually, you'll get rid of that old flick altogether — and good riddance!

## Treating life as an experiment

One good way to cultivate positive thoughts and behaviors is to think about your life as a scientific experiment. It sounds odd, I know, but it's actually very effective!

Here's how to do it: When you're trying to decide whether a thought or behavior is useful or harmful, put on your scientist's hat. Deliberately think the thought or practice the behavior, and analyze the results. After a while, ask yourself: Does this thought or behavior usually work for me and the people around me? Or does it make things worse for me or others? When you identify thoughts and behaviors that enhance your life and the lives of others, focus on turning them into habits.

As you experiment, be aware that the voices in your head will keep trying to tell you that your ingrained negative thoughts are true and useful. But stay in scientist mode! Realize that these thoughts are based on prior, outdated experiences. Test your ideas out, and go where the facts lead you.

Use this same approach if you know that you've messed up at times in your life. Instead of kicking yourself for mistakes you made in the past, decide to practice new and different behaviors. Then measure your results. Did the new behaviors reduce your anxiety and give you a concrete feeling of self-confidence? Then the evidence is clear: You're on the right path.

## Visualizing your happy, healthy inner child and inner adult

In Chapter 7, I outline some powerful visualization techniques you can use to build your self-confidence. Here, I want to introduce you to another technique that can help you stifle the negative voices in your head. Just follow these steps:

1. **Visualize your "inner adult."**

   Picture this adult as happy, healthy, and wise. Ask this person for advice about any problems you're trying to solve.

2. **Visualize your "inner child."**

   Picture the child you were, who wanted love and acceptance. Now, befriend this child. Take her hand, and say things like the following to her:

   - "You are creative and intelligent."
   - "You had to overcome some big problems, but you also had some wonderful experiences."
   - "We're going to get happier and healthier together."

To many people, this exercise seems a little silly at first. But try it, and you'll find that it helps you tap your inner wisdom and heal lingering wounds from childhood.

# Gaining More Control Over Your Life

Life has its ups and downs, and sometimes the ride can get pretty rocky. In difficult times, you need to work hard to avoid self-pity, look at problems rationally, and view the future in a positive way. The approaches I outline in this section can help you succeed.

## Taming self-pity

We all suffer some hard knocks as we go through life. Extroverts often respond to these tough times by reaching outward, finding new friends or trying new activities. Introverts, on the other hand, may reach inward, expressing their hurt in writing or through art.

Both of these approaches are healthy. What's not healthy, however, is getting stuck in self-pity ("Why me?"). I often see this problem in introverts, although extroverted people can fall into the self-pity trap as well.

Here are some of the forms that self-pity can take:

- Feeling sorry for yourself
- Blaming yourself
- Blaming others

Self-pity occurs when you see yourself as the "victim" of others or a situation instead of seeing that you always have a choice — even if it's a choice between less-than-perfect options. Self-pity is one of the hardest habits to break, and it's also one of the most destructive.

To tackle this issue in my clinical practice, I've developed an approach I call the *pity pot,* which allows you to identify your feelings of self-pity and physically "flush" them away. It may strike you as a little weird, but sometimes you need to get creative to silence those negative voices! So try this activity, have fun with it, and feel free to tweak it to suit your own style.

At the outset of this activity, recognize that any emotion you experience is okay. It's what you do with your emotions that matters.

Here's how to use this approach.

1. **Grab a mortar and pestle set.**

   If you don't have a mortar and pestle, just grab a medium-sized bowl (preferably one that can take some punishment) and a wooden spoon or other tool you can "grind" with.

2. **Vent your emotions.**

   Out loud or on paper, express everything you're feeling — no censoring allowed! You may find that this step alone helps you release your self-pity or other negative emotions.

3. **If you're still having trouble releasing your self-pity, repeat all your venting.** (If you wrote out your feelings, simply read your notes out loud.)

4. **Pick up the mortar (or bowl), and imagine dumping all your negative feelings into it. Then take the pestle or wooden spoon and imagine grinding those feelings into a powder.**

5. **When you're done grinding, carry the mortar or bowl into the bathroom, picture yourself dumping all your ground-up feelings into the toilet, and then flush it.**

As you do this exercise, you may find yourself laughing out loud because it seems so darned silly. But think about it: It's even sillier to let yourself be ruled by old negative beliefs and feelings. And after you finish this exercise, you'll probably feel relieved, energized, and much more ready to stop wallowing in self-pity and move forward with your life.

To make these positive changes stick, try doing this activity every day for 21 days to a month. That's how long it takes to create new brain pathways that will help keep your negative voices at bay.

## Taking charge of your problems

Do many of the problems in your life seem to stem from circumstances you have little or no control over? Then fight back by *taking* control. When you do this, you'll avoid the victim trap that can keep you stuck in bad situations.

To take control over a problem, start by analyzing your role in it. Ask yourself these questions:

- ✔ What choices did you make that helped bring about the problem?
- ✔ What choices are you making to continue it?

Now, figure out what you can do about the situation. Even if a solution is 99 percent out of your hands, you can focus on the 1 percent you *can* control. For example, ask yourself the following questions:

- ✔ Is there any action you can take to address this problem?
- ✔ Is there any action you can take to help someone else who's experiencing the same problem?
- ✔ Is there any action you can take to prevent this problem from happening to you or someone else in the future?

When you do, you'll feel less like a victim of circumstances and more like an effective problem solver.

## Cultivating optimism

Many introverts are like Anna, a quiet little girl I know. When her family goes on trips, Anna's mom and dad pack the usual snacks and a few changes of clothes, but Anna stuffs her tiny suitcase full of safety pins, bandages, and other emergency supplies. Ask her why, and she'll say, "You never know what may happen."

Like Anna, many innies tend to spend more time expecting crises than they do anticipating happy times. Studies show that in general, innies are less positive about the future than their extroverted peers.

In addition, introverts are prone to something called *catastrophic thinking*, meaning they focus on the worst possible outcome that could occur. For example, if they're giving a speech, they won't just worry about being a little boring or doing something mildly embarrassing. No, they'll conjure up something spectacularly awful, like freezing up entirely or even tripping and falling while going on stage.

Needless to say, this kind of thinking leads to a lot of unnecessary stress and anxiety. It also causes physical symptoms, including shallow breathing and rapid heartbeat, and it can even lead to panic attacks.

So try to spot pessimistic or catastrophic thoughts when they occur. When you identify them, acknowledge the feelings you're experiencing. By embracing these feelings, you'll actually help neutralize their power over you. Then, ask yourself questions like these:

- ✔ Is the terrible thing I'm imagining really likely to occur?
- ✔ Is it just as likely — or even far more likely — that something good will occur?
- ✔ Have I handled crises successfully in the past? If another crisis actually does occur, can I handle it, too?

And here's another approach to try. First, ask yourself, "What's the worst that could happen?" And then ask yourself, "If that worst-case scenario comes true, what's the worst that could happen then?" Eventually, you'll probably drill down to a negative core belief — for example, "I'm going to fail this test. And if that happens, I'll flunk the course. And if I flunk the course, I won't get into the right college. And that will reinforce my dad's idea that I'm a failure." When you hit that core belief, you can work on it using the dump-sheet-and-flower technique I talk about earlier in this chapter.

To get an even better handle on your pessimistic thoughts, work at consciously cultivating an attitude of optimism. Doing so may be extremely difficult for you as an introvert, especially if your pessimistic thinking is strongly ingrained. Realize that it's an act of courage simply to say to yourself, "Despite possible setbacks and frustrations, I expect things to turn out all right." And it's an even greater act of courage to face tough times and say, "In spite of all I'm going through, at least I'm hanging in there and getting through this one step at a time. And in the end, I'll learn from this experience." But the more you try this, the easier it will get.

As you work toward an attitude of optimism, be aware that optimism doesn't just mean *hoping* that something good will happen. Instead, it means actively *expecting* that something good is likely to happen, and behaving accordingly. When you're optimistic, you have a clear vision of where you are in life — and you set yourself free to imagine being in an even better place.

Realize, however, that becoming more optimistic is a challenge because pessimism is a habit — and it's so *easy*. It's simple to sit around saying, "There's no use trying because I can't win." But it takes guts to say, "I can change my life for the better," and then do it. So don't be surprised if your mind fights this change. But if you persist, you'll be amazed at how much happier your life becomes.

## Swimming to success

To see how powerful expectations can be, one research team told a group of swimmers that they'd received poorer scores in a race than they actually got. Then they asked the athletes to swim again. Pessimists did worse in the second race, while optimists didn't.

The moral of this story? If you catch yourself focusing on worst-case scenarios, see whether you can let yourself believe that something good may happen in the future — no matter what's happened in the past. Then analyze your results, and see if your optimism pays off.

## Harnessing the power of gratitude

Parents are fond of saying, "Count your blessings." And guess what — they're right! Research shows that feeling grateful for the good things in your life can make you happier, and gratitude can also make you less prone to alcoholism, drug abuse, eating disorders, depression, anxiety, and a host of other problems. It can even boost your energy, ease your aches and pains, and help you sleep better!

And here's another reason to actively practice gratitude: It's easy. Often self-improvement is hard work, but not in this case. Here's all you need to do:

✓ When you first wake up in the morning, or before you go to bed at night, think of three people to whom you're grateful and remind yourself of what these people have done for you. You can create your list in your head or write it down.

✓ If you're feeling stressed during the day, stop and think of at least three things you're grateful for in your life — for example, your dog, the tea you're drinking, or the flowers a colleague sent you for your birthday.

✓ At least once a week, tell a friend or family member that you're grateful for something the person has done for you.

✓ Spot ungrateful thoughts and replace them with grateful ones. For example, if you catch yourself thinking, "John never remembers to bring in the trash can," replace that thought with this one: "John always forgets to bring in the trash can, but that's a small issue compared to all the terrific things he does for me and the kids."

## Getting Your Stress Under Control

Life is crazy, and everyone experiences stress at times. But for introverts, stress can be an especially big problem because their nervous systems are already more aroused than outies', and it doesn't take as much to send them into red alert.

Occasional stress is fine, and in fact, a little bit of stress is actually good for you. But constant stress can be bad for both your mind and your body. If stress is a big issue for you, the following sections explore some good ways to cut it down to size.

## Interpreting stressful events accurately

The first step in getting a handle on your stress is to understand the four steps of the stress process:

1. A stressful event

2. The way you interpret that event

3. The way you react emotionally as a result of that interpretation

4. The way you react physically as a result of your emotions

Now, here's the interesting thing: Often, there's not much you can do to prevent a stressful event from happening. What you can do, however, is to change how you *interpret* it.

For example, imagine that you've worked all day in your home office and you're pleased at everything you've accomplished. But your partner comes home from the office, and she's had a bad day. As a result, she's in a foul mood, and she says, "This place is a mess. You didn't even clean up after breakfast."

Most likely, her remark is going to irritate you. After all, you haven't been sitting around all day watching TV and drinking beer! So you have every right to be annoyed at this point.

But here's the question: What are you going to do about it? Consider these three options:

✔ You think, "She always does this to me. No matter what I do right, she finds something to nag me about. She doesn't even care about my feelings." As a result, you get angry yourself, and you say something harsh in return. Before you know it, the two of you are having a full-fledged fight. And by the time you go to bed, your stress level is off the charts.

✔ You have the same thoughts as in the previous option, but instead of acting on them, you hold them inside. As a result, your stress level rises. Your blood pressure shoots up, and you may get an upset stomach or a headache.

✔ You stop and count to ten. Then you think to yourself, "She's really had a lousy day, and right now she's taking it out on me. If I just keep my temper and let her unwind, she'll calm down, and she'll probably apologize for snapping at me." Your irritation quickly passes, and any stress you feel is just a blip on the radar screen.

Clearly, the way you interpret a stressful event can be far more important than the event itself. So when you find your stress levels climbing, take a step back and ask yourself questions like these:

✔ Why is *[my child, my partner, my friend]* saying hurtful things to me right now? Does she really mean them, or is she just upset because she *[lost her soccer game, had a lousy day at work, just broke up with her boyfriend]*?

✔ Why am I stressing out over this *[charity event, family dinner, work project]*? Is it really such a challenging *[event, dinner, project]*, or am I just tired because I'm not getting enough sleep?

One way to boost your ability to interpret stressful situations accurately is to improve your emotional intelligence (see Chapter 5).

## Understanding your stress threshold

Everyone has an innate *stress threshold*. When you cross that line, you're likely to go bonkers at the least provocation — for instance, a minor criticism or a "check engine" light on the car dashboard.

Although your own stress threshold depends in part on your genes and biochemistry, it's not inflexible. In fact, a lot of things can lower your stress threshold, making it easier for you to melt down. For example, if you have a cold, you're getting too little sleep, or your significant other just dumped you, your tolerance for stress may drop like a rock.

Fortunately, you can raise your stress threshold. One excellent approach is to practice mindful meditation (see Chapter 2). Other good ideas include

✔ Exercising

✔ Eating a good diet

✔ Finding things that make you laugh

✔ Writing a journal about your feelings

✔ Pursuing creative interests

✔ Escaping physically — on a vacation, a bike ride, a hike, or a shopping trip

Also, never underestimate the power of play! Adults tend to take life far too seriously, and that's one reason they get so stressed out. So make some time each week for a little fun and games — whether it's throwing a Frisbee with your dog, shooting hoops with your kids, or playing video games with a buddy.

## Considering a personal coach or mental health professional

Sometimes it's very, very hard for people to address negative thoughts and behaviors on their own. If this is the case for you, you may benefit greatly from a little professional help.

Here are some situations in which calling on a personal coach can be a good idea:

- If you have a great deal of trouble setting and sticking with your life goals, a personal coach can help keep you on the right path.

- If bad habits are holding you back, a personal coach can help you replace them with "positive addictions" — good habits that enrich your life rather than interfere with it.

If you have difficulty reaching your goals or overcoming negative behaviors even after working with a coach, you may need the additional expertise of a psychologist or psychiatrist. And seek out a mental health professional if you need help overcoming serious emotional or mental problems. For example, call on a psychologist or psychiatrist for help if you have any of these issues:

- You're frequently sad or depressed.

- You have debilitating anxiety or fears.

- You have emotional issues stemming from a trauma or physical or sexual abuse.

- You have an eating disorder.

If you decide to hire a coach or therapist, look for a results-oriented professional who focuses on changing your current thinking — not solely on delving into your past. Of course, you and your therapist may need to explore your past experiences to understand how they've influenced your current beliefs and behaviors. However, your therapist's goal should be to help you let go of negative past experiences so you can choose to have a brighter future.

Also, insist on a coach or therapist who's licensed. And look for a professional with at least two years of additional training in coaching or the psychology of change, and at least five years of professional experience. Be sure to ask for references and to check them out.

If you're a business owner, you may want to consider hiring a professional coach who can help you with both business and personal issues. For tips on hiring a professional coach, see Chapter 10.

# Making New Friends

Whether you're an introvert or an extrovert, good friendships are vital to your emotional health. If you're an introvert, you don't need a big group of friends, but you do need a few close pals.

However, it's sometimes hard for introverts to strike up friendships. One reason, as I explain in this section, is that the meeting places that work for outies are the very places you try hard to avoid. Luckily, as I explain, the world is full of places where introverts can make new acquaintances.

To succeed at making new friends, you need to get your game face on. In this section, I tell you how — and I also offer ways to get a friendship off the ground and keep it strong.

## Looking for friends in all the right places

For most introverts, a big question is: "Where can I meet people I'll like?" The places where extroverts like to make new friends — for instance, parties and bars — turn most innies off completely.

And face it: You're not likely to meet many new buddies at *your* favorite hangouts. Libraries, for instance, aren't exactly teeming with people wanting to connect with you!

So what's an introvert to do? Here are some great ways to meet people you're likely to enjoy:

> ✔ **Join clubs or groups that center around your interests.** No matter what you're into — restoring old cars, growing organic food, playing chess, even raising chickens — there's a group of fellow enthusiasts out there somewhere. And starting out with a common interest makes it easier to strike up conversations with potential friends.

- ✔ **Take classes.** You can find inexpensive and fun classes at local community centers. One friend of mine met her best friend at a painting class. She was too introverted to ask for a handout when she came in late, but her extroverted friend-to-be noticed her discomfort and grabbed one for her. That was the start of a 20-year friendship!

- ✔ **Volunteer.** Find a cause you believe in, and offer to help with fundraisers and other activities. Volunteering is a great way to meet interesting people, and you'll be doing a good deed for the world as well.

- ✔ **Greet new neighbors with cupcakes or a houseplant.** Also give them your phone number so they can call if they have any questions about their new neighborhood. And if you really like them, invite them over for dinner.

- ✔ **If you have very young children, join a play group.** You'll find plenty to talk about when you're surrounded by other parents dealing with the same teething, bed-wetting, or behavior issues you're coping with.

If you join a group, volunteer, or take a class, stick with it long enough to get to know your fellow participants well. It may take you three or four sessions to start enjoying yourself and building friendships, so be patient.

One other place you can make friends is in the office. In Chapter 4, I offer tips for building workplace relationships.

## Setting realistic goals

If you're a perfectionist, as many introverts are, you're likely to expect far too much from yourself when you're setting out to make new buddies. For example, you may feel like a failure if you go to two or three yoga classes and don't click with anyone.

To avoid falling into this trap, steer clear of goals like "I will make a new friend this month." Instead, set goals like "I will go to four yoga classes this month and enjoy learning some new skills." You're more likely to make friends when you're not keeping score. (For more on dealing with perfectionism, see Chapter 12.)

Also, set teeny-tiny goals for getting to know new people. After all, you cheer a baby when he first learns to walk, even though he takes only a few steps and then falls down. The point is: He took a few steps! That is where to place your own focus: on tiny, step-by-step progress. Remember each step, and celebrate it.

## Breaking the ice

To make new friends, you'll often need to make the first move. That's tricky for most innies, because stepping up to a stranger isn't an introvert's cup of tea. However, here are some ways to make it easier on yourself:

✔ Use coping statements to keep yourself confident when you arrive at an event where you're hoping to make new friends. Here are some good ones:

  • "My nervousness is perfectly normal and okay."

  • "It's brave of me to get out and meet new people."

✔ Breathe! Before walking up to a stranger and introducing yourself, take a few deep breaths to help you relax.

✔ Use the pretend-extrovert tips I outline in Chapter 3. They'll help you look confident and strike up conversations.

After you meet someone you think is a potential friend, make the first move *again*. For example, if you're both taking a class, ask the person whether she'd like to join you later to study. Or if you're in a painting group, suggest that you meet on the beach the next weekend for a sketching session. Choose a small, time-limited activity that's well within your comfort zone. If you're lucky, that small step can lead to years of friendship.

And what if the other person says, "No, thanks"? In this case, don't take it personally. People have a lot of reasons for being unwilling or unable to start new friendships.

For example, my friend Elizabeth tried to invite another member of her Tai Chi class out for lunch, but the woman said no. Being an introvert, Elizabeth immediately wondered if she'd somehow annoyed or offended the woman. Months later, however, she found out that the woman was the sole caregiver for a parent with Alzheimer's and could get out of the house only on rare occasions. The woman hadn't explained this to Elizabeth because — being an introvert herself — she thought it was too much information to offer to a new acquaintance.

So if someone says no to your offer of friendship, don't blame yourself, and don't give up. Instead, keep seeking out other people, and eventually you'll make a great connection.

## Keeping friendships healthy

Because introverts invest so much effort in making a new friend, each real friendship you build is important to you. So you want to cultivate your relationships carefully, but you also want to make sure your friends treat you well. In this section, I tell you how to do both.

### Showing that you care

As an introvert, you're probably not all that fond of telephone calls — or of birthday parties, baby showers, and holiday get-togethers.

But all these things are likely to be important to your friends, especially if they're extroverts. They'll also want you to come to their picnics, invite them over for dinner, or even be in their wedding parties. Now, you may not want to do all these things, but do *most* of them anyway! It's perfectly fine to say no to an occasional social event (and I tell you how to do so in Chapter 13). But saying no to most or all events is unfair to your more extroverted buddies.

Also, open up to your friends, even if you find it a little uncomfortable. Sharing confidences is the fastest way to strengthen bonds. You don't have to tell all your deep, dark secrets, but at least let your friends take a peek into your inner soul.

### Refusing to be a doormat

As an introvert, you're loyal to your friends. And occasionally, you may be loyal to a fault.

While an extrovert can shed friends and still have a lot of buddies, it's harder for you to let go of a friendship you've worked hard to build. As a result, you may put up with people who take advantage of you or don't care much about your needs. And doing so can harm you emotionally or even physically.

To determine whether your friendships are healthy, ask yourself questions like these:

- ✔ Does your friend give as much as he takes?
- ✔ Does your friend forgive you when you make mistakes?
- ✔ Does your friend encourage you to make healthy lifestyle choices?
- ✔ Does your friend typically come through on obligations?
- ✔ Does your friend like and respect you just as you are?
- ✔ Can you trust your friend to keep your secrets?

You don't always need to give up completely on a friendship that's not entirely healthy. If you really like the other person and you think your relationship can change, try taking the following steps to make it work better for you.

✔ **Set limits.** If a friend constantly imposes on you, stand up for yourself and say "no." This is a good way to find out whether the other person is a true friend.

✔ **Make your expectations clear.** Your friend may not realize that he's failing to understand your needs, so express those needs openly. For example, say, "I'm serious about losing ten pounds — so even though I love your homemade bread, please don't bring me any for the next two months."

✔ **Alter your own behavior.** Sometimes you can change a friendship for the better by redefining your own expectations. For example, if your friend is a great guy but he can't keep your secrets, share your confidences with someone else.

Often, you can salvage a friendship with a little work and a big dose of honesty. But if your relationship continues to bring you more pain than joy, ask yourself if it's time to ditch your faux friend and start hunting for better ones. *Remember:* As a smart, loyal, witty, kind innie, you don't need to settle for less than the best!

# Chapter 12

# Falling in Love and Staying in Love

*In This Chapter*

▶ Improving your odds of meeting that special someone

▶ Building a deeper relationship with a partner

▶ Managing innie-outie differences in a relationship

▶ Splitting up in a harmonious way

**1**s finding someone to love high on your agenda? Or are you in a relationship that you want to make stronger and happier? In either case, you'll find a lot of help in this chapter.

First, I offer tips for that crazy game called dating. Next, I talk about what to expect if you enter into a romantic relationship with an extrovert or another introvert. After that, I tackle some of the biggest issues that can arise between innies and outies in love. And finally, I provide advice for handling things gracefully if a breakup occurs.

## Navigating the Dating Scene

Dating can be exciting, frustrating, fun, boring, or anything in between. But one thing's for sure: It's hard work! As the saying goes, you have to kiss a lot of frogs before you find a prince (or princess). And for introverts in particular, all that frog-kissing can be a real chore.

In this section, I offer advice for finding that Mister or Miss Right who's out there somewhere in that giant frog pond. In addition, I discuss how to get things off on the right foot when you do meet someone you're attracted to.

### Spotting people you'd like to date

In Chapter 11, I offer a list of good places to make friends — from charity events to classes and clubs (and more). You may also find people you're attracted to romantically at these places, so give that chapter a quick skim if you're not sure where to start looking for a soul mate.

In addition to these real-world locales, introverts have another terrific tool when it comes to finding romance: Internet dating sites. These sites offer a number of benefits if you're an innie, including the following:

- ✔ They allow you to get to know something about people before you meet them face-to-face, which makes starting a conversation a whole lot easier when you do get together.

- ✔ They help you determine how introverted or extroverted a potential date is. For example, extroverts typically want to dive into a phone call or a date after exchanging a few e-mails. Introverts, on the other hand, generally want to exchange more e-mails and have one or two phone calls before agreeing to an in-person date.

- ✔ They often allow you to determine quickly whether you're compatible with someone, saving you from an awkward evening if you're not.

- ✔ If a date doesn't work out, odds are you'll never see the person again. So it's less upsetting than having a bad date with someone you see every day at the office or in your apartment complex.

It's true that online dating has its risks as well. As an introvert who's wise at spotting dangers, you probably know this already, but here are a few cautions just in case:

- ✔ Don't give an online contact your personal e-mail address. If you want to communicate outside of the dating service's site, create a generic e-mail address that doesn't include your last name.

- ✔ If you want to exchange calls, give the person your cellphone number, not your home phone number.

- ✔ Make sure your first two or three dates are at a public place, and let other people know where you're going and when you expect to be home.

And here are some other tips for succeeding at online dating:

- ✔ Don't start a chat with more than one person at a time. It infuriates other people when you start a live chat or accept an invitation to chat, only to vanish because you're chatting with someone else.

- ✔ Treat a chat like a phone call. If you need to end the conversation, don't just quit. Instead, say something like "Oops! Something just came up, and I need to sign off. I'm sorry." And if you like the person and want to chat more, say so.

- ✔ If you're worried about your nerves getting in the way during your first phone call, consider doing the "dump sheet" exercise in Chapter 11 before the call. This exercise will help you calm down and overcome your fears. Also, it's fine to be upfront about your nervousness when you're on the phone. Just say something like, "I'm new to this whole thing, and I'm not sure how it works." People are likely to cut you some slack — and if they don't, they're probably not a good match for you anyway.

✔ Don't send out "form letter" e-mails to a lot of people at once. (Other people can tell if you do this, and they'll hold it against you or perhaps even block your account and complain to the website.)

✔ Fill out at least half of the profile the dating service sends you. Most of the questions they ask are innocuous. If you're paranoid about answering them, most likely Internet dating isn't for you.

## Making a first date work

Is there *anything* more awkward than a first date? Probably not, especially if you're an introvert. In fact, you may have no idea what to do after you say "hello." What's the solution? Read these tips:

✔ **Try to get to know the person over the phone before you plan a date.** If you do, you'll have a pretty good idea whether the two of you will click, and you'll know enough about the other person to have some conversational topics in mind.

✔ **Consider alternatives to a restaurant date because making small talk over a long dinner can be exhausting.** Instead, suggest a few other options, such as coffee or another activity. You can suggest an idea other than dinner by saying something like, "Would you like to meet for coffee or dinner — or do you ice skate? You do? Then how about a skating date?"

✔ **Pick an event with a definite ending time.** You'll feel more at ease if you have a pretty good idea how long your date will last.

✔ **Go easy on the alcohol.** If you're somewhere where drinks are being served, set a firm limit for yourself. One glass of wine may ease your anxiety and make the conversation flow more easily, but three or four may make you do or say things you'll regret later.

## Addressing expectations

If you're an introvert, you like to build relationships slowly. When you're dating another innie, that's usually not a problem. But when sparks fly on a date with an extrovert, you and your date may have different expectations about what's to follow.

Frequently, outies are ready to jump into hugs and kisses (and more) while innies are still warming up. As a result, extroverts may think they're getting the brush-off while introverts can feel pressured to move too quickly. And this can cause a budding relationship to wilt quickly.

Here are a few good tricks for preventing this problem:

- ✔ **Plan the timing and location of your first few dates carefully.** For example, suggest a daytime baseball game for your first date rather than a romantic dinner, and state upfront that you have another obligation later that day. Doing so will signal that you're not planning on getting intimate right away.

- ✔ **When you're prepared for intimacy, make your expectations clear.** If you're ready for kissing and cuddling but not ready to go further, let your date know. For example, say, "I'm a little old-fashioned, and I like to take things very slowly." But if you're ready to take your romance to the next level, let your remarks and body language show that you're in the mood. (Some candles and sexy music can send a clear message, too!)

- ✔ **When you're really getting serious, open up emotionally to the other person.** Introverted people are often afraid to say "I love you," but extroverts (just like introverts) need to hear these words. So if you're ready to commit to a serious relationship, spit out those three little words — it's not as hard as you think!

# Enjoying a Deep and Healthy Relationship

When you're dating casually, getting along is usually pretty easy . But when you're sharing a home and a bed, things tend to get a whole lot more complicated. And that means you'll need to work at keeping your relationship strong.

In this section, I take a peek at the dynamics of healthy relationships. After that, I explore the pros and cons of pairing up with an outie or an innie. And finally, I look at smart ways to handle the classic conflicts that pop up in relationships between introverts and extroverts.

## Grasping the basics of a good relationship

A friend of mine says that a healthy relationship requires what she calls the three Ls: *like, love,* and *lust.* And that's a good list! If you truly like the other person as a friend, feel a deep love for the person as well, and have good chemistry between you, you have all the essentials in place. Even two out of three is a good start — or sometimes enough — so don't worry if it takes time for love or friendship to grow or for chemistry to kick in. (But if it doesn't happen over time, ask yourself whether you need more.)

Personally, I find that couples are likely to be successful if they have two additional things going for them: mutual respect and mutual trust. In fact, I consider these to be "musts" for a successful relationship.

Feelings alone aren't enough to cement a relationship, though. Translating your feelings into actions is also important. When I work with couples, I rely a great deal on a model developed by the famous psychologist John Gottman. He listed these seven principles of a positive relationship:

- ✔ Creating mental "love maps" where you store information about your partner's dreams, hopes, fears, and feelings so you can understand the person on a deeper level

  For example, your love map may look like this:

  - John is deeply committed to creating a safer world for the children he works with as a therapist.

  - He has dreams of us having a big family ourselves.

  - He's afraid that he can't live up to his parents' expectations for him.

  - He acts assertive, but inside he's insecure and has trouble expressing his needs.

- ✔ Nurturing your fondness and admiration for your partner, and respecting the fact that your partner is different from you

- ✔ Turning toward your partner rather than away; in other words, responding positively to your partner's attempts to make physical or verbal connections with you rather than giving him the brushoff

- ✔ Letting your partner influence you by letting go of the belief that you're completely right about things and open yourself up to your partner's ideas

- ✔ Working together to solve any problems that are solvable

- ✔ Empathizing with your partner's views even when you can't solve a problem

- ✔ Creating shared meaning through activities such as establishing family traditions

And here's something else that's absolutely crucial for a successful relationship: sharing core values. For example, successful couples may share values like these:

- ✔ We both agree that financial security is an important goal.

- ✔ We both think lifelong learning is important.

- ✔ We both place a high value on remaining physically fit.

Shared values lead directly to shared behaviors, which help solidify a relationship. For example, if you both place a high priority on fitness, you'll encourage each other to exercise and eat right. If you agree that financial security is critical to a happy life, you'll both behave in fiscally smart ways. And if you both value lifelong learning, you'll have fun sharing anything from museum visits to martial arts classes. As a result, you'll savor each other's company, and you'll deeply respect your partner instead of thinking, "He's kind of a jerk."

If your core values differ from your partner's, on the other hand, getting along can be very difficult. For example, I know one woman who defines her core values as "truth" and "emotional validation." Her partner, on the other hand, defines his core value as "peace." The woman in this relationship is unhappy because she's constantly bugging her partner to be open and truthful about his feelings, but he prefers to avoid conflict or to think quietly about touchy issues before discussing them with her.

Depending on how strong your core values are, it can be a deal breaker if your partner doesn't share them. So talking about these values very early in your relationship is crucial.

## Recognizing how different personalities mesh in relationships

In addition to understanding the ground rules for a strong relationship, considering how different personalities can affect that relationship is important. As you can guess, one of the most interesting things to consider is how introverted or extroverted each member of a couple is.

Often, people assume that partners with similar personalities will get along best. But one study suggests that over the long run, just the opposite is often true. The researchers studied 67 couples, all middle-aged or older, asking them how satisfied they were with their marriages. They found that in middle age, those who had very similar scores for introversion or extroversion were less satisfied than couples who weren't as similar.

Why? The researchers suggest that couples with differing interests and abilities may find it easier to divvy up tasks. For example, an extroverted partner may be better at coaching kids' soccer games or handling squabbles with neighbors, while an introverted partner may excel at keeping the checkbook balanced and helping the kids with their homework.

## How different is too different?

Over the years, I've had happy romantic relationships with both introverts and extroverts. But one thing I've found is that it can be a challenge to make things work out if the two of you have *very* different ideas about socializing.

For example, I once went to Cozumel, Mexico, with a great guy I really liked. I thought we'd have a terrific time together, but instead we quickly ran into trouble. Things started to go wrong when I told him I wanted to take a two-hour boat trip over to Cancun, and he said he didn't want to go. So I said, "No problem; just relax by the pool, and I'll go by myself." Well, you'd think I was abandoning him forever! He was such an extrovert that the idea of being left alone for a few hours really upset him.

By the way, he got the last laugh. I did go by myself, but I got violently seasick on the hydroplane and spent the entire trip to Cancun throwing up. I recovered from my seasickness (and wisely took a plane back to Cozumel rather than a boat), but our relationship was never as strong after that experience.

On the other hand, another study suggests that a matchup of an extroverted woman and an introverted man can sometimes lead to extra conflict. One reason, the researchers suggest, is that this pairing goes against the norm in many cultures. Of course, many matchups between introverted men and extroverted women work out beautifully — and so do many innie-innie and outie-outie relationships. We've all met happy bookworm couples and outgoing couples who spend all their time traveling and partying.

The bottom line? If you and your partner respect each other's needs and share the core values that I talk about earlier in this chapter, you're likely to be happy whether you're both introverts, both extroverts, or an innie-outie mix.

# Handling Innie-Outie Differences Successfully

As the research shows, introvert-extrovert couples have a great shot at achieving long-term happiness together. However, their different personalities can also make life challenging at times. If you're in an innie-outie relationship, here are some tips to help you and your partner stay satisfied and happy with each other.

# Identifying each other's needs and interests

People in relationships often expect their partners to be mind readers. But even the closest of couples often have no clue what's going on in each other's head — especially at the start of a relationship when people are still getting to know each other. I often tell couples, "When it comes to good relationships, there's no such thing as ESP."

Now, if you're an introvert who's paired up with an extrovert, your partner deserves a little extra sympathy here. Most likely, you find it hard to open up about your feelings, especially when a relationship is just getting off the ground. So your loved one is likely to be completely in the dark when it comes to understanding what you like and need. This is frustrating for your outie, and it can cause the following problems:

- ✔ Your partner may "fill in the blanks" with false assumptions about your needs and desires.

- ✔ Your partner may stop asking for your input and start making decisions without including you.

- ✔ Your partner may become more demanding and bossy because you're not weighing in with your own ideas and opinions.

Meanwhile, your extroverted partner may talk frequently about his interests and expectations. And this may lead you to think, "All he talks about is himself. What about me?"

If so, it may surprise you to know that your outie partner may not *like* taking the reins all the time. From his point of view, you're creating a vacuum he has to fill.

Luckily, there's an easy way to remedy this situation. But here's the thing: If you're the introvert in the relationship, the ball is in your court. That's because *you're* the one who's withholding vital information.

So open up, even if it's uncomfortable for you. Let your partner know what you like, what you don't like, and what you're expecting out of your life and your relationship. Also, let him share the same information with you.

Here's a good way to start this conversation. Pick a quiet time and pose questions like these for each of you to answer:

- ✔ What's your idea of a perfect vacation? A perfect weekend?

- ✔ What's your biggest career goal?

✔ What's the biggest problem you want to solve in your life?

✔ If you had an extra free hour in each day, what would you do with it?

✔ What worries you the most about your future? What excites you the most about your future?

Also, share details about your pasts. Exploring your partner's early life can help you understand his needs and goals today. For example, you may discover that your partner is leery about having children because he grew up in an abusive family and worries that he won't be a good dad himself. If so, you can address this issue in a sensitive and understanding way.

## Figuring out how to talk with each other

Sometimes introverts and extroverts seem to speak different languages. And in a sense, they do! That's because they have very different communication styles, which can lead to big trouble. Here are some of the problems that commonly occur when innie-outie couples talk:

✔ The extrovert may bounce quickly from subject to subject without giving the introvert an opportunity to think about each topic.

✔ The introvert may listen quietly without showing much emotion, leading the extrovert to think that she's bored.

✔ The extrovert may get so excited about the conversation that he interrupts the introvert, who needs time to ponder what she wants to say.

✔ The introvert may tune out the extrovert's small talk, making him feel angry when he realizes that she's not listening.

✔ The introvert may talk at length about a topic that fascinates her, such as string theory or the evolution of horses' brains, while the extrovert wonders, "Will she ever shut up and let me talk about something more interesting?" (Of course, other introverts who aren't into that topic will think the same thing!)

✔ The extrovert may come home from work or school bubbling over with news about the day, while the introvert may need some quiet time to decompress before he's willing to jump into a conversation.

✔ The extrovert may respond to an introvert's silence by talking too much simply to fill in the vacuum. When this happens, the introvert may resent or be exhausted by the extrovert's nonstop conversation.

Luckily, there are ways for the two of you to get on the same page when you're talking together. Here are some good guidelines if you're the introvert in your relationship:

- ✔ Cut your outie partner a little slack when it comes to small talk. It's like food and oxygen to him, so pretend like you're interested even when you aren't!

- ✔ When your extrovert is talking, let your interest show on your face and in your voice. Smile, lean into the conversation, and express enthusiasm with phrases like "No way — he really did that?" or "That's amazing!"

- ✔ If your partner is itching to share his news but you need a little time to charge your battery before a long conversation, be honest but sensitive. For example, say, "I really want to hear about that. But can you give me a few minutes to clear my head and get dinner started? Then we can sit down with a glass of wine and you can tell me all about it."

- ✔ When you get on a roll about one of your favorite topics, watch your partner's body language. If he looks confused, sketch out some of your ideas on paper for him. If he starts looking bored, on the other hand, consider wrapping it up and switching to a different subject.

- ✔ Remember that extroverts tend to be "big picture" people. Unless it's crucial to give your outie partner a lot of details, focus on your major points.

Also, help your extroverted partner understand how to communicate with you more effectively. For example:

- ✔ Ask him if he can slow down a little so you can digest what he's saying.

- ✔ If he has a tendency to interrupt you, let him know that you need a little time to finish your thoughts before he jumps in. (And be patient with him as he overcomes his urge to butt in. This bad habit takes a while to break.)

- ✔ If he can't help talking a mile a minute, gently put on the brakes by asking for examples. For instance, if he's a teacher and he's ranting about the word problems in the district's new math program, ask him to describe some of those problems to you.

Also, as the two of you become closer, see whether you can both work on *matching* and *pacing* during conversations — talking at a similar speed and emotional intensity as the other person. See Chapter 7 for more on matching and pacing.

Emotional "matching" is especially important when one of you is upset. Often, one person in a couple talks very excitedly about something that's made him mad while the other person replies with something like, "Okay, I can see why that upset you, but just calm down." To understand why this is maddening, imagine calling a company and saying "The vacuum cleaner I bought from you yesterday just caught on fire!" and having the person respond, "Oh, yes. I understand. But just calm down."

Instead, try to respond in situations like this with enough emotion to show that you're concerned and you have empathy. Doing so will make your partner feel heard and help him get his own emotions under control.

# Looking for win-win solutions

In any relationship, you'll have issues to iron out. And dealing with these issues can be especially challenging if you and your partner have very different personalities. To succeed in finding solutions, the two of you need to start out as allies, not adversaries.

So when you find yourselves on opposite sides of an issue, remember that your goal isn't for you to "win" and your partner to "lose." Instead, look for solutions that work for both of you. Here's how to do it:

1. **Identify all the areas you agree in, and write them down.**

2. **Identify the specific areas you disagree in.**

   Often, you'll find that what initially looks like a huge disagreement is actually a fairly small one.

3. **Look for any signs of a breakthrough in your discussion, even tiny ones. Reinforce each other positively with a kind comment, a hug, or a "thank you" when you make some progress in coming to an agreement.**

4. **Realize that the two of you may approach problems in different ways.**

   Introverts have a tendency to focus on the glass being half empty, while extroverts may focus on what's going right. Because of this, an innie may be too pessimistic about solving a problem, while an outie may gloss over serious issues. If you're both aware of this, it'll be easier for you both to meet in the middle.

In particular, look for win-win solutions when you're planning social activities. As an innie, you have the right to say no to an over-filled social calendar. But your extroverted partner also has the right to charge his battery by mingling with other people. So sit down together when you're planning your social calendar and ask questions like these:

✔ How many commitments do the two of you already have?

✔ What upcoming social events does your extroverted partner consider to be "must attend" activities to add to the calendar?

✔ Is that list doable for you? If not, can your partner attend some events alone?

✔ When you do attend events together, can you commit to having at least a few conversations with people rather than just sitting in a corner or watching TV?

✔ When can you schedule some quiet, intimate time together to meet your needs?

When you finally agree on your social commitments, odds are you'll each get only part of what you want. But you'll both get what you *need,* which is a chance to recharge your batteries in your own ways.

For example, my friend Diane — an extrovert through and through — lets her husband hang out in his "man cave" for hours every week. In return, he agrees to go on more trips than he'd like, which keeps Diane and her travel-loving family content. She's had to work hard to understand his need for quiet and privacy, while he's had to move outside of his comfort zone more often than he'd prefer, but as a result, they have a strong and happy relationship.

## Analyzing your different arguing styles

As a psychologist, I get to listen to a lot of people arguing. (Some days, I think I deserve combat pay!) And one thing I know from experience is that introverts and extroverts fight in different ways (although culture and gender will also play a role in their behavior).

Typically, the extrovert will wade into the battle, talking a mile a minute and gesturing broadly. The introvert, on the other hand, is likely to shut down completely. He may stop talking, and he may lock himself in a bathroom or even leave the house. This is particularly true for men, who are often raised to walk away from an argument so they won't appear threatening. (Men who are big in build are especially likely to do this.)

Also, extroverts tend to get over arguments more quickly. Introverts, on the other hand, may nurse a grudge for quite a while.

Needless to say, introvert-extrovert arguments can get a little crazy. Here are some good ways to help keep things sane.

✔ When your extroverted partner gets in your face, go ahead and run away if you need to — but only *temporarily.* Say something like this: "I hear what you're saying, but I need a little time to absorb it. So if it's okay with you, I'm going to go in the other room and think about it. Then in 15 minutes, let's get back together and see whether we can find a way to resolve this that works for both of us."

✔ Pick a time when you're both calm and happy and have a conversation about your different perspectives on issues in your relationship. For example, say, "We've been enjoying each other a lot lately. And it's interesting that we do sometimes see the same situation in very different ways. Would this be a good time to talk about what we need from each other when a disagreement does come up?"

✔ Work on letting go of grudges so you can avoid arguments or get over them quickly. Forgiveness isn't just good for the person you forgive; it's healthy for you, too.

✔ If you find that you squabble over chores — for example, if you get angry when the dishes aren't done when you get home, while your partner says that you're a nag — consider using a "honey do" list instead. Simply post a list of chores you'd like the other person to do. This technique works especially well with men, and it can help you avoid a lot of arguments.

One good way to keep a spat from turning into an all-out battle is to write down your feelings instead of yelling at each other. Here's how to do it:

1. **Agree that each of you will write out your perceptions about what the situation is and how you feel about it.**

   When you do this, each of you will need to accept your own responsibility for creating the situation instead of simply blaming the other person.

   Be aware that extroverts will tend to write a lot, while introverts may be more concise. That's fine. Each partner should allow the other person to decide how much to share and should respect that decision.

2. **Write down your hopes for resolving the situation. Describe the changes you want to see, and be clear about your needs.**

3. **As you share what you've written, acknowledge each other's efforts to come to an agreement.**

   Don't wait until you've resolved your issues completely; instead, celebrate each step! Doing so will keep you both motivated to continue seeking a solution.

If arguments are seriously affecting your relationship, consider working with a licensed clergyperson or licensed therapist who can help you find more effective ways of resolving your differences. Here are several therapy techniques that can be helpful:

✔ Role-playing can help each of you spot the negative behaviors that you exhibit during disagreements and come up with better approaches.

✔ If one of you tends to steamroll over the other in arguments, a therapist may have the more dominant person in your relationship sit back while the quieter person speaks uninterrupted.

✔ In therapy, you can practice using "I" statements (such as "I feel scared when we argue") rather than "you" statements (such as "You scare me when you yell"). This technique is very useful for keeping arguments calm, because it makes your partner feel less defensive. In addition, it helps you remember that your partner isn't causing *you* to do or say anything. Instead, *you* are reacting to a situation based on your own history and experiences. (In other words, if your partner pushes your buttons, remember that you're the one who has those buttons in the first place!)

✔ A therapist can help you match each other's pace when you're arguing, which will help you get more in tune with each other.

## Being wary of perfectionism

Fran, an outgoing friend of mine who's married to an introvert, dreads tax time every year. She says, "On the first day of March, Bob drags out his file of perfectly organized receipts. Then he says, 'Where are your receipts?' And I say, 'Uh . . . in that shoebox in the closet?' And he gives me *the look*."

Like Bob, many introverts hold both themselves and their partners to high standards when it comes to everything from financial organization to house-keeping. (Quite a few extroverts are perfectionists as well, but this may be a bigger issue for innies.)

Now, sometimes, a tiny touch of perfectionism is a good thing. For example, while Fran teases Bob about his receipt-keeping, she admits, "He's the only reason we get our tax return done on time." However, continually holding yourself or your partner to unrealistic standards can lead to anger, stress, and frustration — and for many partners, it's a deal breaker.

For example, I once knew a woman who worked two part-time jobs, had three young children, and still insisted on keeping her house and garage absolutely spotless. Her husband, who worked long hours at a high-stress job, resented the fact that they spent nearly all their free time mopping floors and cleaning bathrooms. Eventually, he issued an ultimatum: It's me or the house. (Luckily, she chose him — and a maid service.)

If you're an introvert who thinks that perfectionism may be a problem for you, here are some tips:

✔ Ask yourself whether reducing your demands for perfection could enhance your relationship. For example, would you have fewer arguments, and would you have more time to enjoy each other?

## How to argue around kids

If you're a quiet and peace-loving introvert with children, you may be tempted to avoid arguing with a partner while your kids are watching. But it's important to show children that it's okay to disagree — and that even when you're arguing, you're fundamentally aligned in your efforts to find a solution.

So don't feel like a bad parent if you occasionally get into a feud in front of the kids. When this happens, do your best to keep things calm and respectful. If the two of you are really upset and you don't feel like you can fight fair, say something like this: "Right now, the two of us don't see eye to eye about this. So we're going to go discuss it by ourselves. We'll let you know what we decide."

Also, look for win-win solutions when your partner is arguing with one of your kids. For example, imagine that you're all going to a neighbor's house for dinner and your teen refuses to change his grungy clothes. If you hear your partner bickering with him about this, take your partner aside and ask, "Would you be okay with those pants if he puts on a clean shirt?" The two of you can brainstorm a solution and then present it to your child jointly by saying, "We both decided. . . ." This helps your kids (and you) recognize that parenting is a team effort, and it makes it more difficult for your child to play one of you against the other.

✔ Identify one specific area where you could "lighten up" when it comes to your own behavior or your partner's. For example, if you currently insist on cooking a gourmet dinner every night, try letting yourself off the hook and serve hamburgers or chili once in a while. Or if you expect your partner to mow the lawn every week, ask yourself whether it's fine for him to do this chore every other week.

✔ If you really feel strongly that it's necessary for your partner to do a chore perfectly, think about whether you can pitch in or hire someone to do it for him. Or ask yourself, "What other area am I willing to compromise in to make it easier for him to do this?"

✔ Ask yourself if you're focusing too much on looking for things that are wrong in your relationship. If you realize that this is an issue, actively focus every day on identifying things that are going *right*.

Also, try this experiment. Pick two or three areas you're willing to back off on, and weigh the results. Odds are, you'll discover that both you and your partner are happier and more satisfied with your relationship.

## Identifying the real source of your issues

To handle a problem successfully, you need to get to the root of it. And sometimes the issues you chalk up to your introvert-extrovert differences can actually stem from other causes.

For one thing, adults often unconsciously pick up beliefs and behaviors from their own families. For example, if your dad swore like a pirate while your partner's father never said anything stronger than "phooey," the two of you may have very different ideas about whether cursing in your household is okay. Those ideas will probably have very little to do with your personality and a whole lot to do with how you were raised. That's one reason sharing information about your families and your childhoods can help you understand and respect your differences more easily.

Also, the problems that people attribute to personality clashes can sometimes signal something more serious: a mental disorder. If your relationship is very troubled — or if either of you exhibits worrisome or alarming behaviors — you may be dealing with one of these problems:

- Depression
- An anxiety disorder
- Attention deficit hyperactivity disorder (ADHD) or attention deficit disorder (ADD)
- A personality disorder
- Post traumatic stress disorder (PTSD)
- A substance abuse problem
- An eating disorder

If you suspect that problems in your relationship stem from any of these issues, consult either a psychologist or a psychiatrist. The right diagnosis and treatment can make a world of difference!

# Splitting Up Sanely

As the song goes, "there must be 50 ways to leave your lover." But that doesn't mean that it's ever *easy* to break up. Whether you're the person saying goodbye or the person getting dumped, a split-up can be a very traumatic experience.

A breakup can be especially traumatic if you're an introvert because you invest a great deal of yourself into each of your relationships. In addition, you're prone to blame yourself when things go badly. So when a relationship ends, you may spend days or weeks wondering what you did wrong. (Extroverts may blame themselves, too, but they'll typically get over it faster.)

Fortunately, you can make a breakup easier on you and on your former partner. One good approach is to do the exercises in Chapter 11 for combatting negative self-talk. Also, try the tips in the following sections.

## *When you're getting dumped*

If your partner is the one initiating a breakup, handle the news in this way:

- ✔ **Avoid the urge to beg the person to stay.** If your partner says the relationship is over, it's over.

- ✔ **Try to avoid blaming yourself or your partner.** Human beings aren't perfect, and most likely you both made mistakes. If you find yourself trapped in self-blaming, try the dump sheet activity and other activities in Chapter 11.

- ✔ **Find an outlet for your emotions.** As an introvert, you may find it difficult to talk with your friends and family about a breakup. So express yourself through journaling, painting, or music — or work out your hurt and anger physically with a sport, like kickboxing or tennis.

- ✔ **Understand that it takes time to get over a breakup.** If your lover says goodbye to you, you'll go through the classic grief cycle of denial, anger, bargaining, depression, and acceptance.

  When this happens, be aware that your emotions won't necessarily follow in this tidy sequence. They may appear in any order, or appear in rapid succession, or even occur all at the same time. And even when you think you're past one part of this cycle, you may slip back into it temporarily. Give yourself time to complete this process, and understand that it's a perfectly normal and healthy path to recovery.

At some point, even after a breakup that deeply saddens you, you're likely to find yourself "whitewashing" the situation — that is, saying, "It's all for the best that we've split up." Although whitewashing can be a problem in some areas of life, it's a perfectly fine response in this situation if it helps you move on. It's much better than ruminating over the breakup or holding a grudge, which can keep you stuck where you are.

# When you're doing the dumping

If you're the person initiating the breakup, follow these guidelines:

- **Be sure you really *do* want to break up.** If you've just had a fight, give yourself several days to calm down and think things through rationally. Also, be aware that introverts sometimes respond to personal difficulties or tragedies by pushing their strongest supporters away. Make sure you're not making this mistake yourself.

- **Wait for the right moment.** Avoid saying "it's over" in the middle of an argument, and don't blindside your partner during a happy moment. Instead, wait for a neutral time when you're both relaxed and calm. And if your relationship is more than a month or two old, don't break up via a text message or an e-mail! Even though breaking up in person is difficult, doing so shows that you have respect for the other individual, and it will be appreciated.

- **Pick the right place.** In general, it's best to announce your intentions in private, not in public. But there's an exception to this rule: If you're afraid the other person may become hostile or even violent, meet in a public place with exits you can reach easily, and bring a friend or two along with you.

- **Expect some blowback.** If your partner isn't ready to quit your relationship, she's likely to be very hurt or angry. As a result, she may say some cruel things. Keep your cool, and let her vent without fighting back. (And yes, I know how hard this is! To make it easier, focus on your breathing and on coping statements like "this will be over soon" or "I am proud of myself for being strong and not melting down.")

- **Don't back down.** Once you've made your decision, stick to it.

If you're splitting up after a brief relationship, you may find it easy to get your life back on track. But if you're leaving a serious, long-term relationship, it may be wise to get some counseling. A good therapist can help you work through any lingering anger or self-doubt so you'll be well prepared to enter a new, healthy relationship.

# Chapter 13

# "Cheers!" Taking the Stress Out of Big Social Events

*In This Chapter*

▶ Identifying why you dread social events

▶ Coping when you're a guest at a big event

▶ Staying sane when you're the host

▶ Accepting or declining invitations

Debbie, an introverted friend of mine, still blushes with embarrassment when she talks about something that happened to her years ago. She was hurrying down a hallway at work, totally lost in her own thoughts, when a coworker — someone she considered to be an office buddy but not a close friend — rushed up to her, beaming with joy.

Out of the blue, the coworker said, "Guess what, I'm getting married! Do you want to be one of my bridesmaids?" And before Debbie could stop herself, she heard herself say, "No!" (Luckily, she immediately covered up her faux pas by pretending that she was joking, and her outie coworker never caught on. And, yes, she did wind up in the bridal party.)

Normally, introverts are better at hiding their dismay when they get an invitation to a big social event. But it's true that for most innies, the festive occasions that everyone else looks forward to — Thanksgiving, weddings, New Year's Eve parties — can be a source of annoyance or even dread.

In this chapter, I look at why these events are so stressful for introverts, and then I offer tips for making them more innie-friendly, whether you're a guest or the host. In addition, I suggest ways to escape for a few minutes when you need to get out of the hustle-and-bustle of a party. And finally, I talk about ways to graciously say "no" to an invitation when you desperately need to stay home and recharge your batteries.

# Understanding Why Social Occasions Stress You Out

Do you find yourself saying "ugh" when you get a wedding invitation in the mail, and does your heart sink when a friend calls and says, "What are you doing on New Year's Eve?"

If so, don't feel guilty. (And don't feel like you're alone!) Innies are wired to enjoy intimate social occasions like small dinner parties, but they're simply not designed to cope well in a sea of people, especially when many of those people are strangers. So it's very natural for introverts to dread those big occasions.

Here are just some of the reasons large social events aren't ideal for you as an innie:

- ✔ You have to make a lot of small talk — something that isn't your forte.
- ✔ You're expected to keep your "happy face" on for hours.
- ✔ You have to deal with a lot of noise and commotion.
- ✔ It's hard to take a break or to make your escape quickly.

Big family events can be especially stressful for innies if a lot of emotional undercurrents exist. (And doesn't that describe just about *all* big family gatherings?) Innies are often extra-sensitive to other people's feelings, so the unspoken tensions around the table at Thanksgiving can quickly sap their energy.

How exhausting can big social events be for introverts? One innie I know jokingly compares them to vampire attacks. He says, "It's like the extroverts in the room are sucking the lifeblood out of the rest of us."

 Because social occasions are so draining for introverts, don't feel like you're doing something wrong when you try to sneak out early. Instead, give yourself a pat on the back for showing up at all. You're probably doing it just to make your friends or relatives happy, and isn't that noble of you?

# Coping When You're an Innie Guest

Although big social events will never be a piece of cake for innies, you can do a few things to make them more manageable. (Note that I didn't say "fun"; I said "manageable." I want to be realistic!) In the following sections, I discuss some things that work well for the innies I know.

# Planning ahead

As soon as you get an invitation, start planning your escape strategy. Figure out how long you're willing to stay at the event, and think of a good reason you can leave early. If you have a partner, come up with a plan that will work for both of you. (See Chapter 12 for more info on dealing with social events if you have an extroverted partner.)

If you're like most innies, the very act of forming your escape plan will cause your stress levels to drop. Also, having a strategy ahead of time will help you avoid offending your hosts. When you R.S.V.P., you can say something like, "Unfortunately, we'll need to duck out a little early because we accepted another invitation on the same day. But there's no way we'd miss your event, even if we can't stay for the entire evening."

And what about those big events that stretch out forever, like weddings where the bride and groom plan four days of activities for the bridal party? First, decide whether you really need to be on hand *every* day and for *every* activity. If not, make up an excellent excuse for skipping a few less-important activities. For example, if you're flying in for a wedding, tell the bride that you can't get off work the first day. Sure, it may be a white lie, but sometimes a tiny bit of dishonesty can save your sanity.

# Escaping the crowd

After you arrive at a party, greet your hosts and do some mingling, but when you feel your battery running low, look for excuses to avoid the small talk. Here are some good tricks:

- **Bring a camera or video camera, and appoint yourself as the unofficial party photographer.** When you're hiding behind a lens, being quiet is much easier. And if you take some great shots and send them to your hosts the next day, they'll be very grateful!

- **Volunteer to help with the dishes.** And when you make this offer, don't take no for an answer. Most hosts will politely say, "Oh, no, just go enjoy yourself" — but simply ignore them, and start ferrying dirty plates from the dining room or putting glasses in the dishwasher. Secretly, your hosts will love you for it.

- **Offer to play with the kids.** Often, you'll find a scattering of babies or young children at an event. If you enjoy hanging out with little tykes, volunteer to change diapers or play hopscotch, and parents will happily hand their tots off to you. Ask the host if there's a quiet spot where you can supervise them, and voilà! — you've found your hide-out.

✔ **Hang out with some of the older guests.** Often the older generation feel a bit overlooked at parties and other events, so they'll be grateful for your quiet attention — and they frequently make more interesting conversation than the younger generations.

## Breaking the ice

Many innies find it awkward to make small talk with strangers. In Chapter 3, I offer tips on starting a conversation. Here are some additional ways to break the ice at a party:

✔ **Wear a conversation starter.** Whether it's a special piece of jewelry or an interesting tie, make sure to wear something striking that people will notice and comment on.

✔ **Look for something interesting in your host's home to point out, such as an unusual sofa, a portrait on the wall, or even the appetizers.** For instance, say to your host, "I love this painting; can you tell me more about it?" Open-ended questions like this can start a good conversation.

✔ **Talk to one guest at a time.** Look around for someone else who's alone, and start there.

Also, see whether you can get your host to provide you with some information about the other guests ahead of time. If you know a little about them, jumping into a conversation with them will be easier.

## Scheduling some unwinding time — before, during, and after

Before you head for a party, schedule a little alone time. If you can spend an hour or two quietly recharging your batteries before an event, you'll last longer when you get there.

As soon as you arrive, scout out the house and look for innie hidey-holes. For instance, you may be able to duck out into the garden, or you may find a quiet corner in the living room. And make sure you pack a magazine or a paperback so you can sneak into the bathroom from time to time for a quick reading break.

Also, treat yourself to something special (and quiet) when you get home. For example, watch a favorite movie, take a bubble bath, or download some new music. Trust me — you've earned it.

# Coping When You're an Innie Host

Attending someone else's party is stressful enough. But what about those times when you have to host an event yourself? No matter how introverted you are, you'll occasionally need to invite people over to your place for a party, baby shower, wedding reception, or holiday dinner. The following sections explore some ways to cut these stressful social events down to size.

## Taking the focus off yourself

When you're planning an event, one great idea is to center it around an activity that takes the spotlight off of you. For example, one friend of mine started a tradition called "bad movie night." Once or twice a year, he'd invite a bunch of friends over for chips and dips and a showing of the movies they all nominated because they were "so bad they're good." Everyone always had a great time, and the guests all focused on the movies and the munchies, not on my introverted friend.

Here are other good activities that can reduce the pressure on you as the host:

- **Parties that center around special events:** Of course, the Super Bowl and the Emmy Awards show are obvious choices. But plenty of other good options exist. For example, one introverted friend of mine always invites her friends over to watch one of the ice-skating finals of the Olympics. It's a fun tradition for them now, and because the Winter Olympics happens only once every four years, she doesn't need to host this event very often!

- **Parties that center around hands-on activities:** For example, host a tamale-making party or a poker night.

- **Parties that center around other people:** One introverted friend of mine hosts what she calls "chef nights." Once or twice a year, she pays a local chef to come to her house and show her guests how to make a fabulous meal, and everyone has a ball getting cooking tips and eating gourmet food.

- **Parties at fun places:** Instead of inviting people to your home, consider treating them to a picnic at the beach or booking a dining room at a trendy new restaurant.

## Creating innie sanctuaries

When you're hosting an event at your own home, look for ways to create quiet zones within the chaos. Think of activities that will allow a few introverts (including you!) to break off from the main group part of the time. Here are some examples:

✔ If you're hosting Thanksgiving dinner, set up a table in one corner of the living room and put a jigsaw puzzle, a chess board, or some fun games on it. If you set up a puzzle, let your guests know that they're welcome to finish it.

✔ If your furniture arrangement is flexible, create physical oases at the edges of a party by placing one or two chairs and an end table in each corner. Put a few photo albums, books, or magazines on the tables so innies can take a reading break.

✔ Spread your parties out. For example, instead of seating everyone at a huge table at a dinner party, set up smaller tables that seat four to six people.

✔ Set up multiple activities in different rooms as well as some outdoor activities if you can. This way, your introverted guests (and you) can gravitate toward less-crowded spots.

## Teaming up with a cohost

Do you have an extroverted friend who's a real party animal? If so, ask that person to cohost your event with you. That way, you can focus on keeping everyone plied with food and drink, while your extroverted buddy keeps them entertained.

Another option is to cohost your party with an introverted friend so you can tag-team. When one of you needs a break, the other one can step in and keep things rolling while you escape for a while. (You'd be amazed at how easy it is to sneak off from your own party for 10 or 15 minutes without anyone noticing!)

If you can't round up a cohost, make sure you invite at least one or two extra-sociable people to your party. In effect, these people often become unofficial cohosts, taking much of the pressure off you.

## Recharging your batteries

When you're hosting a long event, you may simply run out of steam partway through. If that happens, you'll probably start feeling tired and foggy, and you'll find it harder and harder to make conversation.

In this case, your first option (and I'm guessing you know this already!) is to retreat to the bathroom for a few minutes. This escape will work once or twice, but eventually your guests are going to start wondering whether you have an overactive bladder. So it's a good idea to have some extra tricks up your sleeve, such as the following:

- ✔ **Make a grocery store run.** Say, "Oh, goodness, we're getting low on ice, so I'm just going to dash around the corner and buy a bag." Then move really fast, before someone else offers to run this errand for you. Spend five or ten minutes wandering around the store before you head back home, so you can clear your head. (Just remember to buy the ice while you're there!)

- ✔ **Walk the dog or tuck in the kids.** If you have young children or pets, think of them as built-in excuses. Mention to your guests that you need to walk the puppy around the block or that you need to tell your little ones a bedtime story. Then stretch out that walk or bedtime ritual as long as you can.

- ✔ **Practice mini-meditation.** In Chapter 2, I outline the steps of mindful meditation. Normally, this activity takes some time. But ducking into a bedroom and doing even five or ten minutes of meditation can help you de-stress and clear your mind.

## Getting those last guests to go home

When you host an event, some guests simply won't get the hint when it's time to pack up and leave. (I talk more about this in Chapter 18.) You'll go from enjoying these guests, to politely yawning and glancing at your watch, to looking daggers at them — and *they still won't leave!* It's a never-ending source of amazement to introverts that guests can be so clueless.

How can you stop people like this from overstaying their welcome? Here are some tricks that often work:

- ✔ **Have an iron-clad ending time.** Simply saying, "We're having a party from six to nine" isn't good enough. Instead, when you invite your guests, say something like this: "We'd love to have you over for dinner on Friday. Can you make it at six? Bob and I need to stop by his mother's house at nine to make sure she's fine after her surgery, but that will give us three hours to have fun." Make it clear that at nine o'clock sharp, you're heading out the door — and they'll need to scoot as well.

- ✔ **Make the first move.** Stand up and say, "Wow, this was really fun; thank you so much for coming! I need to get to bed before I keel over, but let's do this again soon."

- ✔ **Hand them their leftovers.** If you're throwing a dinner party, plan on cooking more food than you need. Then, when you're ready to call it a night, pop into the kitchen and package up the remaining goodies for your guests. Make sure you include some leftovers that need refrigeration, so your guests will have a strong incentive to get home quickly.

✔ **Turn up the lights.** At restaurants and bars, the staff starts turning on additional lights as closing time nears. If you do the same thing, you'll send a strong signal that the party's over.

✔ **Stop offering drink refills.** Also, clear away any snack plates, so people won't be tempted to stay and nibble.

If you discover that certain friends are chronic offenders when it comes to lingering, consider inviting those people to restaurants or movies instead of entertaining them at your home. This way, you can ditch them quickly when you're ready to say adios.

# Deciding Whether to Say Yes or No to an Invitation

Ah, guilt. Introverts experience this emotion nearly every time they think about turning down an invitation to a party, a wedding, or a baby shower. They don't want to hurt people's feelings, so often they wind up dragging themselves to events they don't want to attend — only to stand around feeling miserable for hours.

If this sounds like you, it's time to jettison the guilt trip. You're perfectly right to say yes to some invitations and no to others. And better yet, you can turn down an invitation without jeopardizing a relationship. The following sections explain how to decide which invitations require a "yes" and how to bow out of the others gracefully.

## Determining which invitations to accept

If you're a strong introvert, you'll secretly want to decline nearly every social invitation that comes your way. Of course, in the real world, that won't work. Here are some questions that can help you decide whether an event is a must-go occasion or one you can skip.

✔ **How important is this event to the person who's inviting you?** If it's a good friend's wedding, suck it up and go. Declining this invitation could damage your friendship forever. But if it's a casual holiday party and the host won't miss you all that much, feel free to make an excuse.

✔ **Is this event important to your career or to your partner's career?** If the answer is yes, plan to attend, even if it's just for an hour or two. If not, consider taking a pass.

✔ **What type of event is it?** If you're invited to something you're pretty sure you'll hate — for example, a huge party where nearly everyone will be a stranger — you may be better off skipping it. However, it's not a good idea to turn down every invitation. So consider accepting invites to occasions that are more up your alley, such as intimate dinner parties with good friends.

✔ **How many events are you already committed to?** Pacing yourself is key, especially during the holiday season. If you've already said yes to two or three big events, that can be a good enough reason to say no to the next invitation.

Also, ask yourself how many times you've accepted previous invitations from the person who's hosting the event. If you've begged off the last two parties, you probably should go to the next one. But if you've attended the host's previous parties faithfully, you've earned a pass.

## Declining invitations tactfully

As a caring innie, you may fret that you'll offend a friend or family member if you say no to an invitation. But unless the event is very important, you can usually beg off without ruffling any feathers. Here are some tips for making your "no" as friendly as possible:

✔ Offer a sincere "thank you." Even if you're going to decline an invitation, let the person know that you're very grateful that he wanted you to come.

✔ If you're caught off-guard by an invitation, simply say that you'll need to check your schedule. This delay will give you a little time to plan your excuse.

✔ Say that you want to attend, but you have a prior commitment. This is the all-time favorite excuse, and it typically works pretty well.

✔ R.S.V.P. quickly when you're saying no. Doing so gives your host time to invite someone else in your place.

✔ If you're invited to a birthday party or a wedding shower, send an extra-nice gift and a card. Or send flowers on the day of the party.

✔ If possible, make an alternate plan. For example, say, "I'm so sorry I can't come to the party on Sunday, but would you like to go to lunch next week?" This invitation lets the other person know that you value your relationship, even though you're skipping the festivities.

✔ If the host is a very good friend, be honest. It's perfectly okay to tell someone, "I love spending time with you. But I'm so introverted that great big parties are hell on earth for me. Will it offend you if I don't come?"

By the way, the people you're really close to probably won't be as surprised as you think when you beg off. In fact, if they're familiar with your innie nature, they may be shocked if you actually say yes!

# Part IV
# Supporting Introverts

## Five Ways to Help Your Introverted Young Child Make Friends

- ✔ Start scheduling play dates when your child is very young. Set up one-on-one play dates instead of large group ones, and notice which kids your child likes the most so you can invite those children frequently.

- ✔ Look for community activities that match your child's interests. For example, if your introverted son loves gardening, locate a community garden where little kids can help with the harvesting.

- ✔ Plan events that take advantage of your child's interests and skills. For example, if your child loves horses and she's a skilled rider, ask whether she wants to invite a couple of schoolmates for a horseback ride. When she's in a setting where she's knowledgeable and confident, she'll be more likely to relax.

- ✔ Come up with a signal your child can send you if she's getting overwhelmed at a social activity but may not know how to tell her friends. When you see that signal, step in and offer her an excuse to take a quick break.

- ✔ Hone your child's social skills. Make sure she knows how to share, take turns, say "please" and "thank you," and be a polite host. (Also, make sure she knows how to apologize if she misbehaves or hurts another child.)

Visit www.dummies.com/extras/successasanintrovert for tips on helping your introverted child in school.

# In this part . . .

- ✔ Discover how to support your innie friends by accepting them just as they are and acknowledging their strengths and need for "alone" time.

- ✔ Socialize with your introverted pals by getting their prospective on events and understanding that they may want to leave early or decline entirely.

- ✔ Identify whether your child is introverted, and find ways to create an innie-friendly home.

- ✔ Help your introverted child develop friendships, a healthy self-image, and a positive school experience.

# Chapter 14

# Being an Understanding Friend to an Introvert

. . . . . . . . . . . . . . . . . . . . . . . . . . . . . . . . . . . . . . . . . . .

*In This Chapter*

▶ Recognizing that introversion is normal

▶ Getting along with the introverts you know

▶ Understanding an introvert's rules for socializing

. . . . . . . . . . . . . . . . . . . . . . . . . . . . . . . . . . . . . . . . . . .

As you can guess from the title of this book, much of it is for introverts. But this chapter is specifically for a different audience: all you extroverts!

If you're an extrovert, I'm guessing that your introverted friends and relatives frequently puzzle you. What makes them tick? Is there something *wrong* with them? Why do they act the way they do? And how can you get along more easily with them?

In this chapter, I tackle all these questions. First, I clear up a big misconception: the idea that introverts are somehow "wrong." Instead, as I explain, both introverts and extroverts are perfectly fine just the way they are.

After that, I offer tips for understanding and coexisting happily with the innies in your life. And finally, I tackle a topic that often brings introverts and extroverts into open warfare: those social activities that you love and they dread.

***Note:*** If you have an introverted child, you'll find a lot of helpful info in Chapter 15. And if you're an extrovert who's in a romantic relationship with an introvert, be sure to check out Chapter 12.

# Accepting Innies Just as They Are

It's a fact: Most people think that the people around them are nutty in some ways. Men think that women are nuts. Women think that men are nuts. People in different political parties think that their opponents are nuts.

And I'm guessing that if you're an extrovert, you think introverts are a little nutty as well (and vice versa). But as I explain in this section, introverts aren't crazy; they're just *different* from you. And recognizing this fact is the first step to getting along with them because it helps you get over the desire to change their behavior and allows you to appreciate their strengths instead.

## Recognizing that introversion is healthy

If you're an extrovert with a wide circle of friends, a love of parties, and a zest for new adventures, thinking that there's something very wrong with your quieter friends can be tempting. As a result, you may get the urge to say things like these:

- ✔ "You really need to get out of your shell."
- ✔ "You'd enjoy parties more if you just tried harder."
- ✔ "You're too serious. Lighten up."
- ✔ "It's not healthy for you to spend all day in your room reading books."

You'll probably have the best of intentions if you say these things. But all of these comments have one big flaw: They assume that the introvert's approach to life is wrong, and yours is right. However, in reality, both you and your introverted buddies are perfectly fine.

If you're an extrovert who's living in a world that's designed for you (and not for your innie friends), understanding that introverted behavior is normal can be difficult. One of the best ways to grasp the truth about introverts — and why they *don't* need fixing — is to think about left-handers.

In general, we live in a world that's geared to right-handers rather than lefties. As a result, people in earlier centuries often labeled left-handedness as "wrong" and tried to "fix" it. For example, many kindergarten teachers made lefties sit on their left hands while writing with their right hands. More than a few lefties actually got smacked with a teacher's pointer for daring to break this rule!

Luckily, people eventually came to their senses. These days, we understand that both lefties and righties are perfectly fine. In fact, we now realize that left-handers have some big advantages in certain activities (tennis, for example, which is why quite a few Wimbledon champs are lefties).

Similarly, society is finally beginning to realize that introversion is a natural and normal personality trait. In fact, we're beginning to appreciate the unique talents that make innies wonderful.

## Recognizing the special strengths of the innies you know

In Chapter 1, I talk about some of the remarkable assets that introverts bring to the table. Here's a quick look at these talents, and how they relate to you specifically as an extroverted friend:

- ✔ **Introverts form strong friendships.** Because they don't have loads of casual friends like extroverts, introverts invest a great deal emotionally into each friendship they make. So if an introvert chooses you as a buddy, you can expect that person to be a true and loyal friend.

- ✔ **Introverts tend to listen more than they speak.** As a result, they won't interrupt you with their own issues when you want to talk about your feelings or discuss life crises.

- ✔ **Introverts are deep thinkers.** Need smart advice about a complex topic? Then turn to your introverted friends. They'll be glad to research your issue and offer informed opinions.

- ✔ **Introverts are a bit more risk-averse than extroverts.** In other words, your innie friends may be able to help you avoid making dangerous mistakes.

- ✔ **Introverts let their friends sparkle.** As an extrovert, you probably like to take center stage at parties or other events. And with an innie by your side, you can! In fact, your introverted friend will be grateful if you place yourself in the limelight and let him stay in the shadows.

## Making an Innie-Outie Relationship Work

Both introverts and extroverts are wonderful, but it's true that they have different ways of approaching the world. The good news is that with a little give-and-take on both sides, you and your introverted friends can get along beautifully.

In this section, I offer advice for keeping your introverted buddies happy while meeting your own needs in a relationship. (Also check out Chapter 18, where I offer some good tips for avoiding innies' biggest hot buttons, and Chapter 12, where I discuss intimate relationships.)

## Respecting an introvert's need for "alone" time

The biggest difference between you and your introverted friends is that innies need to spend a lot of time by themselves. Being alone with their own thoughts refreshes and relaxes them, because they recharge their batteries by turning inward.

As an extrovert, you're just the opposite. You recharge your batteries by turning outward, and that means you draw energy from people and activities. As a result, you may feel surprised or even hurt when an innie friend turns down your invitation to a party or a night on the town. But realize that your friend's inner battery, just like the battery in a cellphone, needs time to recharge. And for an innie, that takes peace and quiet.

So don't be upset if your introverted friend sometimes chooses an evening alone with a book over your delightful company. And don't take it personally, either. It's just how introverts are.

On the other hand, don't let your introverted buddy off the hook *all* the time. One of your biggest assets as an extroverted friend is that you'll introduce your quiet friend to activities that will enrich his life (even if you have to drag him to them). In addition, you'll help him expand his circle of friends — something that can be a challenge for innies.

And besides, your introverted friend needs to respect *your* needs as well! Otherwise, your relationship won't be a satisfying one.

So see whether the two of you can work out compromises. For example, talk your buddy into attending a tailgate party one Saturday, and then spend the next weekend at his house playing video games or watching movies. Or better yet, look for activities you both enjoy. For example, meet at the gym where you can participate in a group workout while your introverted friend tackles the treadmill — with earbuds on, naturally!

## Allowing an introvert to think before talking

As an extrovert, you think quickly, and you may talk quickly, too. But introverts are deep thinkers who typically need to mull their ideas over before saying them out loud. As a result, they often talk slowly and deliberately.

Because you move at a faster pace, you may be tempted to interrupt your introverted friend or finish his sentences for him. You may also grow frustrated because you have a lot of interesting ideas and you're afraid you'll forget them while you're waiting for your innie buddy to say what he wants. However, you can't speed introverts up. When it comes to innie communication, it takes as long as it takes. And if you interrupt introverts while they're thinking, they'll get irritated and shut down. They also hate it if you criticize them for taking time to ponder their thoughts before they speak. Nothing makes an introvert angrier than saying something like "You're overanalyzing this."

Instead, when you're talking with an introvert, try to match his slower pace (see Chapter 12 for more on matching and pacing). For example, after offering your thoughts on a topic, say, "What do you think?" Then wait quietly while your introverted friend prepares his answer. This exchange takes a little patience, I know! But in the long run, it'll make your friend respect you more and feel more comfortable talking with you, which will make your conversations far more rewarding.

## Minimizing multitasking demands

Introverts are very good at focusing deeply on one thing at a time. But ask them to juggle several tasks at once, and they may implode.

So if your introverted friend is writing a blog post and you rush in and say, "Let's talk about our camping trip," he may snap back, "Not now!" Give him a few minutes to reach a stopping point, and you'll have much better luck getting him to listen to you.

Also, try not to overload your friend with a huge to-do list. For example, if you have an introverted roommate, avoid saying, "Today, let's clean the kitchen and paint that ugly closet door and rearrange the pantry." Instead, suggest one activity at a time so you don't overload your innie friend's circuits.

## Understanding an introvert's desire to stay out of the spotlight

Mary, an extroverted acquaintance of mine, is totally into fashion — bold colors, huge earrings, designer purses, you name it. Her introverted best friend Jenelle, on the other hand, dresses as if she's in the witness protection program. Most of the time she's decked out in a gray T-shirt, faded blue jeans, and plain sneakers.

## Shopping for an introverted friend

A while ago, I bought what I thought was the perfect gift for a friend: a goofy pair of boxer shorts. Later, I found out that my introverted buddy would wear the boxers at home but never to work. It finally dawned on me that he was afraid that his male coworkers might — oh, the horror! — catch a glimpse of them when he was in the restroom.

I mentioned this realization to another introverted friend of mine, and she chuckled. It turns out that her husband is fond of buying her T-shirts with silly slogans on them. He's never noticed that she wears these shirts when she's scrubbing floors or cooking dinner but won't even venture outside to the mailbox in them.

The message? Go ahead and try to stretch your introverted friend's fashion horizons if you must, but don't be surprised or hurt if your eye-catching gift winds up in the Goodwill bag. Similarly, be wary about giving perfumes, aftershaves, bright fingernail polish or lipstick, or other attention-attracting gifts unless you know your introverted friend likes them.

It's hilarious to watch the two of them shop together, because Mary will hold up a flaming yellow dress or a gaudy hat and say "This is *perfect* for you," and Jenelle will actually shudder. Then Mary will roll her eyes dramatically as Jenelle heads back to the gray T-shirt section.

Like Jenelle, many introverts shy away from clothes that make them stand out in a crowd. By nature, innies prefer to observe the world, not have the world observe *them*.

For the same reason, most introverts aren't keen on activities that put them in the spotlight. For example, when Mary and Jenelle went to a magic show in Las Vegas recently and the magician asked for audience volunteers, Mary immediately leaped up and waved her hand. Jenelle, on the other hand, stayed firmly planted in her chair.

If you're an extrovert, your innie friends' desire to watch life from the sidelines can be frustrating at times. You may think they're missing out on all the fun! But realize that for them, observing quietly *is* fun. So don't pester them to join in. Instead, let them blend happily into the scenery while you take center stage.

Of course, sometimes your introverted friends will *need* to be in the spotlight, and here's where you can help them out. For example, if an innie friend needs to make a speech, you can help him practice and give him tips on his performance. And if he's nervous about a job interview, you can role-play it with him. Extroverts can be great "coaches" for introverts in situations like these.

## Grasping an introvert's approach to new activities

As an extrovert, you're probably always ready for a new adventure. So if I say "I want to try that new sushi place" or "I'm going rock climbing," you'll probably say, "Great — take me with you!"

Introverts tend to be more wary about new adventures, even little ones. Why? Because they're wired differently from you. Their nervous systems are already on high alert, so they're not all that keen on even more stimulation. (I talk more about this in Chapter 3.)

So don't be surprised if you say, "Let's go hot-air ballooning" or "Do you want to try skiing?" and your introverted friend looks at you in horror and says, "No!" After some thought, he may decide that your idea is fun. But introverts typically need to ponder a new activity before opting in.

 And by the way, if your introverted buddy says that a new activity is simply too dangerous, stop and think before you engage in it yourself. As a cautious and deep-thinking introvert, he may very well be right!

# Partying in Ways That Suit You Both

Extroverts thrive on action and crowds, while introverts crave quiet moments. This means that innies and outies will never be on the same page when it comes to parties and other big social occasions. Luckily, as I explain in this section, you can narrow the gulf between you and your introverted friends if you know what to expect from them.

## Getting the introvert's perspective on social occasions

When you go to a party with an introverted friend or invite him over to your house for Thanksgiving, you may be expecting him to mingle happily with your other guests. However, you're likely to find that he sits quietly in a corner peeking at his watch instead. Here's why introverts behave differently from extroverts at social occasions:

- ✔ They don't like small talk.
- ✔ It takes them time to warm up to strangers.

✔ They're great at one-on-one relationships but tend to shut down in groups.

✔ Their batteries run down quickly when they're in a crowd, and they need to find a quiet place to recharge them.

When you keep all these things in mind, you'll find it easier to help an innie friend enjoy himself at a social occasion. Here are some tips:

✔ Introduce him to a small group of people and then stick around for a while until he gets comfortable with them.

✔ Provide activities that make it easy for him to fit in. After Thanksgiving dinner, for example, encourage him to park in front of the TV and watch a football game with fellow fans. In this situation, it'll be easy for him to make small talk.

✔ Help him out with some conversation starters. For example, say something like "Jerry's an artist, too. He even had a show at that new gallery downtown."

✔ Let him hide out when he needs a break. For example, if you're holding a wedding reception at your house, say, "Feel free to duck into my office any time you need a little peace and quiet."

✔ If the party is at your house, give your friend useful chores to do, such as setting up tables or taking photos. (For more on this, see Chapter 13.) A specific task will give him an excuse to escape from the chatter.

## Being okay with early departures

If you're an extrovert, you like to wring every last drop of pleasure from a social event. And if you're *really* extroverted, you're probably the final guest to leave a party. However, introverts can handle only a couple of hours at a social event before they start to flag. So your introverted friends or relatives are likely to duck out early from parties. (I have one introverted friend who says, "I've never seen the end of a single party except the ones I've thrown. And I'd leave my *own* parties early if I could.")

So don't get upset if your introverted friends skip out early from a party, even if it's one you're hosting. It's no reflection on the party itself; it's just how they are. And don't question whatever excuse they come up with for escaping quickly. Be kind, and just pretend that you believe it.

Also, don't be too surprised if your introverted friends R.S.V.P. for your events and then cancel at the last minute with some lame excuse. Often, they'll initially accept an invitation because they care about you and don't want to hurt your feelings. But as the event approaches, their introverted nature will kick in and they'll start looking for a way to escape.

Mind you, I'm not condoning this behavior — shame on you, introverts! — but remember that parties drain introverts' batteries, so they're biologically wired to want to avoid them. So even though innies shouldn't do this, don't take it as an insult, because it truly isn't. And if it makes you feel any better, realize that your introverted friends generally aren't canceling because they've been invited to another party that they think may be even better. (That's an extroverted behavior — shame on you, extroverts!)

As an aside, one good way to make your occasions work for introverts is to plan the "must-see" activities, such as the arrival of the cake at an anniversary party, early in the event. That way, even the innies who sneak out early can get to see the main events. Of course, you'll need to weigh the needs of your extroverted guests and decide whether they'll be okay with this plan.

## Accepting an introvert's right to skip some events

Extroverts love it when their calendar is filled to the brim with parties and social events. But introverts need to balance their social obligations with their strong need for quiet time, so they'll often decline invitations.

When they do, don't criticize them or label them as "party poopers." Instead, recognize that oversocializing exhausts them, and it's smart for them to guard their energy.

By the way, you'll have more luck getting your introverted friends to attend your own events if you plan innie-friendly activities. For info on the kinds of social events that introverts enjoy, see Chapter 13.

# Chapter 15

# Parenting an Introverted Child

## In This Chapter

▶ Spotting introversion in a child

▶ Identifying issues that can masquerade as introversion

▶ Making a happy home, school, and social life for a young introvert

▶ Helping an introverted child or teenager thrive

▶ Dealing with Bullies

Are you raising an introverted child? If so, you have an exciting road ahead of you! Your wonderful child is likely to fascinate, frustrate, puzzle, impress, and delight you — sometimes all at the same time.

Introverted children are a joy to raise, but they can also test your parenting skills. In this chapter, I take a look at the fun and the challenges of being mom or dad to an introverted child or teen.

Of course, the first question to ask yourself is "Am I *really* raising an innie?" I help you answer that question by discussing what introversion looks like in a young person (and I also look at a few issues people sometimes mistake for introversion). Then I talk about how to make life as happy, healthy, and stress-free as possible for your innie child or teen. And finally, I look at ways to protect your child from a common danger for introverts: bullying.

## Identifying Introversion in a Child

In many ways, introverted kids are a lot like introverted adults. So if you think your child is an innie, Chapter 2 can help you decide whether you're right. You can also spot a lot of clues about your child's personality just by watching him or her. For example, there's a good chance your child is an innie if any of the following are true:

 ✔ Your child watches other children from the sidelines for a long time before joining an activity.

- ✔ Your child can talk nonstop to family and close friends about her interests, but she clams up in a group.

- ✔ Your child is cautious and hesitant to try new activities.

- ✔ Your child's teacher says things like "She's so smart and talented, but she won't speak up in class."

- ✔ Your child can focus intently for hours on a project or a book.

- ✔ Your child happily spends a lot of time alone in her room.

- ✔ Your child tends to zone out or even melt down at big social events.

- ✔ Your child exhibits "quiet" body language at school or at social events, but at home, her gestures may be very animated.

- ✔ Your child has a small group of friends, and within that group, she may be very influential.

- ✔ Your child needs to think before she talks.

- ✔ Your child gets upset if you schedule a lot of after-school or weekend activities for her.

- ✔ Your child prefers not to be the center of attention.

- ✔ Your child sometimes gives other kids the impression that she's "stuck up."

- ✔ Your child's not big on flashy clothes and prefers muted colors that allow her to blend in.

- ✔ Your child would rather work on school projects alone than in a group.

Young innies, like introverted adults, are often labeled as shy (for more on shyness, see Chapter 2), and many children are both shy and introverted. But many innie children *aren't* shy. They just prefer small doses of socializing, because they recharge their batteries by turning inward rather than outward. If you aren't sure whether your child is shy, take the shyness test in Chapter 2 and answer the way you think your child would.

Some (but not all) introverted children are also highly sensitive. These children can react strongly to sights, smells, noises, tastes, textures, emotions, and physical pain. For more information on high sensitivity, see Chapter 2.

# Distinguishing Between Introversion and Medical Conditions

Introversion is a normal, healthy personality trait. But sometimes, kids are mistaken for being introverted when they actually have something very different going on, such as ADD, ADHD, or autism. The following sections explain how these three conditions can mimic introversion in some ways.

# Considering ADD and ADHD

Most likely, you know at least a few kids who have a diagnosis of attention deficit disorder (ADD) or attention deficit hyperactivity disorder (ADHD). Both of these conditions are very common.

Kids with ADD exhibit symptoms like these:

- ✔ They have trouble focusing and concentrating.
- ✔ They're easily distracted.
- ✔ They may find finishing tests or homework difficult, and their work may be messy.
- ✔ They tend to forget things, such as their lunch or their jacket.
- ✔ They have trouble listening to others and following conversations.

Kids with ADHD exhibit additional symptoms like these:

- ✔ They fidget and squirm more than other kids.
- ✔ They have trouble staying in their seats and tend to run about when they should be sitting or standing still.
- ✔ They talk excessively and have trouble staying quiet.
- ✔ They're always on the go.
- ✔ They often have trouble controlling negative emotions and tend to blurt out their feelings

Some kids with ADHD also are impulsive. These kids interrupt others, blurt out answers before they're called on, and have trouble waiting for their turn.

 Because of their rich inner life and a tendency to daydream, introverts can sometimes appear to have ADD or ADHD when they don't. This confusion is even more likely if they're gifted innies who are bored and fidgety in class because they've already mastered the material. And introverted kids can also have trouble focusing if they're overwhelmed by multitasking demands. Because they like to focus deeply on one thing, they can get frustrated and shut down if a teacher asks them to bounce from task to task.

On the other hand, some kids with ADD or ADHD can look like they're introverted when they aren't. And some kids are introverted *and* have ADD or ADHD.

To gain some insight as to whether your child may have ADHD or ADD, consider these questions:

- ✔ Is your child struggling to learn in school?

- ✔ Does your child have a great deal of trouble following directions, remembering to do chores, or paying attention to you at home?

- ✔ Is it hard for your child to focus on one thing at a time, such as reading an entire book chapter or watching a half-hour TV show without zoning out?

- ✔ Do you find your child's behavior hard to control?

- ✔ Is your child always on the move, and does she find it very hard to sit still?

If you spot issues like these, your child may have ADD or ADHD (or a combination of ADD or ADHD and introversion). A doctor can refer you to a psychologist for thorough testing to determine whether an ADD or ADHD diagnosis is appropriate.

By the way, I recommend steering clear of family physicians who make a diagnosis of ADD or ADHD without referring a child for psychological testing. ADD and ADHD are overdiagnosed these days, and it takes a thorough evaluation to determine whether a child really has one of these conditions. Also, different types of ADD and ADHD exist, and it's important to distinguish between them.

If your child does get an ADD or ADHD diagnosis, be aware that kids with these conditions often get overmedicated when they need only a small dose of medication. And some children do just as well with therapy alone or with alternative treatments (such as dietary changes).

## *Ruling out autism spectrum disorders*

In general, telling autism from normal introversion is pretty easy. But in very young children, it can be a little tricky to differentiate between mild autism and introverted behavior.

If you're concerned that a young child may have an autism spectrum disorder, ask yourself these questions:

- ✔ Does your child have extreme difficulty making eye contact with people?

- ✔ Are your child's speech and language delayed or abnormal?

- ✔ Does your child have difficulty with pretend play, such as pretending that a block is a truck or pretending to cook with toy food?

- ✔ Is your child unable to play in an age-appropriate way with other children?

- ✔ Is your child unable to point to something she wants to show you?

✔ Does your child exhibit repetitive behaviors or unusual preoccupations?

✔ Is your child abnormally sensitive to certain textures or noises?

If you answer *yes* to many of these questions, ask your doctor for a referral for testing. Identifying autism quickly is important, because early intervention can be highly effective. But if you answer *no* to all or nearly all these questions, you're probably looking at normal, garden-variety introversion.

# Creating an Innie-Friendly Home for Your Child

Introverted children encounter a lot of challenges in the outside world — crowded classrooms, noisy birthday parties, even run-ins with schoolyard bullies. So it's critical for them to have a supportive, understanding family and an innie-friendly home where they can relax, feel accepted, and recharge their batteries. In this section, I talk about ways to make your child's home life cozy and happy.

## Appreciating your child's innie-ness

If you want to make a good home for an innie child, the first step is to search your own soul. Why? Because your child's happiness as an introvert begins with you accepting her just as she is.

If you're an extrovert, it may be difficult for you to understand the way your introverted child thinks and behaves. But it's vital to recognize that her approach to life isn't wrong; it's just *different*. In Chapter 1, I explain why introversion, just like extroversion, is a normal, healthy way of approaching life.

So be careful not to hold your child to outie expectations. Understand that she'll probably form a few rich friendships instead of being a social butterfly. Let her have the quiet time she needs to charge her batteries, and be empathetic if she's overwhelmed by activities that you loved as a child.

And what if you're an introvert yourself? On one hand, you'll be able to understand where your child is coming from. But on the other hand, you may look back on the challenges you faced as a young innie and project your own emotional baggage onto your child. If you catch yourself doing this, realize that your child isn't you. As an introvert, she'll encounter some of the same challenges you did, but she may respond to them in very different ways. So take care to separate your feelings from hers.

And whether you're an introverted or extroverted parent, avoid the urge to try to change your child's personality. As I explain in Chapter 3, pressuring an innie to become more extroverted is a mistake. Your child may someday decide on her own to develop some outie behaviors, but that choice has to be hers. And if she decides that she's perfectly fine as a full-fledged innie, that's an equally good choice.

Do let your little introvert know that you expect her to be part of the family, though. Make your rules clear on this front; for example, tell her that you expect her to eat dinner with the family every night. Set rules about participation in family activities early, hold to them faithfully (although you can tweak them as your child ages), and model them yourself.

## Steering clear of the overscheduling trap

Kids today often have schedules even more hectic than their parents'. For example, they may run from play dates to soccer practice to music lessons. That's great if those kids are high-energy extroverts who love careening from one activity to another. But for introverted kids, this kind of schedule can be highly stressful and lead to meltdowns.

Young innies need time to recharge their batteries by retreating inward. So give your kid a break! Expose your innie to new experiences, but do it without overwhelming her. Here are some tips:

✔ If your introvert is very young, pick only one activity at a time, and allow her to ease into the activity slowly. For example, if you sign up your 4-year-old for a tap dance class, ask the teacher whether it's okay for your child to observe the first session quietly from the sidelines (unless she wants to join in). Then let her participate more and more over the next few sessions, going at her own pace.

✔ Let your child discover which activities she likes instead of pressuring her to stick with an activity that doesn't interest her. Also, allow her to blossom slowly when she tries a new activity, and celebrate her baby steps.

✔ Avoid scheduling back-to-back activities. When an activity ends, make sure your child has some quiet down time afterward so she can recharge. For example, if a coach says "We're all going out for pizza after the game," allow your child to say no if it's too much for her.

✔ Consider signing your child up for an activity twice in a row. She may enjoy it far more the second time around, when she knows exactly what's expected of her.

✔ Offer your child a choice of activities. When she gets to make a choice, she'll be more willing to try something new.

✔ If you're parenting an older child or teen, let your child set the pace when it comes to extracurricular activities. And if she's excited about activities she does alone — for example, painting or playing the violin — respect her interests and give her the supplies she needs to pursue her hobbies.

✔ Avoid the trap of thinking that your child needs to participate in the activities you enjoyed as a child (especially if you're an extrovert).

Whether you're planning activities for a younger innie child or an older one, be aware that it can be difficult for these kids to separate from their parents or leave their homes for long stretches. Quiet toddlers often experience more separation anxiety than their outie peers, while older kids or teens may stress out if they need to go away to summer camp or attend an out-of-town band concert.

To ease innie kids through these times, prepare them upfront. For example, if you sign your tot up for a gymnastics class, take her to the building ahead of time and show her pictures of other kids doing gymnastics so she'll know what to expect. If an older innie is fretting about going to camp, show her brochures about the camp and describe the activities she'll be doing.

Above all, make your child's early experiences with social activities as positive as possible. A young innie who's constantly overstimulated may become even more reluctant to try new activities. And an introverted child who's pushed into demanding social activities that she's not ready to handle may experience failure and become wary of social events in the future. So schedule wisely, and plan activities that don't ask too much of your quiet child.

## Helping your innie child handle change

Extroverted kids typically deal with changes pretty well, but for young innies, unpredictability can be overwhelming. However, life is full of change and surprises, so it's important to help an innie child cope with new schedules, new people, and new experiences. The following sections show you how.

### Helping a young child deal with change

Young innies can melt down if they need to handle a lot of changes at once. So one of the best ways to help a young innie handle change is to minimize it. Here are a couple ways you can do that:

✔ Create predictable routines that help your child stay anchored in the shifting sea of life. For example, if you're parenting a toddler, try to keep her naps and mealtimes as consistent as possible. Create predictable bedtimes as well — for example, a nightly story hour and back rub. These consistent activities will reassure her if other parts of her life get stressful or chaotic.

✔ When changes do occur, prepare your child as much as possible. For example, if you're divorced and your custody agreement changes, immediately let your child know exactly what her new schedule will be. If she's old enough, create a calendar so she can clearly see when she'll be at your house or your ex's.

### Teaching an older child or teen to handle unpredictability

Older introverts can handle changes to their schedules, and they need to develop this skill because life doesn't always follow a set plan! So show your introverted child or teen some tricks, such as the following, for adjusting to change smoothly.

✔ Modify the visualization exercises I outline in Chapter 7 so your child can use them. For example, if she's moving from elementary school to middle school, take her on a quick tour of the school so she'll know what it looks like. Then have her visualize herself being successful in different areas of the school — chatting happily with one new friend and eventually several friends in the hallway, hitting a home run on the softball field, or giving a confident presentation in class.

✔ Teach your child how to overcome catastrophic thinking. (For more info, see Chapter 11.) For example, if your child is terrified of moving to a new town and says, "I'll never make new friends," ask her questions like these:

• Did you feel really scared when we moved to this town five years ago?

• Did you make new friends here?

• Is it possible that you'll love the new town and make friends there?

You'll find many other activities in Chapter 11 that can help your young introvert cope when life changes pop up. Focus specifically on the activities that will help your child overcome negative thinking and pessimism.

Also, encourage your child to find some "transferable" hobbies and activities that will help her adjust if she switches schools or neighborhoods (especially if you move frequently). For example, an interest in computers or basketball may help your child ease into a new situation and meet other kids with similar interests.

# Bridging the communication gap

If you're an extrovert and your child is an introvert, the two of you may have different ways of communicating and very different body language. This gap can sometimes make sending the right messages difficult — and it can also result in misunderstandings and hurt feelings. (These things can happen if you're an innie as well, but it's a bigger risk in an outie-innie combo.)

For example, if you're a big hugger, does your child enjoy your bear hugs, or are they a little overwhelming for her? If you give her a huge hug and she flinches or pushes you away, don't take it personally. Instead, see whether she responds better to a smile or a pat on the shoulder.

And does your child follow through easily when you describe her weekend chores verbally, or does she do better when you give her a written list? When you match her communication style, you'll help set her up for success.

Here are more tips for bridging the outie-innie communication gap:

✔ Try talking to your innie more slowly. It's not that introverts themselves are slow; in fact, quite the opposite is true. Introverts tend to think deeply about what you're saying, and they need time to absorb your comments and mull them over.

✔ When you're chatting, give your innie time to think about what she wants to say. Be careful not to interrupt her or "fill in the blanks" in her sentences. (By the way, introverts frequently do better in this area than extroverts. While outies tend to cut you off when you're talking on the assumption that they already know what you're going to say, innies typically listen patiently and ask questions to make sure they understand you. If you're an extrovert, try this technique yourself and you'll find that it makes conversations much more meaningful.)

✔ Focus on one topic at a time. Doing so will make it easier for your innie to follow your conversation.

# Keeping sibling relationships positive

If you have two or more kids, your family dynamics can get interesting, or even a little crazy! And that's especially true if you're parenting a mix of innies and outies.

As it turns out, extroverted siblings are actually a blessing for innies. Outies can stand up for innies if they're being bullied, and they bring crowds of friends home, increasing the odds that the innies will find new buddies.

However, problems can often crop up in an innie-outie sibling relationship. Here are some ways to make this mix work:

✔ Innies tend to value their privacy more than outies, so let your innie draw clear lines. For example, allow her to post a "keep out" sign on her door when she wants her sibling to give her some space.

✔ Make sure your introvert respects your extrovert as well. For example, make it clear that you expect your innie to go to some of your outie's soccer games or parties even if she'd rather stay in her room and read a book.

One friend of mine insisted that her introverted son David go to his brother's music recital. When David balked, she said, "Alex watched you play football; now you need to return the favor." As it turned out, David learned a lot from watching his brother perform under pressure in front of a judge. As a result, he gained a new admiration for Alex that strengthened their relationship.

✔ Don't let your outie bully your innie. Sibling bullying is a real and serious problem, affecting up to a third of kids. One recent study found that sibling bullying can lead to significant mental distress, including depression and anxiety.

On the other hand, don't be too protective of your introvert! An extroverted sibling's gentle teasing or arguing can help toughen up a quiet introvert so she's better prepared for the real world. Just keep a tight rein on this behavior, and make sure your innie is handling it well. If you spot your innie retreating or engaging in passive-aggressive behavior (such as "accidentally" breaking one of the sibling's toys), talk with both kids about what's okay and what's not okay when it comes to teasing and arguing.

✔ Teach your introverted child effective ways of responding to a sibling's teasing if it gets too mean. (For more on this, see the section "Teaching your child ways to handle bullies," at the end of this chapter.)

✔ Appreciate your children's differences. Talk with them individually and then as a family about their innie and outie traits, and explain why each type of personality is valuable.

For example, say something like this: "Jordan is such a great big brother because he really listens to you and cares about what you say. It's nice to have a brother who's such a good listener, isn't it? And you're a great little sister, because you get him interested in new activities. Thanks to you, he loves tennis and soccer now." As they grow up, keep reminding your kids that their different personality traits are terrific and that they can benefit from each other's strengths.

## Giving your innie her own private space

Introverted kids often like to hole up somewhere, especially when they're feeling down. So if your child doesn't have a room to herself, make her a little space — maybe a corner of the living room — that's all her own. Give her a cozy chair and a table, and let her shut out the world when she's in her spot. (Or consider providing a tent or a treehouse in your yard.)

Also, respect your innie's privacy if she creates her own little hideaway. For example, one little girl I know likes to hide out in her closet when she's feeling stressed out. She's placed a little chair and a reading light in there, and she sits and reads until she's feeling ready to face the world again.

Providing private spots for your child will benefit both you and her. A moody introvert can spread her negativity to the rest of the family, and she'll sense your negative mood in return, making her even moodier. By allowing her to "quarantine" herself when she needs some alone time, you'll stop this cycle in its tracks.

Be aware, however, that your innie may sometimes hide out in her private space just to manipulate *your* behavior. For example, the little girl with the closet hideaway will sometimes sit there for hours after her mother scolds her, just to make her mom feel guilty. If your introvert tries the same trick, remember that she *likes* being alone, so skip the guilt trip and just leave her on her own until she's ready to rejoin the family.

Also, don't let her escape from social or family obligations by hiding herself away. Say something like, "You can stay in your room until 6:00, and then it's dinnertime."

# Encouraging Friendships

Young extroverts make friends easily — on the playground, in the classroom, on the football field, at parties — but for introverted kids, it's not that easy. Luckily, you can lend a hand. In this section, I explore tricks for helping an innie child or teen find the few good friends she needs.

## Helping a younger child make friends

Like adult introverts, young innies aren't great at small talk, and they don't warm up easily to strangers. So as an innie's parent, you need to do a little extra work to help your sweetie make friends. Here are some approaches that can work well:

✔ Start scheduling play dates when your child is very young. Set up one-on-one play dates instead of large ones, and notice which kids your child likes the most so you can invite those children frequently. Plan fun activities, such as cookie baking or video games, that can lead naturally to conversations.

✔ Look for community activities that match your child's interests. For example, one mom's introverted son loved gardening. So she located a community garden where little kids could help with the harvesting, and that's where her son met the tyke who's now his best friend.

✔ Plan events that take advantage of your child's interests and skills. For example, if your child loves horses and she's a skilled rider, ask whether she wants to invite a couple of schoolmates for a horseback ride. When she's in a setting where she's knowledgeable and confident, she'll be more likely to relax.

✔ Come up with a signal your child can send you if she's getting over-whelmed at a social activity. When you see that signal, step in and offer her an excuse to take a quick break. For example, say, "Emily, could you go upstairs and see whether your brother is still napping?" Let her practice giving you this signal several times so she'll be comfortable using it when she needs a little break from playing.

✔ Hone your child's social skills. Make sure she knows how to share, take turns, say "please" and "thank you," and be a polite host. (Also, make sure she knows how to apologize if she misbehaves or hurts another child. Apologizing is an important social skill that too many parents neglect.) Use role-playing to practice social skills until your child has them down pat.

If your child finds it especially difficult to make friends, consider using a *social script*. In this approach, you actually write out a script that focuses on a specific social situation. For example, you can use a social script like the following to help a young child prepare for a birthday party:

> "I am having a birthday party on Saturday. Four kids from my class will come. They will bring me presents. We will have cake. I will blow out the candles on the cake, and everyone will sing 'Happy Birthday' to me. Then I will open my presents. I will say 'thank you' when I open each person's present. We will all play for a couple of hours, and I will share my new toys with the other kids. Then my friends will go home, and I will be able to play with my toys by myself."

Rehearse your social script every day for a week or so before an event. This way, your child will know what to expect on the big day and how to act appropriately — and that will translate into a better shot at making friends.

## Helping an older child or teen make friends

The middle-school and high-school years are often tough for introverts. Teens can be cruel and catty, and they tend to divide into cliques that exclude quiet kids. As a result, building new friendships can be difficult for innies.

If your child develops close friendships early in life (see tips in the previous section) and doesn't move around a lot, she'll likely have the circle of friends she needs to be happy as a teen. But here are a few additional ways you can help your child find friends at this vulnerable stage of life:

- ✔ Encourage your child to get involved in volunteer work. Kids who volunteer tend to be kinder and more innie-friendly than other teens. (But don't bill this activity as a friend-making effort. Instead, focus on the work she'll be doing and how it benefits her community. That way, she won't feel pressured to make friends.)

- ✔ Encourage your child to join clubs that match up with her interests. Introverted kids often find it easier to open up and talk to other people when they're sharing information about their favorite pastimes.

- ✔ Let your teen think outside the box when it comes to choosing friends. For example, if she wants to hang out with the younger kid next door or she enjoys talking about cats with the grandma down the street, that's fine. Although introverts tend to have fewer friends than outies, they're also more open to forming bonds with people of different ages.

   As a young introvert, I made friends with the girl next door who was one year younger than me. Okay, I admit it: It was partly because her mom let her read comic books, while mine didn't approve of them! But we enjoyed each other's company all summer, even though my mom thought she was "too young" for me.

- ✔ See whether you can get your child interested in activities, such as martial arts, self-defense, acting, and dance, that will raise her self-esteem and promote assertive body language. These activities can boost her confidence so she's more willing to seek out new friends, and they can also help protect her against bullying.

Above all, don't worry if your child falls in with a group of kids that other children label as "uncool" or "nerds." Often, these kids are really the coolest kids in the school; it's just that nobody knows it yet. (They'll find out later in life, when these nerdy kids follow in the footsteps of Bill Gates!)

Do be concerned, however, if your teen doesn't have any good friends at all, especially if she seems depressed (see nearby sidebar "Is your introverted kid okay, or is she depressed?"). In this situation, you may want to look into therapy or social skills groups.

## Is your introverted kid okay, or is she depressed?

Introverted kids commonly spend hours and hours in their bedrooms, and it's perfectly fine if your introvert does, too, as long as she's happy. But if she isn't, ask yourself if she's showing signs of depression.

Currently, doctors look for these symptoms when they assess kids for major depression:

✔ Feelings of sadness, emptiness, or irritability (or tearfulness in young children) nearly every day, for a large part of the day

✔ Reduced interest in activities they used to enjoy

✔ Feelings of worthlessness or guilt

✔ Fatigue

✔ Changes in eating or sleeping patterns

✔ Marked restlessness or under-activity

✔ Poor concentration

✔ Thoughts of suicide

✔ A combination of depressive symptoms and anxiety

*Warning:* If you spot these red flags, be sure to talk with your child's doctor. And if your child mentions any thoughts about suicide, seek help *immediately!*

## *Helping an introverted teen handle romance — or the lack of it*

Often, introverted teens start dating much later than their outie peers. Moreover, when they do begin to date, they may get off to a rocky start because teens these days sometimes expect to get intimate pretty quickly, while introverts need time to build relationships.

As a result, your innie teen may spend a lot of Friday and Saturday nights at home. If that's the case, don't make a big deal of it. As long as your child is happy and has a friend or two, dating can wait. (In fact, loads of parents would love to trade places with you!)

If your teen does get into a serious relationship that results in a breakup, she's likely to take it very hard. If this happens, gently ask her about it. Avoid saying glib things like, "There are plenty of other guys out there" or "I didn't like him much anyway." Introverted kids hate dismissive comments like these, and they often respond by becoming sarcastic and cynical. (I talk more about this in the section "Acknowledging your child's emotions," later in this chapter.)

Instead, understand that your child's pain is real, and respect it. But do see whether you can ease her woe a little bit with some innie interests, such as a book by her favorite author or the new box of watercolors she's been wanting.

---

## Are texting and IMing good for innies?

If your teenager spends hours texting, you may be tempted to say "Knock it off!" But as it turns out, texting and instant messaging can sometimes be very helpful for introverted adolescents.

A recent study examined teens' text and IM messages and found that teens who were distressed when they started texting or IMing tended to feel relieved by the end of their chats. This effect was more pronounced for introverted teens than for their extroverted peers.

The researchers concluded that for innies in particular, texting and IMing can improve well-being.

*Tip:* It's important to draw limits when it comes to texting. Introverted kids (and extroverted ones as well) still need to learn and practice real-life social skills. And they need to know that texting during family meals or conversations, or when company is present, isn't okay — so set limits and stick to them.

---

# Enhancing Your Child's Self-Image

Introverted children are wonderful just the way they are, but they don't always hear that message from the people around them. In fact, in an extroverted world, they're likely to feel like square pegs in round holes. So one of your most important jobs as a parent is to let your child know that being an introvert is cool. The following sections provide some ways to do so.

## Explaining introversion to your child

Innie kids and teens need to know that their feelings and behavior are perfectly normal. So sit your young introvert down and talk about introversion and extroversion. Let her know that both innies and outies are terrific, and that both of them have special talents.

To prove that innies are terrific, ask your child to list her favorite movie or book characters. Odds are, she'll pick a lot of introverts. For example, if she's young, she may love Roald Dahl's smart, quiet Matilda. If she's older, she may go for Batman, Katniss Everdeen in *The Hunger Games,* Wolverine in *X-Men,* Mr. Darcy in *Pride and Prejudice,* or one of those intense and brooding vampires that girls drool over these days.

After your child lists some favorite innie characters, ask her why she likes them. She'll probably say something like "They're quiet instead of noisy, and they're loyal to their friends, and they think hard about what's right and wrong." Then you can point out that the traits she listed are innie traits and that she can be proud because she's like that herself!

Also, talk about innie adults she admires, such as a favorite neighbor or relative. Then have her think about innie actors, comedians, or musicians who she thinks are great. (For some ideas, see Chapter 16.)

And to reinforce the message that both innies and outies are fabulous, ask her to name extroverted people and outie fictional characters she admires as well.

## Avoiding the urge to praise outie behaviors

Some days, your young introvert will be all innie. On other days, however, she may reveal a slightly more extroverted side of her nature. When she does, you may be tempted to say, "You were so sociable today; I really enjoyed seeing you come out of your shell."

If you feel that urge, bite your tongue. Otherwise, you'll send your child the message that extroverted behavior is better than introverted behavior. And that can make her feel inadequate or even guilty when she goes back to being her innie self.

Similarly, avoid criticizing your child's innie behaviors. For example, don't say things like "try to be more sociable when your cousins are here." Instead, say something neutral or positive like "Could you take your cousin Teddy out to see the kittens when he comes? I think he'd really enjoy that." This approach will accomplish your goal without making your child feel bad.

And after the visit, don't criticize your child if she was quiet or praise her if she was outgoing. Instead, say something like, "I noticed that you played with Teddy and both his sisters today. Do you like them?" And if she says yes, then say, "Great! What did you guys do that you really liked?" This way, you can help her explore her feelings without inserting your own judgments.

## Acknowledging your child's emotions

Little innies tend to worry a lot. (For example, one quiet little boy I knew used to fret constantly about volcanoes — not really a big threat in his home town of Phoenix!) In addition, innies may become deeply sad or upset if other children tease them, if they get a bad grade on a test, or if something embarrassing happens to them.

If you're an extroverted parent (or even if you're an introverted one) you may tend to dismiss these emotions with a wave of the hand and a comment like "we don't have volcanoes here" or "you'll do better on next week's test" or "just ignore those kids; you don't need them as friends." But these responses aren't the best approach for consoling an introverted child.

Instead of trying to brush your child's feelings away, acknowledge them. For example, if your child is upset about not getting a party invitation, you can say something like this: "That must make you feel very sad. I'm so sorry. Is there something I can do to help you feel better?" If she can't think of anything, offer some suggestions (such as going shopping for some new school clothes or going to a movie with a friend).

This approach tells your child that her emotions are valid and worthy of respect, making it easier for her to share those emotions and thus gain control over them.

My sister and I, both extreme introverts as kids, grew up with a mom who used this approach. For example, if she found us crying because a friend didn't invite us to a sleepover, she'd say something like "Well, just don't worry about it. We'll go do something else fun instead." I know she believed that this approach was helpful, but it was actually very frustrating and painful for us because it sent the message that our emotions were silly and trivial.

And here's an even worse story I heard from a friend named Sally. When Sally was little, the girl in the house next door didn't invite Sally to her birthday party. So on the day of the party, Sally's mom set up her own picnic table in the backyard and put out sandwiches and potato chips. Then she and Sally had their own "party," with Sally's mom exclaiming loudly, "Isn't this fun?"

Well, it wasn't fun for little introverted Sally, who could look right into the neighbor's yard and see the kids at the birthday party staring back at her! I'm sure Sally's mom thought she was doing the right thing, but Sally still cringes when she remembers that day.

# Helping Your Young Innie Have a Good School Experience

Introverted kids are deep thinkers. They love to learn, and they're typically very conscientious when it comes to doing schoolwork. So you'd think schools would adore them, but surprisingly, that's not always the case.

Why? It's not that these kids are rowdy or noisy or disobedient. In fact, they're usually just the opposite: They're quiet.

Unfortunately, most schools these days don't think of "quiet" as a virtue. In fact, teachers often base a child's grade largely on class participation. As a result, bright introverts often lose out to talkative outies. In addition, today's classrooms focus on teamwork — something that's not a young introvert's forte.

Worse yet, research reveals that some teachers have a bias against introverted students. In a recent study, teachers who read about imaginary students rated the quiet ones as less intelligent than the noisy ones, and predicted that they would do worse in school. That's ironic, because innies are frequently gifted (something I talk about in the sidebar "School and the gifted innie," later in this chapter).

So how can you help your quiet introvert succeed in school? By working with his teachers to create a classroom where he can thrive or, if that doesn't work, by finding a different setting for your child. I explore some options in the following sections.

## Working with your child's school and teachers

Today's schools know that kids learn in different ways. As a result, they're good at tailoring their material to reach children with different learning styles and kids from different backgrounds. But sometimes, they overlook another important form of diversity: the innie-outie difference.

In this situation, you can be a strong advocate for your child. Get to know your child's teacher early on in the school year, and make her aware that your child is an introvert. Then ask her to actively work with you to find ways to make your child's classroom innie-friendly.

Be sure to be cooperative and not adversarial. For example, say something like this: "Mindy is so excited about being in your class this year. We've heard great things about you from other parents, and I know you work very hard to help every child succeed. That's why I wanted to tell you a little about Mindy. I'm hoping we can brainstorm some ways to help her do her best."

Here are some ideas you can bounce around:

- ✔ Ask whether the teacher can create some quiet spaces in the classroom (such as reading nooks) where innie students can escape for a bit.

- ✔ Suggest letting students write their ideas down on paper before asking them to discuss these ideas out loud.

- ✔ Ask whether the teacher can base a good part of her grading on written reports or assignments.

Also, offer to give your child's teacher information on introversion and the needs of introverted children. (This book is a good start!)

---

## Helping an introverted child cope with a learning disability

School is a little tough for any kid with a learning disability, but it can be especially challenging for an introvert. An innie may not be ready to handle the curious questions of other kids, such as, "Why do you go to a different room for reading?" or "Is there something wrong with your brain?"

If your little innie is dealing with a learning disability, be sure to prepare her for these kinds of questions. Years ago, I heard about a great way to do this. I was attending a speech by a successful realtor who'd conquered a childhood reading disability. He told the audience that his parents took a smart approach to his disability: They told him, "You don't have a problem, you have a *uniqueness*." So when his friends asked why he left class to work with a resource teacher, he told them, "There's nothing wrong; I just read *differently*." As a result, nobody made a big deal of it.

---

In addition, volunteer in your child's classroom if you can. Doing so will allow you to observe her interaction with her teacher and with other students. If you spot any issues, you can bring them up with her teacher and search together for solutions.

One thing to pay attention to is how your child responds to requests to read out loud. Children often are hesitant to read out loud if they're introverted. They may also fear reading out loud if they have a learning disability, so it's critical not to automatically dismiss this as a sign of introversion. If your child hates to read out loud, make sure you have her checked for a learning disability that may be holding her back and ask the teacher to minimize any demands in this area until you get the results of the testing.

## *Considering alternatives to public schools*

Many schools are very understanding about the needs of introverted children, but unfortunately, some aren't. And if you're stuck with a school that isn't willing to become innie-friendly, you may need to look for a new setting.

These days, more options are available than ever when it comes to schooling. Depending on your lifestyle and where you live, here are environments that may work for your child:

- ✔ **Charter schools:** These schools, financed by public funds and private donations, are free of charge. They're required to follow many of the rules that apply to public schools, but they're often much more flexible, which can translate into a more innie-friendly approach.

- **Magnet schools:** These schools are public schools that focus on special programs. For example, they may teach advanced classes in drama, science, art, or foreign languages. In a magnet school, a gifted introvert may be able to delve more deeply into the topics that fascinate her.

- **Private schools:** The drawback to these schools, of course, is that they're pricy. However, they're typically very committed to helping each child succeed, so they often do a good job of helping introverted students reach their full potential.

- **Online schools:** Some online schools are self-pacing, which is a particularly good option for gifted introverts (see the nearby sidebar "School and the gifted innie" for more details).

- **Home-schooling:** These days, more and more parents are teaching their children at home. They're also teaming up with other home-schoolers and with school districts to provide a wide-ranging curriculum and opportunities for socialization.

If one of these settings appeals to you, check it out. Charter schools, magnet schools, and private schools are always willing to give tours and answer questions. Many communities also have home-schooling organizations that can arrange for you to meet with families who are pursuing this option.

When you check out schools, ask questions like these:

- How much of your grading is based on a student's verbal performance? How much is based on a student's performance on tests, homework, and classroom assignments?

- How often do students work in teams, and how often do they work independently?

- Does your school offer some quiet time so introverted children can recharge their batteries?

- Do you have spaces where students can work alone?

- How do you protect students from bullying? (I talk more about this in the later section "Making sure your child's school has an anti-bullying plan.")

If you talk with home-school groups, ask questions like these:

- What advantages do you think home-schooling offers for introverted children? What disadvantages does it have?

- What opportunities does your child have to socialize with other children?

Take your child along on your visits, and let her ask questions herself. Afterward, ask her what she thought about each setting. Innies are very observant and often wise, so even a young introvert is likely to have good ideas about the right school setting for her.

## School and the gifted innie

As I noted in Chapter 1, 50 percent of gifted kids are introverts. And three-quarters of "super-gifted" kids — children with IQs above 160 — are innies.

You'd think these brilliant kids would flourish in school, but frequently, they don't. Instead, they may spend hours bored to tears as their teachers go over material they already know. They may also get into trouble for ignoring classroom assignments and pursuing their own interests instead. Worse yet, these children's remarkable talents often go undeveloped.

That's why smart parents often seek better options for them. If you think your introverted child is gifted, ask for a professional evaluation by a psychologist. If testing confirms your opinion, ask your school what services it offers for gifted children. Some schools have excellent programs for very bright children, while others fall far short.

If your child's current school can't fully meet her needs, explore other options. Some communities have magnet schools specifically designed for gifted children. Your child may also enjoy a math, science, or arts camp during the summer. And museums, nature centers, and recreation centers frequently offer programs that will excite your innie.

Additionally, consider supplementing your child's education with online courses on her favorite topics. Often, these courses allow students to learn at their own pace, so instead of twiddling her thumbs while she waits for her classmates to catch up, your child can go full steam ahead. The Khan Academy (www.khanacademy.org) and other free online educational sites can also be great resources.

If your child is far more advanced than other kids her age, her school may suggest moving her up an extra grade. But be aware that gifted innies who are way ahead of the pack intellectually may still need to be around same-age peers to learn social skills. So if this option comes up, consider your child's overall social and intellectual development and ask yourself if she's truly ready to study — and play — with older children.

Another issue to keep in mind is that the higher a child's IQ is, the greater the chances are that the child will also have a learning disability. If your child is gifted but still struggles in some areas, make sure you explore this possibility.

# Protecting Your Child from Bullies

Introverted kids are often the victims of bullies. Bullying is a serious issue, because bullied kids can become depressed, anxious, fearful, or even suicidal. In the following sections, I show you steps you can take to help protect your child against this all-too-common childhood threat.

## Making sure your child's school has an anti-bullying plan

These days, most schools are aware that bullying is a huge problem, and they have programs in place to protect students. Make sure your own child's school has an anti-bullying program, and ask to see the details. Here are elements of an effective school anti-bullying program:

- ✔ **It starts with an assessment of the problem.** Often, schools are shocked to find out that they have a much bigger bullying problem than they thought. Accurate information can help them plan an effective response.

- ✔ **It's an ongoing, multifaceted program.** The more ways a school spreads the anti-bullying message, the more effective it will be. So having an occasional assembly isn't enough. Instead, your child's school should plan a variety of activities, including assemblies, classroom activities, newsletter articles, and parent meetings.

- ✔ **It includes teacher and parent training.** Caring adults want to protect kids against bullying, but often they don't know how. A good school program will offer training from experts.

- ✔ **It's zero-tolerance.** The best way to reduce bullying to a minimum is to punish it every time it occurs. Schools need to lay out specific policies about the behavior they will and won't tolerate and spell out the consequences of breaking their anti-bullying rules. Then they need to apply those consequences in every case.

- ✔ **It includes a safe system for reporting bullies.** Kids who are being bullied need a way to talk to teachers or other school professionals privately and confidentially, so they don't need to fear repercussions.

- ✔ **It includes visual monitoring.** Schools should identify bullying "danger zones" — such as bathrooms and isolated playground areas — and place staff members there to keep an eye on things.

- ✔ **It includes student leadership.** Schools should establish student-led committees to tackle the problem of bullying. Often, these committees can come up with more realistic solutions than adults can.

If you decide to work with your child's school to create an anti-bullying program, an excellent free resource is `www.bullying.gov`.

## Teaching your child ways to handle bullies

No matter how good your school's anti-bullying program is, it won't stop every bully. So as a parent, you need to take steps to help your child defend herself if a bully comes after her. The following sections explain ways to do so.

## *Communicate with your child*

The most important action you can take is to open the lines of communication between you and your child.

✔ **Encourage your child to talk to you or her teacher if she's being bullied.** Kids are often ashamed to tell a teacher or a parent if they're a victim of a bully. Make sure your child knows that it's important to talk to an adult in this situation.

✔ **Do some probing.** Even if you talk with your child about bullying, she may still be reluctant to open up to you if she's being bullied. One good trick is to approach the topic indirectly with questions like these:

   • What's it like to ride the school bus? How do the kids act at the bus stop? (You can substitute the lunchroom or the playground here.)

   • What do you like most about school? What do you like least?

   • Who are some of the nicest kids in your school? Who are some of the meanest kids? What do the mean kids do?

   • Which kids are the most likely to be bullies at your school — the girls or the boys? What kinds of things do they do to bully other kids?

If your child does reveal that she's being victimized by a bully, contact the school immediately. If the bullying is severe enough, consider contacting the police as well.

By the way, don't blame yourself if your child becomes the target of a bully. Kids tend to pick on introverted peers in particular, and protecting your child 24/7 isn't possible.

## *Teach assertive communication*

The good news is that you can teach your child some skills that can help make her "bully-proof." Of course, you'll need to intervene when serious bullying occurs, but it's also critical for your child to learn to stand up for herself.

One of the most important skills you can teach your child is assertive communication. It's not enough to say "stand up for yourself," because most kids (especially innies) won't know how to do that. Instead, offer specific instructions.

I saw a great demonstration of assertive communication early in my career. I'd gone to a party in the park with some colleagues, including a social worker named Marcus. As we were talking, a little boy ran past crying.

Marcus stopped the boy and said, "Bobby, what's wrong?" Bobby replied, "Those kids took my ball away and started teasing me and hitting me with it."

Marcus replied, "That's not right. And this is what you're going to do. Go back, stand about six feet away from them, and tell them: 'This is my ball. I'm more than willing to let you play with it, but you need to ask my permission.

You have no right to throw things at me or say mean things to me. And if you continue to do it, I will tell an adult.'"

Marcus had Bobby repeat this speech back to him a couple of times until he had it down pat. Then he sent Bobby off, saying, "I'll watch, but you have to stand up for yourself." And Bobby did. The other kids were so surprised that they gave the ball back and went away.

This same approach can be effective in many bullying situations. So have your child practice variations of this conversation until you sense that she's confident enough to stick up for herself verbally.

Also, help your child become more bully-proof by focusing on these areas:

- ✔ **Have her practice confident body language.** Kids who get bullied often respond by developing defensive body language. They keep their eyes on the ground, hunch their shoulders, and try to make themselves invisible. The result, unfortunately, is that they look even more like prey.

  So help your child develop assertive body language. Have her practice standing up straight, walking confidently, looking people in the eye, and holding her arms at her sides rather than crossed in front of her. If she's old enough to drive, teach her to carry her car keys threaded through her fingers as she walks to her car.

  If she has difficulty with her body language, ask her to think of her favorite assertive movie character and move like that person. (For additional tips on assertive body language, see Chapter 3.)

- ✔ **Help her find ways to stay out of a bully's way.** Ask your child if she can take a route that avoids the bully's favorite zones. If the bully is attacking her and taking her lunch money, try sending in a homemade lunch. And if a bully is going after her at the bus stop in the morning, drive her to school for a while.

- ✔ **See if she can team up with other children.** Bullies prefer to attack kids who are alone, so see if your child can find several buddies to hook up with when she's walking around school.

- ✔ **Help her avoid cyber-bullying.** Cyber-bullying is one of the most dangerous forms of bullying because it can humiliate a child in front of an entire school. To help protect against it, teach your child the basic rules of Internet safety. Also tell her to inform you immediately if someone posts negative or embarrassing information about her, so you can take action quickly. Depending on how serious the cyber-bullying is, your actions can include anything from talking with the other child's parents, to contacting the school, to calling the police.

If your child undergoes a very traumatic bullying incident, consider getting psychological counseling for her. Introverted kids may ruminate over being bullied or even blame themselves. Therapy can help them get past these negative thoughts and focus on the good things in their lives.

# Part V
# The Part of Tens

the part of tens

Enjoy an additional Part of Tens chapter online at
www.dummies.com/extras/successasanintrovert.

# In this part . . .

✔ Get to know some famous introverts, from scholars to actors and comics to presidents.

✔ Discover ways to network effectively as an introvert.

✔ Find out ten things you should never say to introverts.

✔ Make your workplace more friendly for introverts.

# Chapter 16

# Ten Notable Innies

*In This Chapter*

▶ Introducing famous innie scholars

▶ Recognizing noted innie actors and comics

▶ Acknowledging introverted presidents

*A*lthough innies gain energy from their inner world, that doesn't stop them from making their mark on the outside world as well. In fact, you'll find famous introverts in every walk of life. In this chapter, you meet ten well-known innies who've done everything from winning Oscars to walking on the moon.

Now, if you're an extrovert, some of the people included in this chapter will surprise you, and I hope they do! People often equate *introverted* with *quiet, shy,* or *overly analytical*. But in reality, introverts come in a lot of different styles, shapes, and sizes, as you find out in the following pages.

## Charles Darwin

This quiet scientist wasn't at all frightened by the giant tortoises and other strange creatures he met on the Galápagos Islands. No, what scared the heck out of him were the meetings and social events he had to attend when he got back to England.

Like many introverts, Darwin hated the limelight but sparkled when it came to being a family man. One of his daughters wrote, "To all of us, he was the most delightful play-fellow." His favorite pastime was lying on the sofa while his wife, Emma, read Jane Austen's novels to him.

Speaking of his wife, Darwin didn't just get down on bended knee and propose to her on a whim one day. Instead, he drew up a list with columns headed "Marry" and "Not Marry." In the pro-marriage column, he listed, "constant companion and a friend in old age . . . better than a dog anyhow." And in the con side? He wrote "less money for books" and "terrible loss of time." I promise you, an extroverted person wouldn't make a list like this!

Darwin was a deep thinker, able to think for hours about complex ideas. As a child, he once was so deep in thought that he walked right off an 8-foot-high wall. And his favorite hobbies? Reading, fishing, and hiking — an innie trifecta.

## Neil Armstrong

To Americans, he was a larger-than-life hero, the astronaut who made history with one giant leap for mankind. But on Earth, Neil Armstrong was a true-blue innie who hated the attention that followed his epic journey.

It's not that he was shy; in fact, the people who knew him said he was a gifted public speaker and could easily hold his own in a conversation. Instead, they describe him as humble and private to a fault. Because of his intense desire for privacy, he turned down almost all requests for interviews and deliberately removed himself from the limelight after his obligatory welcome-home tour.

Also, like any introvert, Armstrong tended to think deeply about everything, from engineering to golf. At his funeral, Treasury Secretary John Snow, one of his golfing buddies, said, "You'd wait for him to putt. He'd survey the line to the hole. He'd measure the dew on the green. You sometimes wondered, 'Neil, are you ever going to hit the ball?'" This ability to keep others waiting while deeply analyzing a situation is a true hallmark of introverts, as the extroverts who have to wait for them can tell you!

## Elizabeth Barrett Browning

Back in the 1800s, people on both sides of the Atlantic Ocean swooned over this poet's beautiful love sonnets, but Elizabeth hardly ever met any of her doting fans in person. Instead, she spent most of her time at her desk in her bedroom at her family's home, writing poems.

Although Elizabeth didn't seek out her fans, they sought her out. One of them was extroverted poet Robert Browning, who wrote, "I love your verses with all my heart, dear Miss Barrett. I do, as I say, love these books with all my heart — and I love you, too." A cousin of Elizabeth's arranged for Robert to meet her at her home, and sparks flew between the brilliant innie and the worldly outie.

Over the next two years, Robert and Elizabeth wrote more than 500 letters to each other, and she dedicated one of her most famous works, *Sonnets from the Portuguese,* to him. Hiding their relationship from her tyrannical father, they courted and married secretly; afterward, Robert whisked her off to Italy, where they lived happily ever after. Who says innies and outies can't make beautiful music (or poetry) together?

# Johnny Depp

We think of Hollywood megastars as over-the-top outies, racing wildly from party to party. But Johnny Depp has a very different reputation in Tinseltown.

Depp's friends and fellow celebs say he's a family man who loves hanging out at home with his kids. He also does tons of research for each role (a very innie behavior). What's more, he thinks before he talks, which most introverted celebrities do. Watch him in an interview, and you'll see that he ponders each question carefully before answering.

Want more evidence that everyone's favorite big-screen pirate is an innie? Back when he was still living in France, the actor — twice named *People* magazine's sexiest man alive — sometimes didn't leave his home for months at a time.

And this will resonate with you if you're an innie: When Johnny Depp buys a property, he typically looks for a lot that's more than 30 acres in size, because that's about how far away a *real* introvert wants his neighbors to be!

# Eddie Murphy

This *Beverly Hills Cop* star is such a rare sight at Hollywood parties that Barbara Walters once accused him of being a recluse. Not true, he says. Instead, he describes himself as a misunderstood introvert who loves hanging out at home. (And if you take a peek at some of his homes on the Internet, you can certainly see why.)

Also, although he's wild and crazy in his standup comedy routines, Murphy is a deep thinker (a classic innie trait) when he leaves the stage. In his rare interviews, he's as likely to talk about the future of the world as he is to discuss the movie biz.

# Johnny Carson

For three decades, Americans tuned in every night to watch Johnny Carson on the *Tonight Show*. To his audience, he felt like part of the family, the kind of guy who'd be everybody's buddy.

But that was Carson's public face, not his private one. In real life, he was a quiet innie who politely tried to avoid his fans. He didn't like parties either, and he'd duck out as quickly as possible. He was all business on the set, and he usually turned down offers to go out on the town with his celebrity guests after the show.

Carson described himself as a "loner," and his friends said he was happiest when he was at home. And ironically, the man who interviewed the world's most famous people hated being interviewed himself. He once joked, "I will not even talk to myself without an appointment."

# Jerry Seinfeld

Watch Jerry Seinfeld on stage, performing in front of thousands of people, and you may think he's an extrovert. And, in fact, he told Oprah Winfrey that he *is* an extrovert — but only while he's in the spotlight.

Seinfeld told Oprah, "I love people, but I can't talk to them. Onstage, I can." But even then, his trademark style is to toss out observations drawn from his rich, innie-style analytical skills.

You can really see Seinfeld's introverted nature in his early stage routines. They almost always focused on life's oddities and strange situations that people find themselves in — an analytical approach to humor that's very common for introverts. Over time, with lots of practice, he's become more ambiverted as a performer, but it's clear that he's an innie by nature.

And although he's one of the world's most popular people now, Seinfeld didn't hang out with the "in" crowd in school because he didn't feel comfortable around them. Instead, he spent most of his free time in front of the TV, analyzing other comedians' routines and perfecting his own.

All that hard work eventually led to *Seinfeld,* which *TV Guide* named the greatest television show of all time. And that just goes to show that an innie's serious nature can pay off big-time!

# Tom Smith

Are you a movie buff? If so, this man's name will probably ring a bell. That's because Hollywood told his story in the popular movie *Seabiscuit.*

Smith, who trained the legendary racehorse Seabiscuit, was the ultimate introvert. He sometimes slept in the stables with his horses, he often ate meals alone, and he rarely spoke more than a few words to the people around him. The Native Americans who knew him nicknamed him the "Lone Plainsman," and his coworkers called him "Silent Tom."

But put Tom Smith together with a horse, and magic happened. He was a true horse whisperer, with an uncanny ability to get into the minds and hearts of his equine friends. The man who could barely say ten words to other people said, "It's easy to talk to a horse if you understand his language." He sometimes sat for hours, not moving, as he watched his horses to figure out just what they needed from him. In return, they trusted him, and they ran their hearts out for him.

Smith's innie radar also allowed him to spot the winning potential in the least likely of horses, including Seabiscuit — a runty, lazy, goofy-gaited horse that everyone else thought was hopeless. Smith always knew just what Seabiscuit needed: a jockey with a gentle hand on the whip, an extra-long morning nap, even some animal friends (including a dog and a monkey). As a result, the two of them made racing history together, with Seabiscuit hogging the winner's circle year after year and Tom Smith happily and quietly watching in the shadows.

By the way, I include Tom Smith in my illustrious ten because he illustrates that introverts frequently are keen and brilliant observers of their world. They're passionate about what they see "out there," and they can pull this information inward and analyze it in depth. As a result, they can come up with truly innovative ideas and inventions that no one else thinks of.

# Calvin Coolidge

When Americans nicknamed this president "Silent Cal," they weren't kidding. Unlike today's politicians, who can't seem to shut up, Coolidge was a dyed-in-the-wool innie who despised small talk.

Strong introverts sometimes flout proper social conventions, and Cal was no exception. At a dinner party one night, a guest told him that she'd bet a friend that she could get him to say more than two words to her. Coolidge turned to her and said, "You lose."

Rumor also has it that Coolidge said, "Don't you know that four-fifths of all our troubles in this life would disappear if we would just sit down and keep still?" And here's another quote from Cal that innies can identify with: "The things I don't say never get me into trouble."

# *Abraham Lincoln*

Honest Abe was a charismatic speaker who was totally at ease at social events — in fact, people hung on his words at dinner parties — but he was just as happy spending hours with his nose stuck in a book. One of his best friends, Joshua F. Speed, commented that "Mr. Lincoln was a social man, though he did not seek company; it sought him."

As an adult, Lincoln may have been an ambivert (one of those people in the middle of the innie-outie scale). However, as a young boy, he was a classic innie. He'd walk miles just to borrow a book, and people remembered him as "very quiet," "solemn," and "interested in everything." Occasionally, he'd get so wrapped up in his thoughts that people wondered if he was having "spells."

In his young adult years, Abe devoured books on everything from philosophy to astronomy. One acquaintance said, "He read sitting, lying down, and walking in the streets. He was always reading if he had time." As a result, even though he had almost no schooling as a child, he became legendary for his vast knowledge and his brilliant debating skills.

As president, Lincoln gained a reputation for being a deep thinker who made decisions only after weighing the views of people on all sides. And he didn't hesitate to make an unpopular decision when he felt it was the right one, which is why he issued the Emancipation Proclamation even though it alienated many of his strongest supporters.

# Chapter 17

# Ten Tips for Making a Networking Event Work for You

*In This Chapter*

▶ Preparing before you go

▶ Making connections at an event

▶ Following up afterward

**A**re you hunting for a job, moving up the career ladder, or running your own business? If so, networking events are a great way to get ahead. But . . . *ugh*. Can you think of a worse way to spend an evening?

In reality, face-to-face networking will never be a joy for you as an innie. (Surprisingly, even some extroverts hate it.) As a result, you're likely to gravitate toward online networking. And that's fine, because it's a great approach. But meeting people in person is still one of the most powerful ways to make influential connections.

The good news is that there are ways to make networking get-togethers less painful and far more effective. In this chapter, I offer ten of my best tips.

## Be Picky

After you get your nerve up and decide to start networking, you may be tempted to hit as many events as you can. But if you're an introvert, that's probably not the best approach. If you overstretch yourself, you may burn out quickly and give up entirely on your networking plan.

Instead, consider attending one or two networking events each month. To get the most bang for your buck, use your innie research skills to identify the events that are likely to be the most useful to you. As you consider each option, ponder questions like these:

 ✔ What reputation does this group have?

 ✔ Is this group specific enough to meet my needs?

 ✔ Is this a one-time event, or will I have the opportunity to meet with these people again?

 ✔ Does this group seem to be in sync with my goals and personality?

 Often, social networks can be a great source of information about networking events. Go online and see what other people think about each event's sponsors. Ask how useful the events were and whether people plan to attend future events.

# Do Your Homework

Walking into a roomful of strangers is always tough for an introvert. But the more you know about what you're getting into, the more comfortable you'll be.

So before you attend a networking event, go online or call the hosts and see how many details you can find out about it. For example, ask these questions:

 ✔ How many people are likely to be attending?

 ✔ Does the event have a theme?

 ✔ Will people just mingle, or will there be talks or other activities?

 ✔ Will you be asked to stand up in front of the group and introduce yourself?

Also, see whether you can find out a little about the location of the event. Look for photos online, or even visit the site ahead of time. Then visualize yourself successfully networking in the room where the event will occur. (For tips on visualizing success, see Chapter 7.)

Finally, ask whether the event is formal (suit and tie) or casual. If you can't find out, err on the side of being too formal.

# Set SMART Goals for Each Event

In Chapter 9, I talk about SMART goals. These goals are *specific, measurable, actionable, relevant,* and *timely.*

When you're preparing to attend a networking event, set one or two SMART goals for yourself. That way, you'll avoid the trap of expecting too much or too little from yourself.

Here's an example of a SMART goal for a networking event: "I will attend this event for at least two hours and talk with at least seven people." Make sure your goal is a little bit of a stretch, but don't make it too hard or you'll set yourself up for failure.

Also, be careful to avoid creating goals that may involve factors you can't control. For example, avoid goals like "I will have fun" or "I will make five useful contacts." Instead, focus on your own actions and behavior.

# Think about Trout Fishing (Really!)

Here's a simple way to get in the right frame of mind before a networking event: Compare it to a fishing trip.

If you go fishing, do you expect to catch a fish every time you throw in your line? Nope. In fact, some days you may not catch any fish at all. But it doesn't matter — because you know that if you keep trying, you'll eventually come home with some nice trout for dinner. And each time you go fishing, you'll get a little better at it.

Well, networking is a lot like fishing. One day, you may get only one or two nibbles. Another day, you may come away completely empty-handed. But keep trying, and sooner or later you're going to score some big contacts. In the process, you'll find that networking — although you'll probably never enjoy it — keeps getting easier and easier.

So be philosophical if some networking events turn out to be duds. Just keep throwing in your line, and eventually you'll hook some great catches.

# Arrive Early

Introverts usually don't like being the first people to arrive at events. But in this case, showing up early can be a very smart move. That's because it's easier to meet people as they come in one by one than it is to arrive when everyone's already in a group and you have to elbow your way in.

If you do arrive early, break the ice with other guests as they come in. For instance, say, "Hi! It looks like we're the early birds." Then see if you can turn your greeting into a conversation.

# Focus on One Person at a Time

As an introvert, you can sparkle when you're talking one on one. However, you probably find it difficult to break into a crowd. So at networking events, look for a fellow introvert who's on his own and strike up a conversation with him. (For ideas on conversation starters, see my pretend-extrovert tricks in Chapter 3.)

When you hit it off with one person, look for a way to expand your group. For example, say something like, "That guy over there looks like he's hoping for some company; shall we go join him?"

# Grab a Plate

If you hate standing alone looking ill-at-ease, here's a solution: Get in line! If you're lucky, you can strike up a conversation while you're standing in the queue for food or drinks. And if your attempts at small talk fall flat, it's easy to escape as soon as your plate is full.

When you get in a line, try to time your move just right. One good bet is to slide in right behind someone who's alone and looks a little shy or awkward. Odds are, this person will be truly grateful if you make the first conversational move — and if you're lucky, you'll make an instant friend.

It's pretty simple to start the conversational ball rolling when you're in a queue. Just turn to the person next to you and ask, "Have you ever been to one of these events before?" After you exchange a few sentences about the event, take the initiative and introduce yourself. Also tell the other person a little about yourself, such as what company or part of town you're from.

After that, talk about what you're hoping to get out of the event. But don't talk about referrals. Instead, say something like, "I want to hear this speaker because people say he's fantastic."

If you're attending an event with a guest speaker, research the speaker ahead of time on the Internet. If the person has written a book, read it if you have a chance. This will give you a ready-made topic.

After your conversation is rolling along, you can offer a business card. Many people do this upfront, but it's better to make a little small talk first to show that you're interested in getting to know the other person and not just in getting referrals. However, you can break this rule if you're in line or wandering around an event and overhear someone talking about a problem you know you can help solve — not to benefit yourself, but just out of the goodness of your heart. In this case, handing out a card right away and explaining how you can lend a hand is perfectly acceptable.

# Manage Your Leads

As an introvert, you have to step way outside of your comfort zone to make new contacts at a networking event. So don't let those contacts go to waste!

Make sure you keep track of all the business cards you receive at an event. Here's a tip an entertainment lawyer shared with me to help stay organized: Wear a jacket with two pockets. In the right pocket, put your cards to hand out; in the left, put the cards you collect.

When you get home from an event, your head will be swirling with facts about the people you met. To make sure you remember all this information, write it down right away. Use a database, an old-fashioned rolodex, or any system that works well for you. Include the following information:

- **Is this person likely to be a valuable contact?** Make a note to follow up quickly on your strongest leads. (But hang on to all the cards you collect, because you never know.)

- **Is there some way you can help this person?** The ultimate goal of networking is to create a support group of people who pitch in and help each other. If you can make the first move, you'll take a big step toward achieving that goal.

- **What does the person do for a living?** Make notes about where the person works, what her title is, and how long she's been there.

- **Did the person offer you any details about her personal life?** For example, did she talk about her family, her hobbies, or any charities she's involved in? If so, she'll be impressed if you remember this information later.

Also, write down the date and location of the event where you met the person. If you get together again later, write down the date and location of each meeting.

 By the way, it's much easier to remember information about people if you make notes on their business cards while you're at an event. But be cautious, because although writing on business cards is considered perfectly polite in the United States, it's seen as rude in some other cultures.

# Be the One Who Reaches Out

I know, I know — this one totally goes against your innie grain! But it's smart to make the first move when it comes to following up on the contacts you make at networking events.

Here are some good ways to cement the bonds you've started building:

✔ Follow up on your best prospects within 48 hours by sending an e-mail, making a call, or getting in touch via a social networking site.

✔ If you've identified a way in which you can help the person, offer your aid — even if there's no immediate benefit to you.

✔ Offer to introduce the person to other people who can strengthen her network.

After you form a relationship, touch base with the person every few months — even if it's just to say hi. Many people make the mistake of ignoring their networks until they're desperate, which sends the message, "You don't really matter to me." It's far better to keep your ties strong.

# Say Thanks

If you get a lead from someone at a networking event, follow up very quickly — and whether or not the lead pans out, call or write your networking buddy to say thanks. It's especially important to express your gratitude if a lead turns out to be amazing.

And say thanks in active ways as well. If someone gives you a lead, stay extra-alert for clients or business opportunities you can send that person's way. Doing so is critical, because it's ultimately how you'll get more referrals through your network.

When you're sending leads to your networking buddies, don't worry if they don't send tons of leads your way in return. Focus on giving, and you'll get a big payoff somewhere along the line. (One exception: If you feel that people are taking advantage of you, check out Chapter 11 for tips on determining whether a relationship is healthy.)

# Chapter 18

# Ten Things an Introvert Doesn't Want to Hear

*In This Chapter*
▶ Knowing why some comments alarm innies
▶ Coming up with helpful alternatives

$I$f you're an extrovert who hangs out with introverts, you probably try very hard to be innie-friendly. But sometimes it's tricky, because the most innocent things you say can sometimes make them frown or even look at you in terror.

To offer some insight into the innie mindset, here's a list of nice or seemingly harmless things that extroverted people often say to innies — along with the reasons they can backfire. In addition, I offer some alternatives that will keep your introvert smiling.

## *"We were just in the neighborhood and thought we'd drop in."*

Extroverts usually don't mind unexpected company. But introverts do!

Innies see their homes as safe havens where they can escape from people and recharge their batteries alone or with their families. That doesn't mean that they hate guests. However, they want to be forewarned if visitors are coming. And innies don't like sudden changes in plans. If you ambush them when they're looking forward to a cozy dinner or a quiet evening reading a book, they'll put on a brave face — but underneath, they'll be miserable.

So if a quick look of horror passes over the face of your innie friend when you make an unannounced visit, don't be surprised. In fact, don't be surprised if your innie friend doesn't open the door at all. She's probably lurking right behind it, staring through the peephole and trying to be totally quiet so you won't know she's there.

A better idea than dropping in on an innie unannounced is to text or call ahead and ask if you can drop by. Of course, if you call, you may need to leave your message by voicemail because innies aren't all that keen on unexpected phone calls, either! (I talk more about that later in this chapter.) But your message will give your innie friend time to prepare for your visit or to come up with a kind reason to say no.

# "Turn to the person next to you and introduce yourself."

This is a favorite activity at company orientations or conferences. The idea is to break the ice quickly and make everyone feel comfortable. And it works beautifully for extroverts, but not for introverts.

Why? Because innies don't like making small talk with strangers. They hate big get-togethers to begin with, so they're probably already on edge. Expecting them to form an instant friendship with someone they've never met can cause them to shut down completely.

The innies in your group event will be even more distressed if you ask them to reveal something very personal about themselves. For instance, one innie friend of mine went to a team-building activity where the facilitator asked participants to take chocolate bars from baskets at the side of the room. "So far, so good!" my friend thought. But then the facilitator smiled brightly and said, "If you took a bar from the first basket, I want you to tell the person next to you about a scary time in your life. If you took a bar from the second basket, I want you to tell the person next to you about a time you were proud. And if you took a bar from the third basket, I want you to tell the person next to you about the people you're grateful to."

My friend muddled through somehow, but she said, "If I'd known what the facilitator's game was, I would've said, 'Oh, I'm so sorry, I'm allergic to chocolate, and I can't even be in the same room with it.'"

What's a better approach if you want to make innies and outies bond as a team? One idea is to take your group to a sporting event. The outies will love cheering for their team and chatting with their coworkers. And the innies will appreciate the opportunity to warm up to their colleagues at their own speed, while everyone's attention focuses on the game and not on them.

Another nice idea is to host a potluck or cook-off. Again, there's plenty of opportunity for your outies to converse — and you're drawing everyone's eyes to the food, not to your introverts.

# "Guess what — I told the waiter it's your birthday!"

It's so festive when a parade of beaming waiters comes to your table with a little cake and sings "Happy Birthday," isn't it?

If you're an extrovert, the answer is yes. But think of it from an innie's point of view. There she is, happily enjoying a little party with a few friends, when — blammo! — suddenly, all the other diners are staring at her. She has to sit there awkwardly and paste on a fake smile, when in reality she's thinking really, really evil thoughts about you.

Want to give your innie friends a better treat when you take them out for a birthday lunch? Order slices of cake for everyone at your table, but ask the waiter to simply put them on the table, quietly say "Happy birthday from your friend," and leave.

# "We're having so much fun; can we stay with you a few more days?"

I think it was Benjamin Franklin who said that fish and visitors stink after three days. Well, subtract a day or so if you're staying at an introvert's house! But here's a secret: If an introvert knows ahead of time that you'll be staying for three or four days (or even a week), he can prepare himself. As a result, he'll probably be ready to enjoy your visit. However, he's also going to be looking forward to the day you leave. Don't take it personally; it's just how innies are.

So make sure your introverted friend knows your exact timetable, and don't change plans on him. If you decide that your stay was too short, plan to add a day to your next visit — not to this one.

And here's another tip for those times when you're visiting innie friends who live out of town. If you can afford it, spend all or part of your visit in a hotel. Doing so will give you hours and hours to visit with your buddy, and it will give him some private time to recuperate. If you can't afford that, at least plan some expeditions you can take on your own, so your friend can recharge his batteries while you're off exploring.

# "Oh, I just thought of one more great story. . . ."

Imagine that you're at a gathering hosted by an innie friend. The party is heading into its final hour, and most of the guests have already left. Finally, you decide it's time to pack up and go home yourself. But just as you get to the front door, you suddenly think of a terrific story you've been dying to tell. So you stop in the doorway, turn back to the other remaining guests, and say, "Oh, I just have to share this before I go. . . ."

If you're observant, you'll immediately see a deer-in-the-headlights look flash across your innie friend's face. That's because she loves you, she's glad you came, and she hopes you had fun, but right now, she needs you to go. Really. Just go. Even if your incredible story involves winning the Nobel Prize or encountering aliens from Mars, she just doesn't care. At this point, all she wants is for the last few stragglers to leave so she can collapse.

Worse yet, she knows a horrible truth: One story begets another. Your story is guaranteed to lead another guest to say "That reminds me of . . . ," and that will lead to another half-hour of conversation, just when she thought she was nearly free.

So frustrating as it may be, save your story for later. Your friend will enjoy it much more when she's rested and recharged, so don't waste it now when her battery is dead.

# "Surprise!"

Most extroverts simply love surprise parties. When people suddenly leap out from behind the sofa with party horns and confetti, outies typically shriek with joy.

Innies will shriek as well. But in their case, it's a shriek of terror.

Why? Because innies aren't all that big on surprises in general. Their nervous systems are already on higher alert than an outie's, so they don't take well to sudden jolts, even if it's all in the name of fun. That's why most innies also don't care much for practical jokes (and especially pranks that make them look foolish in public).

So is it ever okay to surprise an introvert? Sure, but do it gently. For instance, send flowers when your innie friend won't be expecting them, or surprise an innie football fan with tickets to a big game. Just don't leap out from behind the sofa when you do it.

# "Give your Aunt Ruth a big hug."

Here's a no-no to avoid if you're parenting very young innies. Hardly any kids like getting pawed or kissed by strangers, but innie kids really hate it. And it frequently happens at big events like Thanksgiving, when they're already on the verge of a meltdown.

So it's not surprising that this request sometimes results in a grimace, tears, or even a full-fledged tantrum. That can put a real crimp in your party, and it's hardly going to win Aunt Ruth's heart.

Luckily, there are better ways to introduce your tot to an adult. One is to say something like, "This is Janie. She's the artist in our family. Let me show you some of her paintings on the refrigerator." This way, Aunt Ruth can ooh and ah over the pictures, your little one can feel proud and maybe even a little warm and fuzzy toward her, and nobody has to get hugged.

Another trick is to say something like this: "Aunt Ruth, this is Janie. I'll bet she'd like to show you her new doll. Janie, can you get your dolly?" Typically, innie kids are less likely to balk at showing off a toy than they are at giving a hug.

It's also a good idea to tell your child a little about each of the guests before the big day. If possible, show your tyke photos of each person as well. You can say something nice or interesting about each guest, such as "Aunt Ruth has five kitties, and they all have six toes on each foot!" This way, the visitors will seem a little less intimidating.

# "You're so quiet; what's wrong?"

This comment definitely makes the top-ten list of introverts' pet peeves. Why? Because 99 times out of 100, nothing is wrong at all. Innies just like to think quietly, and when they do, they often tend to have solemn expressions on their faces.

Now, I agree that it's totally unfair to blame you for misinterpreting what you're seeing. After all, when extroverted people look somber, they usually *feel* somber as well. So if you're expecting outie rules to apply to innies, it's easy to get the wrong message.

Luckily, it's easy to avoid irking innies in this situation. If you see your introvert looking pensive, just say "hi" and wait for her to clue you in about how she feels. No matter what mood your innie is in — good or bad — this approach is safe.

# "Yay! Our class reunion is coming up!"

If you're an outie, you probably love reunions. You can't wait to see your old flames and best buddies, and you're brimming over with questions: Is the hot quarterback still gorgeous? Did Todd and Linda ever get married? And will my old classmates be jealous when they see the terrific partner I landed?

However, these happy scenarios don't go through your innie friends' minds when they get invitations to reunions. Typically, innies form only a few very close friendships in high school or college. So for them, a school reunion is a gigantic party filled with people who are mostly strangers. And you know how innies feel about parties — and how they feel about strangers. So even if they do go to the reunion, they'll usually just hang out on the outskirts with a couple of people they know well.

Innies are even less likely to want to attend a class reunion now that it's easy to hook up with old friends on social networking sites like Facebook. When they meet up with former classmates online, they can catch up without actually showing up. And they can reveal as much or as little as they like, which makes them very happy.

So be understanding if your innie friend or partner wants to skip his own reunion. And if you strong-arm him into going to yours, let him take his own car so he can sneak out early.

# "I'm so glad you returned my call; we have a lot to catch up on."

For extroverts, the phone is an emotional lifeline. When outies can't be around people in person, they can still recharge their batteries by calling their friends. Often, they'll spend hours every day on the phone, and enjoy every minute of it.

Introverts, however, have a love-hate relationship with their phones. They're happy to chat for a few minutes (and I do mean a few) with a buddy or coworker, but a long phone call can exhaust them, just like a long conversation at a party.

This truth sometimes creates a problem for innie-outie friend pairs. If the outie loves to talk for an hour on the phone, but the innie's limit is about 15 minutes, then the innie may start avoiding the calls. And this can lead to hurt feelings on the outie's part.

To avoid this problem, try to get a feel for an innie friend's phone limits. You'll probably notice that at some point, she gets less talkative and less vivacious. When that happens, wrap up your call quickly. If you still have more that you want to say, call a day later — or better yet, send a text message or an e-mail.

# Chapter 19

# Ten Ways to Make a Workplace Innie-Friendly

*In This Chapter*

▶ Rearranging your space

▶ Rethinking your meetings

▶ Letting introverts work in their own way

▶ Cultivating an interview style that works for innies

*I*f you run a department or an entire company, you want to get the most from your workers, and you want them to be happy, too. Chances are a large number of your employees are introverts who find it challenging to deal with herds of coworkers, constant chatter, and high noise levels. So doesn't it make sense to design an office that meets their needs as well as those of extroverts? Yes, indeed — and in this chapter, I offer ten tips for doing just that.

## Let Innies Migrate to the Edges of Your Office

For a privacy-loving introvert, being in the center of a cube farm feels a bit like being on display at the zoo. Innies have difficulty concentrating when they're surrounded by other people, and the chaos may give them "brain fuzz," headaches, or stomachaches.

So if your cube assignments are flexible, consider asking your workers — both innie and outie — how they feel about their current locations. Although you won't be able to satisfy everyone's needs, some action-loving extroverts may be delighted to trade spots with quiet-craving introverts, creating a win-win situation.

# Cut Down on Meetings

Everyone grumbles about meetings, but your introverts in particular hate them with a passion. In fact, they think that many of the meetings they attend are nothing but nuisances that cut into their productive work time.

Are your innies right to resent a meeting-heavy schedule? Consider this: A few years ago, a couple of researchers decided to explore how workers felt about meetings. They asked 37 volunteers to keep diaries for 5 workdays. They also surveyed the volunteers after each meeting and at the end of each day.

The researchers discovered that the employees considered meetings to be "hassles" and "interruptions." Worse yet, a heavy schedule of meetings led workers to feel more fatigued and to sense that their workload was heavier. And here's something else: The job satisfaction of goal-oriented workers dropped as the number of meetings they attended rose. But people who didn't care as much about meeting their goals tended to enjoy meetings.

So introverts have some strong facts on their side. A jam-packed meeting schedule may keep your top performers from doing their best while giving your goof-offs an excuse to avoid doing productive work.

What's the answer? Take a hard look at your meetings and decide whether some of them are unnecessary. If so, eliminate them. Your top performers — and especially the introverted ones — will thank you for it!

# Make Your Meetings Better

Even if you slash unneeded meetings, you'll still need to get together with your team pretty often. Luckily, you can make these meetings a less painful experience for your introverts (and make them more useful for your extroverts).

In Chapter 5, I talk about having 15-minute stand-up meetings each morning. If you use this approach, be sure you have a small agenda and a consistent structure so everyone has some idea about what to expect.

A good technique for longer meetings, called the *parking lot approach,* helps you whittle down the length of your get-togethers. Here's how it works:

1. If you're leading a meeting, start by taping a large piece of paper on the wall. On the paper, write a heading like "Post-Meeting To-Do Topics."

2. As people bring up points they want to discuss, ask yourself whether these points are relevant to your group as a whole. If they aren't, let each person talk for a few minutes. Then paraphrase what the person is saying, like so: "If I hear you correctly, George, you're having trouble

with the new log-in system." Then say, "Let's get together and talk about that issue this afternoon." (Think of this step as *parking* the item for a later time.)

Write George's name and issue down on your sheet of paper. Keep doing so for any other topics people bring up that aren't of interest to the overall group.

3. At the end of your meeting, go back to your list. Often, the people who raised the issues you've listed will say, "Oh, I don't think we really need to talk about that after all." If a person still wants to meet, schedule a time to talk with her after the meeting.

This approach can often shave half an hour or more off a meeting, making your innies very happy. And it'll keep your extroverts on target as well, preventing them from getting bored and starting up conversations amongst themselves.

By the way, if you want to make sure a meeting ends on time, schedule it to start an hour or two before lunch. Typically, people will try to wrap things up quickly when they start getting hungry. Do reassure people that if they think of more ideas after the meeting, they can contact you later.

## Provide Privacy Screens

In the old days, most office workers had real offices with — gasp! — actual doors. When they needed to think, they could close those doors to shut out the hustle and bustle.

Of course, those days are long gone. However, you still can give people more privacy. Consider talking with your supplier about including cubicle screens for your cubes' entryways. It's a little pricy, but it'll pay off if it increases your introverted employees' productivity. If you can't afford to purchase cubicle screens for everyone, at least let workers buy their own. (See Chapter 4 for more on privacy issues in the workplace.)

## Ask about Acoustics

Introverts have an even greater need for quiet than extroverts. So if you have some money in your budget for office design, make your office more innie-friendly by meeting with an acoustics specialist. This expert can come up with ways to alter your floors, walls, cubicle panels, or ceilings so they'll absorb more sound.

Even if you're operating on a shoestring budget, a consultant may be able to help. In some cases, simply rearranging your existing furniture or adding sound-masking equipment can make a big difference for a small price tag.

## Create Private Zones

Office space is at a premium in most companies, but see whether you can find at least one small room to set aside for quiet contemplation. Toss in one or two tables and a few chairs, and let your employees use the room to make important phone calls, work on difficult projects, or just sit for a few minutes and clear their heads.

Be aware, too, that most employees hate discussing sensitive issues in public — and that's especially true for introverts. So if you need to share constructive feedback about a problem or discuss some other delicate topic, find a private place where no one else will overhear you. Also, avoid picking one consistent location for your touchy conversations. Otherwise, everyone will know when an employee is having problems.

For example, a while ago I consulted for a police department. Over the first few days, I kept overhearing comments about "the green room." Finally, I asked someone: "What is this green room?" She laughed and led me down a corridor to an ugly pea-green room with a conference table and a couple of chairs. She explained that if a supervisor needed to rake someone over the coals, the supervisor would say, "Could I meet you in the green room at such-and-such a time?" So everyone in the entire department knew that an invitation to the green room was a *very* bad thing.

I asked the department to repaint the room a nice shade of yellow and start using it for all sorts of meetings, from performance reviews to party-planning meetings. As a result, employees didn't need to do the "walk of shame" to the green room anymore.

If you have your own version of the "green room," I suggest using the same strategy to de-stigmatize it. All your employees, and especially the introverts, will be happier if you do.

## Give a Thumbs-Up to Headphones

Some managers think it's rude for workers to wear noise-canceling headphones, and many bosses think that people who listen to music on the job are less productive. As a result, quite a few companies nix the use of headphones in the office.

For introverts, however, headphones can often mean the difference between high anxiety and high productivity. So unless you need to ban headphones for safety reasons, consider making it your official policy to allow them. Also, allow employees to use white noise machines or fans (as long as they don't bother other workers).

# Let Your Workers Telecommute Part of the Time

More and more companies are letting their employees work from home one or two days a week. Doing so is especially helpful for introverted employees, because the quiet at home allows them to recharge their batteries. In fact, you'll often find that they get twice as much done when they're not in the office!

If you're worried about employees under-performing when they're not under your thumb, set very specific work goals for the days they're on their own. If they consistently meet or exceed those goals, you'll know that all is well.

# Offer Innies Opportunities to Work Independently

Many of the world's greatest ideas spring from the minds of introverts. And virtually none of these ideas get blurted out in the middle of a team meeting. (Imagine Albert Einstein saying, "Hold on a sec, Bob — I just had a great thought. Check this out: $E = MC^2$! Write that down on the chalkboard for me, okay?")

Instead, introverts do their best thinking when they're shut away from the rest of the world. It's true that they can work very well in teams, and they can be powerful team leaders, too. But they also need plenty of "alone" time so they can dig deeply into their work.

See whether you can find ways to give your more introverted employees opportunities to work on their own. For example, give them large, long-term projects that require a lot of research and careful organization.

# Rethink Your Interview Process

Interviews are grueling for just about everyone, but they're torture for many introverts. First of all, innies hate being the center of attention. They're also deep thinkers who need time to ponder questions — something they can't do when you're peppering them with rapid-fire queries. And because they're quiet by nature, it's hard for them to come across as confident (even when they are).

As a CEO or manager, you don't want to miss out on good candidates just because they aren't strong in interviews. To make sure you give introverts a fair shot, remember these guidelines:

- **Study every candidate's résumé and portfolio carefully.** Often, introverts are better at outlining their qualifications on paper than they are at doing it verbally.

- **Avoid trick questions.** Studies show that these questions don't really help you identify good candidates, and they'll throw introverts off their stride.

- **Give introverted candidates time to think.** For example, say, "Take your time; we're not in a big rush." And if an introverted candidate freezes up and can't come up with an answer, say, "Don't worry; we'll come back to that question later."

Also, be aware that introverted candidates may be more hesitant than extroverts to ask questions about salaries, vacations, and benefits. They're less talkative to begin with, and by the end of a job interview, they may be more focused on escaping than on getting all the details they need to know. So be sure to give innie job seekers plenty of information about what you're offering.

And when you're making your decision, ask yourself, "Am I placing too much weight on a candidate's ability to talk easily and answer questions fluently?" A lot of people who sparkle in job interviews are actually inflating (or outright lying about) their skills and experience. So look for good "people skills" if they're necessary for your job, but otherwise, don't assume that a smooth talker is better for your position than a quiet, serious candidate.

# Index

## • *Numbers* •

5-HTTLPR gene, significance of, 36

## • *A* •

accountability on teams
  allowing, 85
  creating, 84
  promoting, 84–85
  in storming stage, 87
ADD (attention deficit disorder), 241
ADHD (attention deficit hyperactivity
    disorder), 241
adjourning stage for teams, 99–100
allies, making in workplace, 57–58
ambiverts, explained, 43. *See also*
    extroverts; introverts
amygdala, function in brain, 33
anchoring visualization method,
    practicing, 103
anxiety disorder, social, 24
Armstrong, Neil, 266
assertive communication, teaching
    to children, 259–260. *See also*
    communication styles
assumptive close, explained, 165
audience engagement. *See also* public
    speaking
  asking for input, 123–124
  being sincere, 114
  clarifying expectations, 114
  delaying answers, 115
  ending on time, 115
  eye contact, 114
  handling mistakes, 115–116
  hecklers, 121–123
  matching and pacing, 118
  mobility, 114

offering handouts, 124
persuasion, 118–121
responding to questions, 115
showing concern, 114
staying in moment, 115
stories and humor, 116–117
sustaining, 121
taking mental notes, 115
types of learners, 121
auditory learners, 121
autism spectrum disorders, 242–243

## • *B* •

Barrett Browning, Elizabeth, 266
behavior. *See* personality
behavioral interviewing, 147–148, 172
Bishop, Russell, 84
bosses. *See* manager types
brain, "plastic" quality of, 43
brain chemicals
  dopamine, 32
  impact of genes on, 32
  serotonin, 36
brain regions
  amygdala, 33
  gray matter, 33
  responses to social cues, 33
  white matter, 33
brainstorming, implementing, 70–71
bridging back members, 86
bullies, protecting children from,
    259–262
bullies in workplace, standing up to,
    55–56
business coaches. *See also*
    entrepreneurs
  assessment experience, 176
  cognitive behavior, 176

business coaches *(continued)*
  considering, 175
  finding, 175–176
  interviewing, 176
  time commitment, 176
business plan
  creating, 160
  Six Ps of Motivation, 160

## • C •

career success. *See also* job interviews
  goal-setting, 156–158
  SMART goals, 156–158
careers. *See also* jobs
  assertiveness, 62
  as "callings," 61
  choosing, 61–62
  for innies, 59–60
  level of introversion, 61
  for outies, 60
  tolerance for failure, 61–62
Carson, Johnny, 267–268
CBT (cognitive behavioral therapy),
    24–25
celebrity innies. *See also* innies
  Armstrong, Neil, 266
  Barrett Browning, Elizabeth, 266
  Carson, Johnny, 267–268
  Coolidge, Calvin, 269
  Darwin, Charles, 265–266
  Depp, Johnny, 267
  Lincoln, Abraham, 270
  Murphy, Eddie, 267
  Seinfeld, Jerry, 268
  Smith, Tom, 268–269
changes in life, reaction to, 27
charter schools, considering for kids,
    257–258
Cheat Sheet, downloading, 3
childhood behavior, considering, 17
children. *See also* introverted children
  with ADD (attention deficit disorder),
    241–242

with ADHD (attention deficit
    hyperactivity disorder), 241–242
  autism spectrum disorders, 242–243
  rating sensitivity of, 35
coach, considering, 193–194
coaching. *See* business coaches; peer
    coaching
cognitive behavior, hiring expert in, 176
Cole-Whittaker, Terry, 115
communication styles. *See also* assertive
    communication
confidence, projecting on teams, 86–87
conflict resolution. *See also* problem
    solving
  clarifying problems, 93–94
  constructive feedback, 96–97
  dump sheets, 93
  finding solutions, 95
  normalizing, 96
  preparing mentally, 93
  sandwiching, 96
  seeking areas of agreement, 94–95
  sharing responsibility, 95
conscientiousness, perception of, 27
contracting approach
  Seven Rs, 81
  using with teams, 81–83
conversation practice
  asking for advice, 39
  asking for stories, 39–40
  asking questions, 40
  complimenting others, 40
  schmoozing, 39–40
conversational pace, noticing, 230–231
Coolidge, Calvin, 269
coworkers
  allies, 57–58
  bullies, 55–56
  steamrollers, 56, 86
  time-suckers, 56–57
cubicles, working in, 49, 283
culture, influence of, 35

## • D •

Darwin, Charles, 265–266
dates, first-time, 201
dating. *See also* online dating;
    relationships
  addressing expectations, 201–202
  readiness for intimacy, 202
Davar, Ashok, 161
deep breathing, practicing, 23
Depp, Johnny, 267
DISC personality model. *See also*
    personality
  applying to managers, 129
  conscientious, 90
  decisive, 90
  influential, 90
  stable, 90
dopamine, significance of, 32
dump sheets
  applying to negative self-talk, 181
  preparing for speeches, 106
  using for conflicts, 93
dump-sheet-and-flower-approach,
    180–184

## • E •

education alternatives
  charter schools, 255
  home-schooling, 255
  magnet schools, 255
  online schools, 255
  private schools, 255
  researching, 256
e-mail communication
  capitalization, 55
  clarity, 55
  etiquette, 55
  professionalism, 55
  terseness, 55
  thinking through, 55
  timing, 55
  wordiness, 55

emotional intelligence (EI). *See also* innie
    leaders
  arguments, 73–74
  blowing off steam, 74
  body language, 74
  drivers, 73
  empathy, 74
  explained, 72
  importance in workplace, 72
  MSCEIT, 72
  non-tech leaders, 73
  open-mindedness, 74
  raising, 73–74
  stress triggers, 73
  tech leaders, 73
energized response, considering, 18
entrepreneurs. *See also* business
    coaches
  assumptive close, 165
  avoiding procrastination, 161–162
  behavioral interviewing, 172
  being available, 166
  being influential, 166–169
  building dream team, 171–176
  business coaches, 174–176
  business plans, 160
  client relationships, 167
  contributing to community, 168
  coping with disappointments, 169–171
  creating blogs, 163
  customer service management, 167
  disappearing clients, 170
  expert reputation, 162–164
  face-to-face marketing, 165
  feedback from clients, 167
  hiring staff, 172–173
  Internet marketing, 165
  versus intrapreneurs, 162
  LinkedIn presence, 163
  long-term loyalty, 166–169
  making contacts, 164
  marketing, 165, 169
  morning ritual, 161
  online presence, 165
  overcoming roadblocks, 161
  posting articles on websites, 163

entrepreneurs *(continued)*
  public speaking, 163
  recording videos, 163
  Rule of Seven, 170
  self-marketing, 162–165
  staffs' skills, 173–174
  strengthening skills, 160
  teaming up with, 164
  thanking clients, 168–169
  website design, 174
  writing books, 163
  writing guest posts, 163
environmental awareness,
    considering, 27
expecting versus hoping, 189
expert reputation, creating, 162–164
extroverted parents, dealing with innie
    kids, 245
extroverted personality, converting to,
    42–44
extroverted world, thriving in, 13
extroverts. *See also* ambiverts;
    introverts; outies
  dominance of, 12
  as friends, 10
  identifying in public, 33
  versus introverts, 8
  ratio to introverts, 9
eye contact, making with audiences, 114

fabrics, sensitivity to, 26
faces
  reactions to, 33
  recognizing, 34
facilitative leadership, 65
fainting psychologist story, 37
famous innies. *See also* innies
  Armstrong, Neil, 266
  Barrett Browning, Elizabeth, 266
  Carson, Johnny, 267–268
  Coolidge, Calvin, 269
  Darwin, Charles, 265–266
  Depp, Johnny, 267
  Lincoln, Abraham, 270
  Murphy, Eddie, 267
  Seinfeld, Jerry, 268
  Smith, Tom, 268–269
feelings, hoping versus expecting, 189
flex-time policy, considering, 28
flower exercise
  applying to negative self-talk, 181–183
  revisiting, 183–184
focused conversation
  deciding, 75
  fact-finding, 75
  interpreting, 75
  reflecting, 75
  technique of, 74–75
forming stage for teams
  accountability, 84–85
  bridging back members, 86
  contracting, 81–83
  introducing team members, 87
  projecting confidence, 86–87
friendships, 198. *See also* innie
    friendships; relationships
  altering self behavior, 198
  demonstrating caring for, 197
  determining health of, 197
  encouraging for innie kids, 249–252
  goal-setting, 195
  joining clubs and groups, 194–195
  joining play groups, 195
  looking for, 194–195
  maintaining, 196–198
  making first move, 196
  neighbors, 195
  setting limits, 198
  stating expectations, 198
  taking classes, 195
  volunteering, 195

genes
  5-HTTLPR, 36
  effect on brain chemicals, 32
  impact on dopamine levels, 32

impact on introversion, 32
interaction with upbringing, 36
studies of twins, 32
goodness of fit, 12
Gottman, John, 203
gratitude, harnessing power of, 190

## • *H* •

happiness, cultivating, 189
headphones
  wearing in workplace, 286–287
  wearing noise-canceling, 50
hecklers, handling during speeches,
    121–123
"hiding out," 26
home-schooling, considering, 256
hoping versus expecting, 189
hormone, oxytocin, 41

## • *I* •

IM messages and texting, 251
index cards, using for presentations,
    106–108
"inner adult," visualizing, 185–186
"inner child," visualizing, 185–186
innie "cone of silence," 92
innie friends, shopping for, 234
innie friendships. *See also* friendships;
    social events
  accepting, 230–231
  approach to activities, 235
  conversational pace, 232–233
  multitasking demands, 233
  need for "alone" time, 232
  with outies, 231–235
  social occasions, 235–236
  staying out of spotlight, 233–234
  strengths of, 231
  thinking before talking, 232–233
innie interests questionnaire, 19

innie leaders. *See also* emotional
    intelligence (EI); leadership skills
  delegation, 75–76
  identifying selves as, 76
  pairing with extroverts, 77
  retreats, 77
  scheduling wisely, 76
  wearing "power clothes," 77
innie test, 16–19
innie-friendly workplace. *See also*
    workplace
  acoustics, 285–286
  cubicles, 283
  cutting down on meetings, 284
  headphones, 286–287
  improving meetings, 284–285
  interview process, 288
  privacy screens, 285
  private zones, 286
  telecommuting, 287
  working independently, 287
innies. *See also* famous innies; introverts;
    unwelcome situations
  approach toward work, 61
  career suggestions, 60
  conversion to outies, 43–44
  gray matter in brain, 33
  as independent thinkers, 64–65
  versus outies, 9
  reactions to faces, 33
  response to touch, 33
  terminology, 1
  white matter in brain, 33
interests questionnaire, 19
internalizing traits, explained, 29
Internet dating. *See also* online dating;
    relationships
  benefits, 200
  risks, 200
  succeeding at, 200–201

interviewing for jobs. *See also* career
      success
  asking questions, 152–153
  behavioral interviewing, 147–148
  challenges, 144
  creating portfolio, 145–146
  doing research for, 145
  ending, 151
  handling "no," 153–154
  looking assertive, 150–151
  making wish list, 148
  performing in, 150–151
  by phone, 149
  rehearsing for, 146–148
  strengths, 144
  survival kit, 151
  taking company tour, 153
  weighing pros and cons, 153
  writing down key points, 148
intrapreneurs versus entrepreneurs, 162
introversion
  as internalizing trait, 29
  rubber band theory, 43
  versus shyness, 20–21, 25–26
  situational theory, 43
introverted children. *See also* children
  acknowledging emotions, 254–255
  alternatives to public schools, 257–258
  appreciating, 243–244
  assertive communication, 261–262
  avoiding overscheduling, 244–245
  charter schools, 257–258
  choosing friends, 251
  community activities, 250
  creating routines, 246
  depression, 252
  distinguishing medical conditions,
      240–243
  encouraging friendships, 249–252
  enhancing self-image, 253–255
  explaining introversion to, 253–254
  explaining outie behaviors to, 254
  with extroverted parents, 247
  "gifted" percentage, 259
  giving private space to, 248–249

  handling unpredictability, 246
  home-schooling, 258
  identifying, 239–240
  joining clubs, 251
  learning disabilities, 257
  magnet schools, 258
  older, 250–251
  online schools, 258
  planning events, 250
  private schools, 258
  protecting from bullies, 259–262
  scheduling play dates, 249
  school experience, 255–257
  sensitivity, 240
  shyness, 240
  sibling relationships, 247–248
  social activities, 244–245
  social skills, 250
  teaching to handle change, 245–246
  texting and IM messaging, 253
  volunteer work, 251
  wellness, 252
  working with teachers, 256–257
  younger, 249–250
introverted teens, need for romance, 252
introverts. *See also* ambiverts;
      extroverts; innies
  actors as examples, 10
  benefits, 9
  continuum, 16
  creativity of, 10–11
  expanding comfort zone, 13
  versus extroverts, 8
  as friends, 10
  identifying in public, 33
  as independent thinkers, 11
  as listeners, 10
  as natural leaders, 11
  owning "self," 13
  ratio to extroverts, 9
  self-respect, 13
  socialization characteristics, 13
  standing up for oneself, 13
  studiousness of, 11
  traits, 15

invitations to social events, responding to, 224–226

# • J •

job interviews. *See also* career success
  asking questions, 152–153
  behavioral interviewing, 147–148
  challenges, 144
  creating portfolio, 145–146
  doing research for, 145
  ending, 151
  handling "no," 153–154
  looking assertive, 150–151
  making wish list, 148
  performing in, 150–151
  by phone, 149
  rehearsing for, 146–148
  strengths, 144
  survival kit, 151
  taking company tour, 153
  weighing pros and cons, 153
  writing down key points, 148
job offers
  benefits, 155–156
  negotiating salary, 154–155
  responding to, 154–156
  schedules, 155–156
  start date, 156
  vacations, 155–156
jobs, matching to workplaces, 152–153. *See also* careers; office life; workplace

# • K •

keynote speech, length of, 105
kids. *See also* introverted children
  with ADD (attention deficit disorder), 241–242
  with ADHD (attention deficit hyperactivity disorder), 241–242
  autism spectrum disorders, 242–243
  rating sensitivity of, 35

kinesthetic learners, 121
Laney, Marti, 1
leadership skills. *See also* innie leaders
  building, 67
  decision making, 64
  emotional intelligence (EI), 72–74
  encouraging independence, 64–65
  facilitative leadership, 65
  factual information, 66
  focused conversation, 74–75
  multitasking, 66
  negative reinforcement, 69–70
  "people burnout," 66
  perceptions of, 66
  positive reinforcement, 69–70
  punishment, 70
  reinforcement, 69–70
  research, 64
  self-confidence, 66
  structured brainstorming, 70–71
  transactional leadership, 67
  transformational, 67–69
learner types
  auditory, 121
  kinesthetic, 121
  visual, 121
learning disabilities, coping with, 255
learning style, considering, 17
life
  increasing control over, 186–190
  treating as experiment, 185
life changes, reaction to, 27
Lincoln, Abraham, 270
listeners. *See* audience engagement
loneliness, considering, 22

# • M •

magnet schools, considering, 258
management skills. *See also* innie leaders
  building, 67
  decision making, 64
  emotional intelligence (EI), 72–74
  encouraging independence, 64–65

management skills *(continued)*
facilitative leadership, 65
factual information, 66
focused conversation, 74–75
multitasking, 66
negative reinforcement, 69–70
"people burnout," 66
perceptions of, 66
positive reinforcement, 69–70
punishment, 70
reinforcement, 69–70
research, 64
self-confidence, 66
structured brainstorming, 70–71
transactional leadership, 67
transformational, 67–69
manager types
conscientious, 129
decisive, 129
influential, 129
stable, 129
managers
defending, 133
earning trust of, 132–133
friends and enemies, 132
talking with tactfully, 131
manager's goals, identifying, 130–132
managing up
avoiding pitfalls, 140–141
comfort zone, 135
explained, 11, 127
getting training, 134
growth potential, 134
making habit of, 141
manager's personality, 129
manager's style, 128–130
matching skills, 130
peer coaching, 135–140
problem solving, 135
professional organizations, 134
rules, 141
Six Ps of Motivation, 131
tracking results, 141

matching and pacing, 118, 208
Mayer-Salovey-Caruso Emotional
Intelligence Test (MSCEIT), 72
meditation, trying, 28–29
meeting new people, considering, 18
meetings, considering behavior at, 17
meetings at work
controlling, 86–87
getting agendas, 54
parking lot approach, 284–285
participating in, 54
preparing for, 54
sending input via e-mail, 54–55
mental health professional, considering,
193–194
mindful meditation, trying, 28–29
Mitchell, Michele, 104
mnemonic devices, using, 34
moods of others, response to, 27
MSCEIT (Mayer-Salovey-Caruso
Emotional Intelligence Test), 72
multitasking
considering, 18
dealing with, 66
minimizing, 231
Murphy, Eddie, 267

## • N •

negative reinforcement, practicing, 69–70
negative self-talk. *See also* pessimism;
positive thoughts
breaking habit of, 180–184
dump-sheet-and-flower approach,
180–184
impact of, 180
managing self-pity, 186–187
pity pot approach, 187
reframing thoughts, 184
thought-stopping, 184–185
networking events. *See also* social events
arriving early, 273
being philosophical, 273

being picky, 270–271
business cards, 274–275
doing homework, 272
food line, 274
getting SMART goals, 272–273
making small talk, 274
managing leads, 275
reaching out, 276
researching speakers, 274
single-person focus, 274
thanking others for leads, 276
trout fishing, 273
noise, response to, 26
noise in workplace
    fake "walls," 50
    houseplants, 50
    mirrors, 50
    "No interruptions" sign, 50
    privacy screen, 50
    taking breaks from, 49–50
    wearing headphones, 50
    white noise machine, 50
noisy meetings, response to, 18
normalizing technique, explained, 96–97
norming stage for teams
    building relationships, 98
    key results, 97
    norms and goals, 98

**● O ●**

office design, planning, 51
office life. See also jobs; workplace
    cube farm, 49
    emphasis on teamwork, 48
    emphasizing achievements, 53
    getting credit for projects, 53
    interruptions, 48
    kids and home office, 52
    meetings, 54
    multitasking demands, 48
    noisy workplace, 49–52
    physical exercises, 51
    scheduling "alone" time, 51
    self-promotion, 48
    telecommuting, 52
online dating. See also dating;
        relationships
    benefits, 200
    risks, 200
    succeeding at, 200–201
online schools, considering, 258
optimism, cultivating, 188–189. See also
        pessimism
outie interests questionnaire, 19
outie test, 16–19
outies. See also extroverts; pretend
        extroverts
    approach toward work, 61
    behaving like, 36–37
    career suggestions, 60
    friendships with innies, 230–235
    gray matter in brain, 33
    versus innies, 9
    reactions to faces, 33
    response to touch, 33
    temporary behavior, 36–37
    terminology, 1
oxytocin hormone, significance of, 41

**● P ●**

pain, reaction to, 26
parking lot approach, using for meetings,
        284–285
party behavior
    considering, 16
    evaluating, 18
peer coaching
    goal-setting, 136
    non-judgmental approach, 137
peer-coaching roles
    collaborator, 139–140
    delegator, 140
    educator, 137
    motivator, 138–139
    roles, 137–140
performing stage for teams, 99

personal coach, considering, 193–194
personal feelings, discussing, 22
personality. *See also* DISC personality
    model
  changes over time, 44
  in relationships, 204–205
personality model, DISC, 90–91
persuasive talk
  action steps, 121
  applying pacing, 120
  creating awareness, 119
  outlining issues, 119–120
  visualizing success, 120
pessimism, minimizing, 189. *See also*
    negative self-talk; optimism
pet peeves. *See also* innies
  birthday announcements, 279
  catching up on phone calls, 282
  class reunions, 282
  drop-in guests, 277–278
  excessive storytelling, 280
  exposing quietness, 281
  extended stays of guests, 279
  hugging relatives, 281
  spontaneous introductions, 278
  surprise parties, 280
Pfeiffer, Michelle, 10
phone interview, participating in, 149
pity pot approach, using, 187
pivotal points
  identifying, 104
  visualizing, 104
positive reinforcement, practicing, 69–70
positive thoughts. *See also* negative
    self-talk
  adopting, 187
  cultivating, 185
  cultivating optimism, 188–189
  life as experiment, 185
PowerPoint presentations. *See*
    presentations
presentations. *See also* public speaking;
    speeches
  dump sheets, 106
  index cards, 106–108
  informative, 105

persuasive, 105
recording during planning, 105
technical, 105
pretend extroverts. *See also* outies
  body language, 38
  conversation, 39–40
  eye contact, 38
  gestures, 38
  physical distance, 38
  pros and cons, 41–42
  role-playing, 40
  smiles, 38
  stance, 38
privacy screens, using in
    workplaces, 285
private schools, considering, 256
private zones, creating in workplace, 286
problem solving, considering, 17.
    *See also* conflict resolution
problems
  clarifying for resolution, 93–94
  taking charge of, 187–188
Ps of Motivation, 160
  pleasure, 131
  power, 131
  prestige, 131
  problem solving, 131
  productivity, 131
  profit, 131
psychologist story, fainting, 37
public events. *See also* innie friendships;
    networking events
  cohosting, 222
  coping with, 218–220
  creating inner sanctuaries, 221–222
  early departures from, 236–237
  escaping crowds, 219–220
  hosting, 221–224
  making small talk, 220
  overstayed welcomes, 223–224
  planning ahead, 219
  receiving invitations to, 219
  recharging self during, 222–223
  replaying, 22
  responding to invitations, 224–226
  scheduling unwinding time, 220

skipping, 237
stress associated with, 218
taking focus off self, 221
public schools, alternatives, 257–258
public speakers
  educators, 107
  facilitators, 107
  persuaders, 107
public speaking. *See also* audience
    engagement; presentations;
    speeches
  breathing skills, 112
  connecting with audiences, 112
  dressing for, 113
  at facilities, 110–111
  handouts, 111
  keynote speeches, 105
  mastering material, 104–108
  microphones, 111
  mobility, 112
  in office, 110
  organizing ideas, 104–105
  pauses, 112
  pivoting, 112
  practicing technique, 111–113
  preparation, 102
  projecting, 112
  reaction to, 17
  scheduling breaks, 125
  seminars, 105
  staying true to self, 123
  visualizing success, 102–103
  volume, 112
  workshops, 105

questionnaires
  innies, 19
  outies, 19

reframing thoughts, 184
rejection, worrying about, 22

relationships. *See also* dating;
    friendships; online dating; sibling
    relationships
  arguing around kids, 213
  arguing styles, 210–212
  building, 201–205
  communication styles, 207–209
  differing personalities in, 204–205
  ending, 214–216
  getting professional help, 211–212
  identifying sources of issues, 214
  keys to success, 203–204
  learned behaviors, 214
  like, love, lust (three Ls), 202
  matching and pacing, 208
  mental disorders, 214
  mental "love maps," 203
  mutual respect, 203
  mutual trust, 203
  needs and interests, 206–207
  nurturing partners, 203
  planning social activities, 209–210
  seeking win-win solutions, 209–210
  sharing values, 204
  therapy techniques, 211–212
  wariness of perfectionism, 212–213
  writing down feelings, 211
relatives, responding to calls from, 18
reputation, building as entrepreneur,
    162–164
resource, companion articles, 3
romance. *See* dating; online dating
Rowling, J. K., 10
Rs of contracting
  relationships, 81, 83
  reporting, 81, 83
  resolving, 81, 83
  resources, 81–82
  results, 81
  road map, 81–82
  roles and responsibilities, 81–82
rubber band theory, 43
Rule of Seven, 170

## • *S* •

salary, negotiating, 154–155
Samuel, Mark, 84
sandwiching, applying to conflicts, 96
schmoozing, 39–40
school alternatives
  charter schools, 255
  home-schooling, 255
  magnet schools, 255
  online schools, 255
  private schools, 255
  researching, 256
Seinfeld, Jerry, 268
self-criticism. *See also* pessimism;
    positive thoughts
  breaking habit of, 180–184
  dump-sheet-and-flower approach,
    180–184
  impact of, 180
  managing self-pity, 186–187
  pity pot approach, 187
  reframing thoughts, 184
  thought-stopping, 184–185
self-description, 17–18
self-employment. *See also* business
    coaches
  assumptive close, 165
  avoiding procrastination, 161–162
  behavioral interviewing, 172
  being available, 166
  being influential, 166–169
  building dream team, 171–176
  business coaches, 174–176
  business plans, 160
  client relationships, 167
  contributing to community, 168
  coping with disappointments, 169–171
  creating blogs, 163
  customer service management, 167
  disappearing clients, 170
  expert reputation, 162–164
  face-to-face marketing, 165

  feedback from clients, 167
  hiring staff, 172–173
  Internet marketing, 165
  versus intrapreneurs, 162
  LinkedIn presence, 163
  long-term loyalty, 166–169
  making contacts, 164
  marketing, 165, 169
  morning ritual, 161
  online presence, 165
  overcoming roadblocks, 161
  posting articles on websites, 163
  public speaking, 163
  recording videos, 163
  Rule of Seven, 170
  self-marketing, 162–165
  staffs' skills, 173–174
  strengthening skills, 160
  teaming up with, 164
  thanking clients, 168–169
  website design, 174
  writing books, 163
  writing guest posts, 163
self-pity, overcoming, 186–187
seminar, length of, 105
sensitive issues, managing, 27–28
sensitivity
  as internalizing trait, 29
  internalizing traits, 29
  versus introversion, 25–26
  occurrence in innies, 29
  test, 26–27
serotonin, regulating levels of, 36
Seven Rs of contracting
  relationships, 81, 83
  reporting, 81, 83
  resolving, 81, 83
  resources, 81–82
  results, 81
  road map, 81–82
  roles and responsibilities, 81–82
shirt-folding example, 64–65
shopping behavior, considering, 18

shyness
  avoidant personality disorder, 24–25
  CBT (cognitive behavioral therapy), 24
  dealing with, 23–24
  as internalizing trait, 29
  versus introversion, 20–21
  overcoming, 23–24
  practicing deep breathing, 23
  social anxiety disorder, 24–25
  testing, 21–22
sibling relationships, keeping positive,
      247–248. *See also* relationships
situational theory, 43
Six Ps of Motivation, 160
  pleasure, 131
  power, 131
  prestige, 131
  problem Solving, 131
  productivity, 131
  profit, 131
sleep, regularity of, 28
SMART goals
  actionable, 157
  measurable, 157
  for networking events, 272–273
  relevant, 157
  specific, 157
  timely, 157
smells, sensitivity to, 26
smiling, importance of, 39
Smith, Tom, 268–269
social anxiety disorder, 24–25
social cues, responses to, 33
social events. *See also* innie friendships;
      networking events
  cohosting, 222
  coping with, 218–220
  creating inner sanctuaries, 221–222
  early departures from, 236–237
  escaping crowds, 219–220
  hosting, 221–224
  making small talk, 220
  overstayed welcomes, 223–224

  planning ahead, 219
  receiving invitations to, 219
  recharging self during, 222–223
  replaying, 22
  responding to invitations, 224–226
  scheduling unwinding time, 220
  skipping, 237
  stress associated with, 218
  taking focus off self, 221
social-emotional processing, 33
socialization characteristics, 17, 22
solutions, finding for conflicts, 95
speech patterns, noticing, 34
speeches. *See* presentations; public
      speaking
  audiences, 108
  details, 109
  ending, 109–110
  focusing on priorities, 108–110
  getting buy-in, 109
  information up to date, 109
  key points, 108
  lengths of, 108
  technical information, 109
  titles for, 108
  visual aids, 109
  visualization of scenarios, 109
Spielberg, Steven, 10
steamrollers in workplace
  dealing with, 56
  example, 86
stimulation, response to, 34
storming stage for teams
  analyzing team dynamics, 90–91
  communicating clearly, 92
  emotions in, 87
  innie "cone of silence," 92
  team support agreement, 88–90
  troubleshooting, 92–97
stress at home, dealing with, 28–29
stress threshold, understanding, 192–193
stressful events, interpreting accurately,
      191–192

structured brainstorming, implementing,
    70–71
success, visualizing, 120

 **T**

talks. *See also* public speaking; speeches
  dump sheets, 106
  index cards, 106–108
  informative, 105
  persuasive, 105
  recording during planning, 105
  technical, 105
task complexity, approaching, 17
taste, sensitivity to, 34
team building, considering, 19
team development stages
  adjourning, 80, 99–100
  forming, 80–83
  norming, 80, 97–98
  performing, 80, 99
  storming, 80
team dynamics, analyzing, 90–91
team members
  bridging back, 86
  getting acquainted, 87
team support agreement, creating, 88–90
teens, need for romance, 252
telecommuting, 52
testing, shyness, 21–22
tests
  for innies, 16–19
  for outies, 16–19
  patterns, 19
  sensitivity, 26–27
texting and IM messages, 253
thoughts, reframing, 184
thought-stopping, practicing, 184–185
touch, response to, 33
tragedies in world, reaction to, 27
transactional leadership, 67

transformational skills
  clarifying expectations, 68
  creating inspiring vision, 68
  encouraging staff, 68
  mentoring, 69
  practicing, 68
triggers, identifying, 28
troubleshooting conflict
  clarifying problems, 93–94
  constructive feedback, 96–97
  dump sheets, 93
  finding solutions, 95
  normalizing, 96
  preparing mentally, 93
  sandwiching, 96
  seeking areas of agreement, 94–95
  sharing responsibility, 95
Tuckman, Bruce, 79–80
twins, studies of, 32

**U**

unwelcome situations. *See also* innies
  birthday announcements, 279
  catching up on phone calls, 282
  class reunions, 282
  drop-in guests, 277–278
  excessive storytelling, 280
  exposing quietness, 281
  extended stays of guests, 279
  hugging relatives, 281
  spontaneous introductions, 278
  surprise parties, 280
upbringing, effects of, 35–36

**V**

visual learners, 121
visualizing
  anchoring, 103
  goals, 103

happy inner adult, 185–186
happy inner child, 185–186
mental styles, 103
pivotal point, 104
public speaking, 102–103
scheduling sessions, 103
success, 120

# • W •

website design, importance of, 174
work habits, considering, 16
working conditions. *See* office life
workplace. *See also* innie-friendly
  workplace; jobs; office life
  emotional intelligence in, 72–74
  making allies in, 57–58
  matching jobs to, 152–153
  power of food in, 58

workplace noise
  fake "walls," 50
  houseplants, 50
  mirrors, 50
  "No interruptions" sign, 50
  privacy screen, 50
  taking breaks from, 49–50
  wearing headphones, 50
  white noise machine, 50
workplace troublemakers
  bullies, 55–56
  steamrollers, 56
  time-suckers, 56–57
workshop, length of, 105
world problems, reaction to, 27

# Notes

# Notes

# Notes

# Notes

# Notes

# Notes

# Notes

# Notes

# Notes

# Notes

# Notes

# About the Author

**Joan Pastor, PhD,** is a licensed industrial-organizational (business) and clinical psychologist. Her company, JPA International, Inc. (www.JPA-International.com), has provided management, leadership, and team-development training, consulting, and coaching services to Fortune 500 companies and governments around the world for more than 24 years. Joan's passion is growing organizations while positively transforming people within them so that they can grow to their fullest potential.

The recipient of numerous awards, including the 2013–2014 Gallery of Success award from Temple University, Joan makes her home in the Los Angeles area.

# Dedication

This book is dedicated to Angela and Tony Cox, Travis and Jennifer Thompson, and my personal friends Marcia, Karen, Brenda, and "Mecca," whose personal support and love guides me to become the best person I can be.

# Author's Acknowledgments

This book was fun and wonderful to write, mainly because I had the best team of people around me to help every step of the way. At the top of the list is my wonderful researcher and personal editor Alison Blake. I couldn't have written this book without her. I also must acknowledge Margot Hutchison, my agent at Waterside Productions, for her excellent advice, her faith in me, and for our continued journey to bring the best and most powerful information to the public in an entertaining manner. I must give a huge thank you to John Wiley & Sons Inc., and especially those associated with the *For Dummies* series.

A special acknowledgement goes to my staff and colleagues at JPA International, and especially Pam Anderson (not the actor but our capable office manager). She is a role model for proactive thinking and leadership.

I truly feel that everyone I've acknowledged each played a part for this book to be the result of a high-performing, collaborative team. And isn't that what it's all about?!

## Publisher's Acknowledgments

**Acquisitions Editor:** Tracy Boggier

**Senior Project Editor:** Tim Gallan

**Copy Editor:** Jennette ElNaggar

**Technical Editor:** Lin Ames

**Project Coordinator:** Sheree Montgomery

**Cover Image:** ©iStockphoto.com/blackred

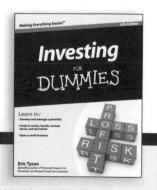
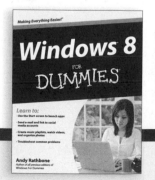

## Math & Science

Algebra I For Dummies,
2nd Edition
978-0-470-55964-2

Anatomy and Physiology
For Dummies,
2nd Edition
978-0-470-92326-9

Astronomy For Dummies,
3rd Edition
978-1-118-37697-3

Biology For Dummies,
2nd Edition
978-0-470-59875-7

Chemistry For Dummies,
2nd Edition
978-1-1180-0730-3

Pre-Algebra Essentials
For Dummies
978-0-470-61838-7

## Microsoft Office

Excel 2013 For Dummies
978-1-118-51012-4

Office 2013 All-in-One
For Dummies
978-1-118-51636-2

PowerPoint 2013
For Dummies
978-1-118-50253-2

Word 2013 For Dummies
978-1-118-49123-2

## Music

Blues Harmonica
For Dummies
978-1-118-25269-7

Guitar For Dummies,
3rd Edition
978-1-118-11554-1

iPod & iTunes
For Dummies,
10th Edition
978-1-118-50864-0

## Programming

Android Application
Development For
Dummies, 2nd Edition
978-1-118-38710-8

iOS 6 Application
Development For Dummies
978-1-118-50880-0

Java For Dummies,
5th Edition
978-0-470-37173-2

## Religion & Inspiration

The Bible For Dummies
978-0-7645-5296-0

Buddhism For Dummies,
2nd Edition
978-1-118-02379-2

Catholicism For Dummies,
2nd Edition
978-1-118-07778-8

## Self-Help & Relationships

Bipolar Disorder
For Dummies,
2nd Edition
978-1-118-33882-7

Meditation For Dummies,
3rd Edition
978-1-118-29144-3

## Seniors

Computers For Seniors
For Dummies,
3rd Edition
978-1-118-11553-4

iPad For Seniors
For Dummies,
5th Edition
978-1-118-49708-1

Social Security
For Dummies
978-1-118-20573-0

## Smartphones & Tablets

Android Phones
For Dummies
978-1-118-16952-0

Kindle Fire HD
For Dummies
978-1-118-42223-6

NOOK HD For Dummies,
Portable Edition
978-1-118-39498-4

Surface For Dummies
978-1-118-49634-3

## Test Prep

ACT For Dummies,
5th Edition
978-1-118-01259-8

ASVAB For Dummies,
3rd Edition
978-0-470-63760-9

GRE For Dummies,
7th Edition
978-0-470-88921-3

Officer Candidate Tests,
For Dummies
978-0-470-59876-4

Physician's Assistant Exam
For Dummies
978-1-118-11556-5

Series 7 Exam
For Dummies
978-0-470-09932-2

## Windows 8

Windows 8 For Dummies
978-1-118-13461-0

Windows 8 For Dummies,
Book + DVD Bundle
978-1-118-27167-4

Windows 8 All-in-One
For Dummies
978-1-118-11920-4

**Available in print and e-book formats.**

# Take Dummies with you everywhere you go!

Whether you're excited about e-books, want more from the web, must have your mobile apps, or swept up in social media, Dummies makes everything easier.

# Dummies products make life easier!

- DIY
- Consumer Electronics
- Crafts

- Software
- Cookware
- Hobbies

- Videos
- Music
- Games
- and More!

For more information, go to **Dummies.com**® and search the store by category.

FOR
DUMMIES

A Wiley Bra